REMEMBERING KILLALOE

About the Author

 Henry Murdoch is a barrister and a chartered engineer. He was born in Cavan in 1938 and educated in Killaloe, County Clare, Crescent College Limerick, Presentation College Cork (1955) and University College Cork (BE 1959). He subsequently studied law at Trinity College Dublin and Kings Inns, and was called to the Bar in 1966. He was conferred with an MBA by Trinity College Dublin in 1972.

He practised as a barrister in the Four Courts in the mid-1980s, when he conceived and wrote *Murdoch's Dictionary of Irish Law*, now in its fifth edition.

He retired in 1999 from FÁS, the Training and Employment Authority, where he was the Assistant Director General – Industry. This was after a 40-year career in the private and public sectors, ranging from engineering, aviation, waste management, training, health services, banking and vocational and medical rehabilitation.

He retired recently as Chairman of the National Rehabilitation Hospital (NRH) after 17 years in that position, but remains Chairman of the NRH Foundation. He is currently a non-executive director of Skillnets Ltd and of the governing board in London of City and Guilds. Up to recently he was an active member of Tenancy Tribunals and Mental Health Tribunals.

REMEMBERING KILLALOE

A Memoir

Henry Murdoch

The Liffey Press

Published by
The Liffey Press Ltd
Raheny Shopping Centre, Second Floor
Raheny, Dublin 5, Ireland
www.theliffeypress.com

A catalogue record of this book is
available from the British Library.

ISBN 978-1-908308-59-7

Printed in Spain by GraphyCems

CONTENTS

PREFACE

In October 2012 at the age of 74, I was walking down from our recently acquired penthouse apartment in Harbour Village Marina in Killaloe, County Clare, when I saw a green An Post van pulling up and the postman getting out. I passed him as he was inserting the mail into the communal letter boxes. I remarked in a friendly way, 'Tommy Grimes didn't have a lovely green van like yours when he was delivering the post on foot in Killaloe over 60 years ago.'

'Did you know Tommy Grimes?' he enquired, a bit surprised.

'Of course I did,' I responded, 'sure didn't he live on the Canal Bank and we lived just up from him in Aillebaun House at the bridge.'

'Well, you must be one of the Murdochs. Your sister Hilary used to ride the horses which my father had out the Ogonnelloe road,' he responded.

Quick as a flash, I said, 'Well, you must be a Quigley.'

And he was – he was Michael Quigley, son of Jack Quigley. I told Michael that I had a photograph of his father Jack with one of those horses. He said that his father, who was then 92, would love to meet me to discuss the Killaloe of the 1950s. I had lived in Killaloe for 10 years, from the age of 11 in 1949 to the age of 21 in 1959 – as a child, a teenager, and a young adult.

I had a number of meetings with Jack Quigley in 2012 at his daughter Mary's house at The Fountain, Ballina, when we mentally walked every street in Killaloe/Ballina and discussed the people who lived there 60 years ago and who now, sadly, are no longer with us. Jack's mind was as sharp as a razor and his memory was formidable. He filled gaps in my own memory. He was highly amused with the photo, taken by me in 1952 and purporting to be of him with my sister and his horse, because it was in fact a photo of his father, Michael. I had neglected to do the sums – the man in the photo would in 2012 have been about 120 years of age!

Jack Quigley was a lovely man. Like many young people in Killaloe at the time, he emigrated to the UK to find work and spent his early adult years there. He returned to Killaloe over 60 years ago, where as a conductor/driver/inspector with CIÉ (the Irish transport company) he got to know everyone in the area.

In my last meeting with Jack around Christmas 2012, he said that I should put pen to paper and record my recollections of Killaloe/Ballina in the 1950s and that he would help me fill in any gaps. Then I became ill for a number of months and, sadly, we never met again. He passed away on 17 July 2013.

Killaloe and its people have had a huge influence on my life – particularly in those formative years. Although my father had a good job as a bank official, my parents had no discretionary income due to the high cost of our education. And we lived in a rambling damp old house which would be condemned as uninhabitable by today's standards.

But we knew that we were privileged to live in such a beautiful place, full of history and full of characters. As kids we lived on boats, fishing on the Shannon and on Lough Derg. We swam at the Pier Head and at the 'Two-Mile-Gate'. We made and flew model airplanes and had an exhibition for An Tóstal in 1953 and 1954. We played hurling and football. In later years, we water skied at the Lakeside Hotel. And many of us emigrated to the UK, to Canada, and to the USA to find work. As teenagers we were fully integrated in the community. We lived in PF Ryan's cinema and we listened to the 'Top Twenty' songs on Radio Luxembourg.

As I have written in the Preface of my companion book *My Killaloe,* we knew everyone, and everyone knew us – after all, Killaloe had a population then of only 901 and Ballina had 134 inhabitants. We were of two communities and counties, divided by a bridge – with Ballina in County Tipperary and Killaloe in County Clare.

Our loyalties were often divided, but those of us who lived in Killaloe regarded Killaloe as being superior – as we then had the bigger population and, after all, didn't we also have Brian Boru, High King of Ireland, who ruled the country over 1,000 years ago from Kincora in Killaloe and who died in 1014 at the battle of Clontarf! We also had the famous Irish tenor Sean Ryan who sang 'Panis Angelicus' at every midnight Mass.

A lot has changed in Killaloe/Ballina since the 1950s. The population of Killaloe has expanded modestly to 1,292, whereas that of Ballina has exploded in recent years to 2,442. With a combined population of just 3,700, the heritage towns have facilities which would be the envy of towns with much larger populations – with a riverside park, an outdoor heated swimming pool, modern marina facilities, two children's playgrounds, speciality shops, a public library and heritage centre, a farmers' market, terrific restaurants and schools, great fishing and waterway activities, including cruises on Lough Derg and excellent facilities for sports.

And all of these facilities are provided against a background of twin towns steeped in history, with people and antiquities to prove it. Today, I cannot look at the Pier Head without seeing the canal being built there in 1799 to bypass the bridge and the rapids downstream, the paddle steamers collecting emigrants in 1852 for their long journey to the USA and Australia, the arrival of the railway at Ballina which lead to the demise of the steamers, and Peter Lacy teaching the girls and boys of Killaloe (including me in the 1950s) how to swim at the Pier Head.

In this book I have endeavoured to capture my personal recollections of living in Killaloe in the 1950s and 1960s, against this historical background, as a child, a teenager, and a young adult.

I would like to thank the following persons who have helped me in all sorts of ways in sourcing material for this book or in jogging my memory: Roy Benson (resident of Killaloe/Ballina), Gerry Collins (The Quiet Man Museum, Cong), Seamus Connolly (former resident of Killaloe), Brian Cullen (resident), Gordon Daly (senior planner, Clare County Council), Sr May Doyle (former resident), Phil and Dick Edmonds (former residents), Liam Gallagher (Central Statistics Office), Fr Paddy Gilligan (Cong), Bobby Gissane (resident), Deirdre McKeogh Griffin (resident), Ivor Hamrock (Mayo County Library), Raymond Heavey, Earle Hitchner (USA), Carmel Hopkins, Aideen Ireland (National Archives), Sean and Una Kierse (residents), John Lefroy (resident), Eoin Little (Lakeside Hotel), Aoife Lynch (boys'national school), Stephen Lynch (resident), Christy McGrath (resident), Professor Des MacHale (UCC writer on *The Quiet Man*), Sean Mac Seoin (Garda Press Office), Chris Minogue (resident), Laurence Murdoch (former resident), Tommy Nolan (resident), Rosemarie Nolan (National Rehabilitation Hospital), Charlie O'Connor (resident), Kieran O'Neill (ESB Press Office), John Phelan (resident), Homan Potterton (former director of National Library), Pat Reddan and his mother (residents), Carmel Ryan (resident) , John Stritch (resident), Dr Ed Walsh, Jimmy Whelan (resident) , Ken Whyte (Presentation College Cork), and the staff of the Killaloe Library, the Clare County Library, Trinity Library Dublin, and the National Library of Ireland.

I am grateful to the following for giving me permission to reproduce text and/or photographs which are subject to copyright protection: An Post (Peter Quinn and Anne O'Neill), Clare County Library (Maureen Comber, Executive Librarian, and Jacqui Dermody),The *Clare Champion* (John Galvin), The *Irish Examiner* (Tom Murphy),The Irish Historical Picture Company (Peter Holder), *The Irish Times* (Kevin O'Sullivan and Lynda O'Keeffe), The *Limerick Leader* (Alan English), The *Connacht Tribune* (David Hickey and Kathleen Ohlstrom), Maxwell Photography, The *Nenagh Guardian* (Pat Ryan), and individual photographers Charlie McGeever (Ballina), Bríd Ní

Luasaigh (Dublin), Sean O'Connell (Cork), Michael G. Stewart (USA) and Steve Williams (UK).

I would particularly like to thank David Givens of The Liffey Press for his very practical advice in getting my printed text and images into a published book.

The author's royalties in respect of this book (and the companion volume *My Killaloe*) will go directly to the charity The NRH Foundation (CHY6750) for the benefit of patients of the National Rehabilitation Hospital (NRH), Dun Laoghaire, County Dublin.

All views expressed in the book are mine and mine alone, as are any errors or omissions.

Henry Murdoch
Glenageary, County Dublin
May 2014

Note:

Where (CCL) appears in a photograph caption, copyright in the photo belongs to Clare County Library from the Killaloe Heritage Centre Collection and is reproduced by their kind permission.

The book is dedicated to:

My parents Greta and Archie Murdoch, who sacrificed so much in Killaloe in order that my siblings and I received an excellent education.

My late brother Bill, who died on 16 April 2008, aged 72 years, and whose ashes are scattered on his beloved Lough Derg.

Jack Quigley of Killaloe/Ballina, who died on 17th July 2013 in his 93rd year and who inspired this and the companion book *My Killaloe.*

My own family – Davida my wife, our adult children Maeve and Breffni, and their spouses and our seven grandchildren.

1

The Journey to Killaloe

'Dear Murdoch. Please report for duty as cashier/
teller at our branch in Killaloe, County Clare, on
Monday ...' – the transfer letter my father dreaded
receiving (1949).

My father, Archie Murdoch, was a bank official with the Provincial Bank of Ireland (later to become AIB – Allied Irish Bank plc). This was to be his fourth transfer in his work location in 16 years of marriage. The typical rural bank at the time had four staff members, with a strict hierarchy – a manager, who was addressed always as 'manager', a clerk and a cashier/teller who were addressed by their surname and never by their first name (or as we called it at the time, their 'Christian' name), and a porter, who was addressed by his first name. And of course all the staff were male.

The Provincial Bank had a strict policy that as an official you were not to get too close to the customer, as this might affect your judgement in your business dealings. So, while the bank encouraged officials to be active in the community, as soon as the official became popular – and particularly if he became very popular – he was moved on to another branch. No

My father Archie and mother Greta in 1930

consideration was given on how a transfer would affect his wife or their children's education or any difficulty in securing accommodation in the new location.

My father, who was born in Cahersiveen, County Kerry in 1904 and raised in Dingle, had his first posting as a clerk to Kanturk, County Cork, in 1921. He subsequently was transferred to Killarney, County Kerry, where he met my mother, Greta Lyons, a teacher, and they got married in 1933.

They were a very popular couple in Killarney, so the policy kicked in, and he was transferred to the bank branch in faraway Cavan, where my sister Hilary, my brother Bill and I were all born in our home in Farnham Street. I have no memory of Cavan as I was only a year old when, in 1939, we were on the move again, this time to Carrick-on-Shannon, County Leitrim where my brother Laurence was born.

My mother often told me that of her four children, I was the happiest. Maybe this is why in later adult life, my brother Bill used to refer to me as 'Happy Harry'. Apparently as a baby, I got great fun throwing items out of my pram, and when people would put them back, I would throw them out again and I thought that this was hilariously funny.

We were to spend the whole of World War II – or 'The Emergency' as it was called in Ireland – in Carrick-on-Shannon, County Leitrim. When the war was over in 1945, we were packing our bags again – this time to Kilkee, County Clare. As kids we really loved Kilkee. It was a brilliant place to grow up in and very different from Carrick-on-Shannon where we had lived for the previous six years.

In Kilkee with my mother Greta in 1946

However, Kilkee was harsh in the winter, being on the Atlantic, and the first port of call for westerly storms. But the summers made up for that, when Kilkee filled with holiday makers, mostly from Limerick city.

We lived in a fine terraced house called 'Lindenlea' in the West End. There were only a few houses between us and America. Further on from us were the Pollock Holes, natural swimming pools which were accessible when the tide was out, and New Found Out, which was facing St Georges Head, and was for serious swimmers, like the Bull Hayes from Limerick who used to swim from there across the bay.

My two brothers, Bill and Laurence, and I went to the boy's national school and my sister Hilary went to the girl's school in the convent. It was a good two mile walk. We used to have great fun on our way to school, trying to miss getting wet by the 'Puffing Hole' just below our house. When the tide was in and it was stormy, the sea would rush into this crevice in the rocks and a shower of water would be thrown into the air and across the footpath and the road.

Our school was a two-teacher, two-classroom school. The principal teacher was Mr Naughton who taught classes four, five and six, all in one big room, and Mr Hayes taught classes one, two and three in the other room. There must have been 50 pupils in each room. Discipline was unbelievable by today's standards. Mr Naughton went around the room swinging a key ring (with a diameter of one foot/30 centimetres) containing the keys to the doors of the school which were about 9 inches/23 centimetres long.

If you stepped out of line, he would give you a belt of the keys across your neck or the back of your head. For three years my brother Bill and I were in the same room. Bill used to take on Naughton by sitting on the outside of the benches we called 'forms' (pronounced 'furms') and nearly challenging Naughton to hit him, which he did frequently. I worked out Naughton's range and always sat in a part of the form which was out of his range. I don't think I ever got hit. Naughton made a huge impression on Bill, because in later life all I had to do to get Bill annoyed would be to mention Naughton's name. Bill would immediately grit his teeth and say 'the beast'.

· · ·

In the summer of 1981, I visited Kilkee with my wife Davida and our two children Maeve (7) and Breffni (6). I brought them to all the places where I had played as a boy. I enquired about Mr Naughton and was told that he was still alive and now in his nineties and that his Swissair flight attendant son was staying with him. Well, I had a great chat with Mr Naughton. He was quite feeble but his brain was razor sharp. He was sitting in front of an electric fire with one bar on, even though it was mid-August. He knew all about my career and my position as a Director with AnCO – the industrial training authority.

Then out of the blue, he said that he read my brother Bill's articles in *The Irish Times* every Saturday. Bill would have been Business Editor in *The Irish Times* at that time. And then he said, 'He writes very well for a fellow who took no interest in school'. Later that day, I sent Bill a postcard from Kilkee and told him what Naughton had said about him. Bill told me that when he read the postcard he gritted his teeth and growled. Well Bill was a superb writer and probably the best financial journalist of his generation. And this was recognised by Naughton.

A short time later Mr Naughton died, as did his great friend Freddie Kerr, a retired bank manager (and a colleague of my father) who was a similar age. When they were in their late eighties they went for a walk every day up the Dunlickey Road, their heads bowed into the usual stormy wind in winter. I think Mr Naughton was a great teacher, handling three classes and over 50 students. I was delighted to have had the opportunity to thank him before he passed away.

· · ·

Two doors down from our house in Kilkee was Sergeant Seevers, a garda sergeant. He had a curragh, a typical west of Ireland light open boat, similar to a canoe, covered in canvas which was freshly tarred every year to keep it waterproof. Sergeant Seevers often brought me out fishing in the bay in the summer. We had no sense of fear and no life jackets.

Typical curragh in 1948 with George's Head and Burn's Cove in background

We were aware from our time in Carrick-on-Shannon that there was a war going on in Europe and that the main players were Germany and Britain. The sentiment in Kilkee definitely was anti-British, which was not surprising, given our history with British occupation for 700 years. The only discernible effect on us from the war was the system of food rationing which was aimed at ensuring that everyone got a fair share of the scarce resources.

Rationing covered such items as bread, tea, clothing, footwear, sweets, chocolate, tobacco, flour, soap and petrol. Elec-

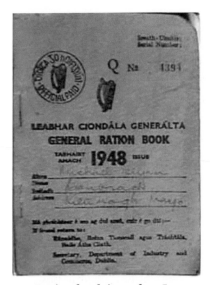

Ration book issued to Jane Harvey, an Irish teacher in Colaiste Mhuire in Ennis in 1948

tricity was available for only a few hours every day. Trains were run on turf (peat), timber and straw. Private cars were rarely used and were replaced by bicycles, by pony and traps, and by horse and carts. Everyone became very thrifty. 'Make do and mend' was the policy for clothes. 'Hand-me-downs' became the order of the day – so I inherited Bill's clothes and Laurence inherited mine. It was hard on the youngest person in large families.

The only persons allowed to use their cars were the priest, the doctor and the taxi or hackney car owner, and their supplies of petrol were severely rationed. My father's car was placed on blocks for the duration of the war and beyond.

Because of the shortage of electricity, we toasted bread on forks with long handles at the fire in the sitting room, and we kept the teapot warm on a stand at the side of the fire. Both my parents smoked at that time, smoking each cigarette to the last millimetre by the use of a needle to support the cigarette. I of-

Dad's car in 1939 with Hilary, Bill and our mother Greta

ten wondered how they did not burn their lips. And paper was in short supply and it was rough, which made its use as toilet paper less desirable but still necessary!

But despite the shortages and the rationing, we always had enough to eat. I remember my mother telling me that she went into her regular shop in O'Curry Street in Kilkee in 1946 and asked for a pound of butter, explaining to the new shop assistant that she has left her food coupons at home but would bring them in next day. The shop assistant retorted in a rather quaint way, 'I'm not believing you'. To which my mother, quick as a flash, responded as she turned on her heels, 'Well, I'll be leaving you'.

Even though the war ended in August 1945 the shortages continued, as did the rationing until 1948 when it became possible again for us kids to buy new tyres for our bikes.

• • •

Our mother Greta was small in stature but a formidable woman in many ways. She was born in 1902 in Ballyhaunis, County Mayo, the youngest of 15 children. Her mother died when she was 13 and so she moved to the home of her elder brother John, who was a dispensary doctor in Kilkelly in County Mayo. He and his very kind wife Mae brought her up and sent her to university. She graduated from UCD with an honours B Comm degree and an H Dip in Education. There were not many female graduates at that time. She was two years older than my father and was very sensitive about it, as she always told us that she was born in 1906.

It was only in 1966 when I ran in the Seanad Éireann elections in

My mother Greta graduating in 1922

the NUI constituency that I got access to the graduate electoral register to learn that she graduated in 1922, which would have made her 16 years of age if her 1906 birthdate was correct!

She was a very intelligent woman, with a fine mathematical brain. When I started to learn calculus for the first time in 1954 as part of the Leaving Certificate honours maths syllabus, she took up my books and learned calculus with me. She often was able to explain concepts which I was unable to understand. I would say that she was a very good teacher, but she had to give up her vocational teacher post when she married my father in 1933. That was the rule at that time, right up to 1973, and was known as the 'marriage bar'. She used to boast that her salary at the time of their marriage was 50 per cent higher than his. We used to joke that she was a 'baby snatcher' in marrying a younger man, but that she must have been in love to give up such a good job!

My parents were very happy in Kilkee. His work in the bank would not have been too taxing. My father did a lot of trout fishing and shooting, mostly snipe and the occasional duck. My parent's social life was playing bridge. The bridge players in Kilkee visited each other's houses to play and when it came to our house, we would be down the stairs first thing next morning to see if there were any ham sandwiches left. Though the bread was by then hard, the sandwiches tasted delicious, as did the drop of Redbreast whiskey in the bottom of the yet unwashed glasses.

A constant bridge player was the local parish priest Canon Grace. He was so absorbed in bridge that my mother said he would be playing an imaginary game while saying Mass. She instanced one occasion, in the Litany of the saints which followed the blessing of the sacrament, in which various saints would be mentioned by the priest, and the congregation would respond by saying 'pray for us', that Canon Grace having correctly said:

'Queen of Heaven,' and everyone responded, 'Pray for us,' followed by:

'Queen of Angels' – 'pray for us.'

'Queen of Hearts' – 'pray for us.'
And then inadvertently said:
'Queen of clubs' – 'pray for us.'
'Queen of spades' – 'pray for us,' before he realised his mistake.

My mother told me this, so it must be true. Canon Grace died in February 1969, aged 90. At his funeral Mass, it was mentioned that he had served as a priest during the reign of seven Popes.

. . .

As kids we were proud of the fact that our house had the same name as the Dorset song 'Linden Lea' by William Barnes (1801–1886), the final lines of which were, 'To where for me, the apple tree; Do lean down low in Linden Lea'. My mother had the sheet music and would regularly play it on our piano. All of the bedrooms in 'Lindenlea' were at the back of the house on the second floor. The front room at that level, with magnificent views of the sea through the French windows, was the drawing room. One night, we were all awoken by the blast of a shotgun and shouting. We ran out of our bedrooms into the corridor to see our dad standing in the doorway

Sketch of 'Lindenlea' by Jeremy Williams, architect, which appeared in Homan Potterton's 2002 book Rathcormick' (© New Island Books). Homan was Director of the National Gallery of Ireland and a regular visitor to 'Lindenlea' as a boy. His father had bought 'Lindenlea' as a holiday home after we left Kilkee.

of the drawing room, with his shotgun. He had been woken by a burglar, had grabbed his shotgun which he kept in the bedroom, and had run out into the hall, and challenged the burglar. The burglar ran into the drawing room, and my dad fired a blast of the shotgun over the burglar's head, as the burglar crashed through the French windows on to the lawn below.

Sergeant Seevers apprehended the burglar next day. He was a young local man who had just been released from prison and had a history of previous burglaries. I'd say he got some shock when he saw my father with the shotgun. The incident was the talk of the town and school. We were so proud of our dad. He was as least as good as John Wayne or the other stars of the western movies at that time.

The Glynn family lived a few houses away from us and their children were our best pals. They had three boys – Robert, John and Willy – all about the same ages as us Murdochs. Their uncle had a flour factory in Kilrush, about eight miles (12.8 kilometres) inland, and their father worked there, so the Glynn boys went to school in Kilrush. When I think of it now, the six of us boys – three Glynns and three Murdochs – were like a gang. We went around like a pack and got up to all kinds of mischief. And there was a certain degree of rivalry between us.

Next door to us lived the Haughs who had a glass house. One day the six of us were sitting on the wall between our house and the Haughs when Willy Glynn threw a stone at the Haugh's glass house breaking a pane. He dared my older brother Bill to do the same. Bill was not going to let the Murdoch side down and threw a stone and broke another pane. The same thing happened with John Glynn and me, and then with Robert Glynn and Laurence, until six panes of glass were broken. I now know that delicate discussions took place between our fathers and Sergeant Seevers, and there was payment of compensation to the Haughs, which prevented us from facing the law. We got a lecture from Sergeant Seevers. And our pocket money was stopped for months – which was very painful and certainly taught us a lesson.

Robert and I were great pals. He was a year younger than me. Neither of us could swim at this stage, so on a particular very sunny day in 1946 when I was 8 years old, the Pollock Holes were out of consideration as the tide was in and the long beautiful beach of Kilkee was too far away. So we decided to go for a dip in the pools in the rocks just below our house. It was very private and could not be seen from the road. Robert said to me, 'Let's go for a swim in the raw'. 'Yea,' said I, 'let's'. So we dropped our swimming togs, and that was when Robert said to me: 'Your wee wee is different from mine'. And it was. 'Well, mine is the same as my brothers,' I said proudly. 'And mine is the same as my brothers,' he retorted, I thought a bit defensively.

When I got home after our swim, I went to the 'fountain of knowledge', my older brother Bill, who as far as I was concerned, knew everything. After all he was 10, a whole two years older than me. He had an immediate answer. 'Do you remember when we lived in Carrick-on-Shannon, the toilet seat would never stay upright and was always falling down. Well, the seat used to crash down and hit our wee wees and that is why our wee wees are different from the Glynns.' To me this seemed a plausible explanation, although I had no recollection of it happening. I must have had some doubts, because a few days later I told my mother what Bill had told me. She burst out laughing and told me that we had all been circumcised at birth for hygiene reasons and that was why we were different from the Glynns.

My mother told Mrs Glynn what Bill had said and everyone had a great laugh and the atmosphere was so improved that the Haugh's glass house incident was forgotten and our pocket money was restored. And Robert and I were glad to find that we were normal after all. And my brother Bill's mischievous side was revealed.

· · ·

About 12 years later in 1958 when I was in University College Cork studying engineering, I had a great friend Kevin O'Brien from Cobh. He was very clever, so much so that after a lecture on nuclear physics, I would emerge with about six pages of notes which I did not understand. He would have about two pages, every bit of which he understood and which he would explain to me. I was not surprised that after graduating he went on to Cal Tech in California, one of the foremost technical universities in the world, and got a Master's degree at the top of the class.

Kevin O'Brien BE in 2009 at the Golden Jubilee of our UCC graduation in 1959

What relevance has that to Kilkee and my story? Well, one day when we were down in the Western Star public house on the Western Road in Cork, downing pints of Guinness, I told Kevin the story about Robert Glynn and myself. Kevin turned to me and said jocosely, 'Henry, you're a grand fellow. The only thing that is wrong with you is that when you were circumcised, they threw away the wrong piece.' You can imagine the raucous laughter which this generated.

Now, it might not have been Kev that said it, but it certainly was one of that drinking group and certainly would tie in with Kev's impish nature and our tendency as students to 'slag' each other. Whoever said it, the remark quickly spread across the whole university with its 1,300 student population at the time. Fellow students would come up to me and say mischievously, 'Sorry for your troubles,' just like they would at a funeral. There was a certain notoriety in it. I did not mind. Kev was and is a great character.

⋅   ⋅   ⋅

We lost touch with the Glynns when we moved to Killaloe in 1949. I never met my friend Robert Glynn again; he died at the age of 17 from leukaemia. Willy Glynn emigrated to the USA and joined the US Marines and fought in the Vietnam war. He is now retired and living back in Kilkee.

Fr John Glynn in 2013

I met up with John Glynn in 1955 at University College Cork where he studied engineering with me. He subsequently left the university early, became a primary school teacher in Papau New Guinea (PNG), was ordained as a priest there in 1980, had a dispute with his bishop in 1997 who refused to allow him to celebrate Mass as 'you are not one of us', even though he had become a citizen of PNG.

In 2000, on the invitation of Bishop Willie Walsh of the Diocese of Killaloe (since retired), Fr John assisted the bishop in relation to the parishes of Kilonena and Toomyvara. Fr John Glynn has since had all his faculties restored by the now retired Archbishop of Port Moresby in PNG, although he still has problems with the present Archbishop.

. . .

My parents were devastated when the transfer letter from the bank arrived in 1949. 'Dear Murdoch. Please report for duty as cashier/teller at our branch in Killaloe, County Clare, on Monday ...' which was in two weeks' time. The letter came out of the blue with no prior discussion or warning. The transfer was to a job at the same grade, so there would be no increase in salary. In all the previous locations we had lived, my parents had rented a house. Kilkee was different. They were putting down roots, so for the first time they had bought the house 'Lindenlea'. It was the first house they owned in their 16 years of marriage. But bank employment at that time was a bit like employment with the gardaí or the army – if you got an order to report for duty in another location in the State, you obeyed the order.

There was nearly a mutiny among us kids. We could not understand how anyone in their right mind could leave the lovely Atlantic to go inland. We believed that all the holiday makers from Limerick who came every year to Kilkee would give their right arm to live in Kilkee. But the bank had to be obeyed. So, in 1949 our father put 'Lindenlea' up for sale and, with sadness, we saw him leave for the Lakeside Hotel in Killaloe, where he would spend the next four months seeking accommodation for us and sorting out schools.

We were not to know then what a brilliant place Killaloe was going to be, how we would quickly be integrated in a new community and make new friends, and how we would come to love our new home, and how it would have such an influence on our young lives.

My brothers Bill and Laurence at Benson's caravan in Kilkee in 1953

We returned for a short holiday to Kilkee in the summer of 1953 when I was 15. We stayed in Mr Benson's caravan which was parked close to the beach. Howard Benson was the owner of the Benson Box Company in Killaloe and had become a great friend of my dad.

My sister Hilary, who was then 19 years of age, was very anxious to go to a dance in the Hydro Hotel. My father agreed provided we all accompanied her. So we all went to the dance. She was very embarrassed as we all gawked at her on the floor with her latest beau.

2

KILLALOE – OUR RETURN TO THE SHANNON RIVER

'Come back from the fire. You will get ABC on your legs' – My mother warning us as we tried to keep warm (1949)

When we arrived in Killaloe in 1949, we moved into a large dilapidated old house at the Killaloe end of the magnificent and historical 13-arch bridge which separates Killaloe in County Clare from its sister town, Ballina, in County Tipperary. It had the grandiose name of Aillebaun House (pronounced 'aisle bawn' rhyming with 'lawn') and meaning 'white cliff' because of the rise of the land from the bridge to the Catholic church at the top of the town on 'The Green'. The house had once been Grace's Hotel, when Killaloe had six hotels during its heyday as a salmon and trout fishery, before the Ardnacrusha Hydro Electric scheme in 1929. That scheme, which was a German engineering triumph of the fledging Irish Free State following independence from Britain in 1922, was to have a major negative impact on Killaloe and its environs.

My father rented the house from Maureen Scanlon, who owned Crotty's bar on Bridge Street and Crotty's general gro-

*Maureen Scanlan at the Killaloe Horse Show in the 1950s, with
Canon Molloy, Dr Sheehy (Limerick), and Fr O'Dwyer (CCL)*

cery store behind the house on Main Street. Crotty's bar was
until recently the Wooden Spoon cafe and Crotty's store was
An Siopa Beag. Our rent was the princely sum of £50 (€64)
per annum.

Half of Aillebaun House was in a derelict state. We lived
in the other part, which was nearly as bad, with dampness
throughout, except in the kitchen which had a range. It was
fired by turf, which was plentiful, and its back boiler gave
us hot water. We lived mostly in that kitchen because it was
warm. And we kids (Bill, Laurence and myself – our sister Hilary was at boarding school in Dublin) had a bath every Saturday night when the range would be especially fired up. But it
was one bath water for the three of us, strictly in age order, So
Bill got the cleanest water, I got the next, and poor Laurence
got the worst.

We had a large sitting room but it was cold and damp. We
would huddle up to the fire for warmth and developed marks
on our legs, which we called 'ABC', but which is now known
as 'fireside tartan'. The four bedrooms were bitterly cold and
damp in winter, with condensation dripping down the walls at
night. Reading a book in bed at night required a frequent inter-

Aillebaun House at the bridge in Killaloe

change of hands from outside to inside the blankets to prevent freezing fingers. And we always had a hot water bottle going to bed, or as I used to say, before I could pronounce it properly, a 'wat hauter bottle'.

The house had a large garden in the front, leading to a railing from which there were panoramic views of the bridge, the Shannon, the Canal, the lockkeepers house (later to be the Killaloe Heritage Centre and Library), Ballina and its old railway station in front, and the Lakeside Hotel to the left. Our neighbours below us, on the Canal Bank, were Peter Lacy, painter/ decorator and swimming instructor, and further down, Tommy Grimes, the local postman. On our right was a vacant site which was previously occupied by the Shannon View Hotel and is now the outdoor area of the Anchor Bar.

The Shannon River and Lough Derg would dominate

Shannon View Hotel before it was demolished (CCL)

17

our lives for the next ten years – in my case, from age 11 to 21. The Shannon River is 360 kilometres (224 miles) long and is the longest river in Ireland and the UK. It rises in a small pool, the Shannon Pot, on the slopes of the Cuileagh Mountains in County Cavan. On its way south, it feeds the large lakes of Lough Allen, Lough Ree and Lough Derg. It passes through towns such as Carrick-on-Shannon, Athlone, Portumna, Killaloe and Limerick, at which point it turns west to empty into the Atlantic Ocean through the 113 kilometres (70 miles) long Shannon Estuary.

St George's Terrace, Carrick-on-Shannon 1940s. Our house was on the left (last one with steps) and the Provincial Bank was on the right

Our love affair with the Shannon started in Carrick-on-Shannon where we spent the six years of the Second World War, 1939 to 1945. We initially lived in a house on the main street where my brother Laurence was born in 1940. We then moved to a house on St George's Terrace, next to Dr Doorley, who was the local dispensary doctor, and just across the road from the Provincial Bank of Ireland. My dad had all of 50 feet (15 metres) to walk to get to work. These two houses later were to become the headquarters of the *Leitrim Observer*.

We were great friends of the children of three families – the Lilleys, who had a newspaper and bookshop at the monument at the end of our street and who were a lot older than us, but they had canoes; the Floods, who owned the general drapers next to the Lilleys and were all about our ages; and the Lowes, who had a grocery and hardware store down the street where my brother Laurence was born. The Flood's shop had a large sign on it 'One Price Warehouse' and proudly proclaimed 'tailors on the premises'.

We had great fun with them all and great fights with the Floods and the Lowes. We built a go-kart using all the resources we could find, but then when we couldn't get agreement on who would get the first 'go'. We Murdochs demanded back the wheels, which we had supplied, and the go-kart never had its maiden voyage.

Our only awareness of the World War was the fact that our dad would go out at night in his Local Security Force uniform and spend the evening looking up into the sky for German war planes. What they would do if they saw one, I don't know. My dad's bronze medal for his service during that time always reminds me of the TV series *Dad's Army*. The medal, which he gave to me before he died in 1996, is interesting. One side has a walking warrior, representing Ireland, holding a sword downwards and with an Irish wolfhound on a leash. Around the top edge is an inscription *Ré na Práinne*, meaning Emergency Period, followed by the designer's name in the smallest of lettering – Lawrence Campbell RHA. The reverse has a laurel spray between the dates 1939 and 1946 and the title of the organisation involved – in my dad's case, *Na Caomnóirí Áitula*, meaning Local Security Force.

My First Communion, on the steps of our house in Carrick-on-Shannon (1945).

My dad's Local Security Force medal

In the winters I used to suffer badly from chilblains. It must have had something to do with cold houses and the lack of fruit in our diet. The chilblains used to particularly attack my ears, so at the Marist Brothers' school which I attended, I was often called 'frosty ears'.

. . .

My initial love of the water sports and 'messing about on the river' was nurtured in Carrick-on-Shannon. Although my parents did not approve, I spent many an hour in one of the Lilley's canoes on the River Shannon. Some 27 years later in July 1972, I returned to Carrick-on-Shannon on my honeymoon with my bride Davida Franklin on my 19 foot (5.6 metres) mini-sailing cruiser *Topaz*, which we launched in Athlone and sailed all the way to Carrick-on-Shannon and onwards to Lough Key. We joined the Shannon Boat Rally.

Our honeymoon boat Topaz in 1972

No sooner had we left Athlone, heading north in Lough Ree, but my Johnson outboard engine broke down. We got a tow to our first nightfall in Lecarrow from Eric Timon, who I knew from water skiing in Howth, and he miraculously took my engine apart and fixed it. Over the next eight days, we sailed to Clondra and attended at the official opening of the canal, we sailed to Carrick-on-Shannon, to the Kilglass River, and then to beautiful Lough Key for two days, then to Leitrim village where we moored under a bridge to escape the rain, and then back to Carrick-on-Shannon for the Rally dinner in the Bush Hotel, then run by Tom Maher.

A few weeks later, I took up an appointment as the first Hospitals' Programme Manager of the newly created North Western Health Board. The Board had taken responsibility for the health services of the three counties of Leitrim, Sligo and Donegal from the Local Authorities. I had responsibility for sixteen institutions – acute hospitals, psychiatric hospitals, welfare homes (then called county homes) and the ambulance service. Naturally, my appointment was positively greeted by the local newspaper, the *Leitrim Observer*, now occupying my previous home in Carrick-on-Shannon, and by the local councillors who were members of the main Health Board and of the local Health Advisory Committee for County Leitrim.

The headquarters of the new Health Board was in Manorhamilton in County Leitrim, completely against the odds. The County Sligo representatives wanted it in Sligo town and the County Donegal representatives wanted it in Donegal town. The vote was by proportional representation. In the first vote, Donegal came first, followed by Sligo, and Manorhamilton a poor third. In the second count, Sligo voted for Manorhamilton to thwart the ambitions of Donegal.

At my first meeting of the local Health Advisory Committee in Carrick-on-Shannon in 1972, I had a rude awakening to local politics. A councillor objected to the fact that I had not been at the previous meeting. The Chairman explained that I had not taken up my appointment until after that meeting and could not have been at the previous one. 'That is not good enough an excuse,' said the councillor. I could see that this was a different world from that of leasing aircraft for Aer Lingus, which was my previous job!

Another eye-opener to me was the openness of the meetings, which were all reported in the local media. In a critical response from me in answer to a question at the Health Board on my assessment of the dental services in County Leitrim, the local paper had a headline: 'Programme Manager says Leitrim men have no teeth.' Enough said!

· · ·

Our link with the Lilleys and the Floods of Carrick-on-Shannon was re-established many years later. Margo Flood (now Keogh) is a member of a book club in Dublin with my wife Davida. Ireland is a small place! And in 1975 our twin children Breffni and Joe were born prematurely in the Rotunda Hospital in Dublin. They were delivered by Dr Edwin Lilley, then the Master of the hospital, whose canoe I often shared as a child in Carrick-on-Shannon some 30 years before. The twins were only three and a half pounds (1.6 kilogrammes) each and were being kept in hospital until they had put on more weight. Unfortunately, after four weeks, Joe died in the hospital in an unexplained 'cot death', but thankfully Breffni survived. We had a seat installed in the grounds of Trinity College Dublin 'in memory of Joseph Henry Murdoch'.

It is about half-way down beside the rugby pitch, looking out over the running track and cricket ground. I sometimes tell people who enquire about our family, that we have a son with a 'seat' in Trinity. This usually sparks off a question, 'Is he in charge of a faculty?' Well, not exactly!

Our son Joe's seat in Trinity College in 2014

So we made it to Killaloe on the Shannon in 1949 from Carrick-on-Shannon, but via Kilkee. Our dad had all of 100 yards (91 metres) to walk to work to the Provincial Bank (now AIB) on Royal Parade. My brother Laurence and I had a short walk to the national school on New Street, where I would join sixth class and Laurence would be in third class. Hilary was in boarding school in Dublin, and Bill was to commence his secondary education with the Jesuits at Crescent College Limerick, some 12 miles away.

3

Jesuit Character Building and Sex Education

*'A Jesuit education will give you a character which
will maintain you for life' – Fr McLaughlin SJ,
Crescent College, Limerick (1949)*

My brother Laurence and I attended the Killaloe boys' national school in 1949. It was then located on New Street and is now a parochial hall. There were two rooms in the school, classes 1 to 3 under Mrs Nora Lynch, and classes 4 to 6 under Mr Michael Lynch (no relation). I was in sixth class in 1949/50 and there were seven pupils in my class – Peter Columby. Michael Gissane, Liam Brown, Tony Horan, Kevin Scanlan, Sean O'Sullivan and myself. Laurence spent four years in the school from third to sixth class from 1949 to 1953. There were fourteen pupils in his fourth year class including Michael Gissane's brother Bobby.

The *Nenagh Guardian* on 12 December 1953 recorded the following:

PRIMARY CERTIFICATES: Congratulations to Mr M J Lynch, Principal, Principal, Killaloe Boys' National School; his assistant Mrs Nora Lynch, and to Masters Pat Carroll, Birdhill; Seamus Connor, St Lua Street; Michael Grimes, Canal Bank; Larry Murdoch, Aillebaun House; and Michael Winkle, Chapel Street, who recently passed their Primary Certificate test.

Pupils of Killaloe boys' national school in 1950/51. Notice, some of the boys have no shoes. My brother Laurence is at far right of second row from front. Back row: Eddie Grimes, Michael McEnerney, Michael Grimes, Bobby Gissane, Michael Winkle, Lua McLaughlan, Tommy Geraghty, Tommy Torpey. Second row: Kevin McDonagh, Billy Ahern, Val Morgan, Jimmy Keogh, Michael McDonagh, Kevin Scanlan, Peter Columby, James Minogue. Third row: Tony Grimes, Gort Burns, Pat Rafferty, Sonny Riordan, Sean Sullivan, Jim Columby, Eric Lynch, Mick Monaghan, Laurence Murdoch. Front row: James O'Connor, Tom Reddan, Anthony Ahern, Tom Addley, Michael Darcy, Michael Gissane, John Keneally, Denis Gissane (CCL)

The school, which had opened in 1902, was very basic. I don't know how the teachers managed three classes at the same time, but they did. In our classroom, which was 1,210 square feet (112 square metres) in area, there was a fireplace at the end of the room. While it might have heated the back of the teacher, when he was seated, it certainly did not heat the room and us 35 pupils. It is no wonder that when winter came, we all seemed to stagger from 'cold' to 'cold'.

The school day began with the roll call, when Mr Lynch would write with chalk on a blackboard, the number in each class, and would tot them up, and put in the total, which on average was about 35 for our three classes. Sometimes we pupils were asked to do the tot. It was a completely different regime from that in the Kilkee national school. I remember pupils being slapped with a cane in Killaloe (including myself), but for misbehaviour or for not doing their homework, but never for inability to answer a question correctly. Mr Naughton in Kilkee did not differentiate between misbehaviour and inability – you got belted for both.

Michael Lynch in Killaloe had a different approach. He was appointed principal of the school in 1917 and retired in 1959 after 42 years as principal. He was a native of Killaloe and lived in a house beside the school. Michael died in 1976 at the age of 80 in England where he then lived with his son.

Nora Rice (later Lynch), the other teacher, was the first female in 1929 to be appointed as a teacher in the school. Her son Eric was a fellow-pupil of my brother Laurence and went on to be a teacher himself. Nora had a very good reputation as a teacher and was very active in the community, as choir mistress in St Flannan's Catholic church and in promoting the Irish language as President of Connradh na Gaeilge. She was a good friend to my mother and visited her in Cork in 1954

Teacher Michael Lynch with our pal Gussie Henchy to his lower right (CCL)

when she was in hospital having been knocked down by a car.

Like Michael Lynch, Nora was a native of Killaloe. When Michael retired in 1959, Nora took over the teaching of the

*Kathleen and Sean Kierse, national
school teachers, in the 1970s
(Reproduced courtesy of Sean Kierse)*

middle-ranking pupils. She was married to Christopher Lynch. She died on 30 March 1981 aged 74, and is buried with her husband, who died ten months later on 30 January 1982, in Killaloe cemetery.

When Michael Lynch retired in 1959 he was replaced by Sean Kierse who was appointed principal. A native of Corofin, Sean had taught in Athlone before his appointment to Killaloe. Sean's wife Kathleen was also a teacher in the school from 1959 until her retirement in 1981. She died on 5 April 2009 aged 83.

Apart from teaching, Sean's two great interests have been local history and the GAA. He has written a number of books on Killaloe, dealing with priests and religious, education, antiquities, the Famine years, an anthology, the GAA, land and people, and portraits. In 1977 he won the 'Listowel Writers' Week' award for his paper on the Great Famine in the parish of Killaloe. He retired from teaching in 1987.

*Crescent College and
Church, Limerick, 1950s*

A new boys' national school was built at the top of Convent Hill and opened in 1965, and an extension added in 1983. Although the new school is now 48 years old, the facilities are excellent.

At Crescent College in Limerick in 1949, Fr Gerard McLaughlin SJ said to my mother, 'A Jesuit education will give you a character which will maintain you for life'. He believed he was interviewing my mother as to whether the Jesuits were going to accept as secondary pupils my older brother Bill (age 13) that year and myself a year later when I would be 12. Bill had completed sixth class in the national school in Kilkee, and I had just entered sixth class in the national school in Killaloe. But my mother believed that she was interviewing McLoughlin to determine whether she would expose her precious charges to a Jesuit education. She was familiar with the Jesuits because she had a nephew who was one – Fr Jim Tarpey SJ, her sister Cissie's son, who used to visit us regularly in Killaloe.

My cousin Fr Jim Tarpey SJ (1952)

Fr McLaughlin was the Prefect of Studies of Crescent College, the college with famous pupils from that time, such as actor Richard Harris of *Camelot* fame, media personality Sir Terry Wogan, and politician Des O'Malley, co-founder of the Progressive Democrats political party. Of course, the Jesuits, as princes of the Church, believed, with a certain degree of credence, that the education they bestowed on their pupils was way ahead of the posse.

Fr Gerard McLaughlin SJ, Prefect of Studies (1952)

There was a three-teacher private secondary school in Killaloe, called St Senan's, located then on the Creeveroe Road. It was established in 1938 (the year I was born) by three brothers, Martin, Edward and Joseph Edmonds, who were natives of Castleconnell, County Limerick. The Edmonds were known as strict disciplinarians and some say in Killaloe that they controlled their children with the use of a whistle, like Captain Von Trapp in the film *The Sound of Music*. When the whistle sounded the children had to return home instantly, and when let out to play they rushed out like greyhounds out of a trap.

Edward Edmonds, or 'Eddie' as he was known, had been a Franciscan novitiate before going into teaching. He died suddenly from a brain tumour at the young age of 45 in 1959 leaving his wife Maura and five children, one of whom, Paddy, worked as a radio officer, the initial career of my brother Bill. Maura and the other children emigrated to the United States to Maura's auntie Sadie. One of the children, 'Phil', who now lives in Providence, Rhode Island, is a regular visitor back to his native Killaloe and has written a personal account of his last visit in 2008 – *Reconnecting with the Soul of Ireland* (2009).

St Senan's did excellent work, but it was essentially a two-storey house, called 'Rose Cottage', and in 1949 had no laboratories or other facilities, so that the study of technical subjects such as chemistry and physics was not possible. My mother believed that the future was in technology, so there was no option but for us to go elsewhere. St Senan's school was eventually amalgamated with St Anne's girls' secondary school in Killaloe in September 1968, and Martin Edmonds was appointed vice-principal.

Of course, my mother believed that Bill and I were brilliant. She did not want us to spend the usual six years doing the Leaving Certificate. Five years would be enough. So she wanted us to start our secondary education in second year – we were good enough to skip first year. Both Bill and I had had only the free public national school education, not the private, fee-paying primary school of the Jesuits at the Crescent. To admit us to the second year would be tantamount to an admission that the national school system was better than the Crescent's own primary school.

'Are you saying, Mrs Murdoch, that the national schools at Kilkee and at Killaloe are better than our junior school here at the Crescent?' asked Fr McLaughlan.

'No, I am not saying that. I am saying that my boys are better than average and should have no difficulty in skipping first year. They don't need six years to do their Leaving Cert,' she responded with conviction.

Fr McLaughlin asked how good was our English. My mother said, 'Excellent'.

'OK Bill,' said Fr McLaughlin, 'what is the plural of house?' Bill replied instantly 'houses'.

'What is the plural of mouse?' asked Fr McLaughlin.

I knew we were in trouble when Bill answered 'mouses'. Of course Bill knew it was 'mice', but this was Bill at his mischievous best. In later life, he always denied this, but I was there, and it reminded me of his bizarre explanation in Kilkee for the fact that our genitalia were different from those of the Glynn boys.

I cannot remember what happened next, but my mother somehow convinced Fr McLaughlin that Bill could start in class 2A2, the lower end of the second year, and I would follow behind him a year later, in 1950. My mother was triumphant. But her best card was yet to come. As we were leaving, Fr McLaughlin said to my mother, 'Mrs Murdoch – when your sons leave this college with a Jesuit education, they may not have passed their exams, but they will leave with a character formed which will sustain them throughout their adult life.'

'Fr McLaughlin,' responded my mother, 'you just get them to pass their exams and you can leave the character building to me!'

We all went to Crescent College, Bill and myself initially and then Laurence. Bill started in 2A2 class in 1949 and I followed him a year later. My mother was right. The national schools in Kilkee and Killaloe were very good. I came first in the 2A2 class exams in 1951, beating all the students who already had done the first year. I was promoted to 3A1 class, the upper tier, the following year and had no difficulty after that.

·   ·   ·

Of course, it was inevitable that I would get the call. All fourth year students in Crescent got the call. A boy from the sixth year would knock on the classroom door, and say, 'Excuse me, Sir, but Fr Stevenson wants to see Leonard O'Brien in his room.' Fr Stevenson SJ was the imparter of sex education. The Jesuits always regarded themselves as way ahead in all matters and why not in sex education as well, even though this was in the conservative 1950s.

Of course, when my turn came in 1952, the usual happened. The teacher said, 'Alright, Henry, away with you.' I rose to a classroom titter, blushed, and made my way to Fr Stevenson's room. He had a set pattern which had always worked in the past. Firstly, he offered you a cigarette, which of course you declined. He would then say, 'You know what we are here to talk about?' to which you would say, 'Yes, Father', and then before you could say anything more he would interject 'girls and babies'. I suppose this was to whet your appetite.

I should clarify that at 14, I very small for my age and looked about 11. But I reckon I knew as much about conception and birth as any teenager could, living as I was in Killaloe, then a small sleepy agricultural village. I had seen calves being born and randy dogs copulating. As kids we frequently threw cold water on top of these dogs to lessen their ardour. I also had an older brother who of course knew everything! I would check his knowledge by pleading total innocence to Fr Stevenson.

This innocence was confirmed when Fr Stevenson asked me, 'Do you know how babies are made and born' and I replied, 'No, Father'. He then asked me to say the 'Hail Mary' prayer.

Dutifully, I said, 'Hail Mary, full of grace, the Lord is with thee, blessed art though among women, and blessed is the fruit of thy womb, Jesus.'

He stopped me suddenly at this point and asked me to repeat the last phrase, 'and blessed is the fruit of thy womb, Jesus'.

He then asked, 'Now, Henry, do you know what a womb is?'

In line with my decided strategy, I replied 'No, Father.'

At that point I could see that Fr Stevenson had come to the conclusion that this unusual childhood innocence should not be blemished by the facts of life. I sensed that he could see a 'halo' over my head and the prospect of a future vocation to the priesthood, preferably to the Jesuits, which he did not want to damage. 'Fine, Henry,' he said, 'and now we will say a prayer for the missions in Africa.'

On my return to the classroom, there again was the classroom titter, my blushes, and then at the break, in response to questioning from my classmates as to what Fr Stevenson had told me, I said with bravado, 'Fr Stevenson told me everything!'

·   ·   ·

Corporal punishment was the norm in boys' schools 50 years ago. Crescent College had a sophisticated approach to such punishment. The Jesuits recognised that to curb excesses, there was a need to divorce the judge from the executioner. Consequently, they had a strict policy that a teacher could not hit a pupil in class. Instead, the pupil was 'sent out' after the class to be punished physically by a single operator, the Prefect of Studies, Fr McLaughlin.

Each teacher had what looked like a cheque book. A chit would be filled out by the teacher with the pupil's name, class, date, description of offence, number of slaps, and would be signed by the teacher, who would also fill out a counterfoil with similar information. The minimum punishment was two slaps on the hand with a leather strap and the maximum was six. And despite the fact that we had in the school such resourceful pupils as Terry Wogan, there was no way around the system, as the chits were regularly checked against the counterfoils to ensure that they were encashed. The fine for failure to 'cash' a chit was double the number of slaps.

Encashment took place at the break times at 11.00 am and 3.00 pm in Fr McLaughlin's office. You joined the queue and when your turn came, Fr McLaughlin administered the punishment in an efficient and non-emotional manner. We all became quite efficient ourselves. The key was to withdraw your hand sufficiently at the last second so that the main impact was on your fingers and not on the palm of your hand. But Fr McLaughlin was no mean operator himself. He had an uncanny knack of being able to detect the slightest movement of your hand, and would adjust the swing of the leather in mid-air and achieve a bulls-eye, which of course was the palm of the hand.

Some teachers had a reputation of 'sending out' someone from every class. Others, never. One particular teacher, Fr fFrench, never sent out anyone. However, having given me repeated warnings not to be talking in class, he eventually flipped and 'sent me out'. When I saw the chit, I laughed. It was for an unheard of one slap. Pupils in the queue also laughed when they saw it. When I got to Fr McLaughlin with a broad grin on my face and gave him the chit, he said, 'So that's what the commotion was all about.'

As he raised the leather, I did my usual last-second hand movement to minimise the impact of the slap. Whether I had lost my touch or whether Fr McLaughlin's mid-air correction failed, I do not know. But I do know that when the leather strap hit the inside of my wrist it wiped the cheeky 'one slap' grin off my face! When I got home that evening, my wrist was all swollen and I could not write or hold a knife in it. When my mother enquired what had happened, I just said that I had fallen in the school yard while playing football and had landed on my wrist. And she believed me.

· · ·

Probably because of her background as a teacher, my mother took a special interest in our education and always wanted to see our homework. Bill used to go to extraordinary lengths to deceive her. He had a particular aversion to Latin and my mother therefore insisted on hearing his translation of his Latin text, Cicero or Virgil or the like. She would be holding the English text while Bill would be reading the Latin text and then translating it into English. What my mother did not know is that Bill would have spent hours beforehand writing above the Latin text the English translation in the tiniest writing in pencil. My mother's eyesight wasn't great – and Bill was a great actor.

'Virgil was … going … no, walking … up the …hill … no, mountain,' Bill hesitantly translated, putting in pauses and mistakes and correcting himself, when in fact he had the correct text in front of him. Every time he corrected himself, my mother would encouragingly say, 'Good boy, very good', and I had to refrain from laughing.

The only relations whom we regularly met in Killaloe were my uncle Fr Laurence, my cousin Fr Jim Tarpey SJ, and my aunties Sal and Eileen. They were all on my mother's side. Auntie Sal was a medical doctor – or a dispensary doctor as they were then called – in Ballygar, County Galway. On one visit in 1952, when I was 14, my mother was pointing out to Auntie Sal the markings of our heights, which were on the whitewashed wall in the kitchen in Aillebaun House. I was very small for my age, and Laurence, who was two years younger, had already passed me out.

'Henry is very small,' said Auntie Sal. At that time adults could talk comfortably about a child as if the child wasn't present. 'There are good goods in small parcels,' responded my mother defensively. 'Now, Greta, if you want Henry to grow, every day when he comes home from school, give him a half pint of milk mixed with a half pint of Guinness,' said Auntie Sal authoritatively. My mother followed Auntie Sal's advice. For the next two years this was my daily diet. It did not do anything for my height, but I was a very happy teenager!

· · ·

When I think back to those years and later, we thought we knew all about sex and sexuality, but we were really very naive. I was 24 years of age before I heard the word 'lesbian' and was told what it meant. And that was after four years in university and two years working in England. We all knew what homosexuality was, and that homosexual acts were then a crime. And we knew that Oscar Wilde was a homosexual. But we did not personally know anyone at university or at work who was a homosexual. And certainly there were no homosexuals in Killaloe or in Ballina! I knew that there was at least one in Cork, because one evening I was in the cinema in Grand Parade watching a movie, when a middle age man sat down beside me, put his raincoat, accidentally, I thought, across my lap as well as his own, until his prowling hand started to come across my thigh. I made a hasty exit to another row in the cinema.

In 1962, I was working with Aer Lingus as an aircraft development engineer and one weekend I travelled to Amsterdam to visit my university friend Kevin O'Brien who was then working there for the Fokker Aircraft company. One night we were in a night club with a group of Kevin's Amsterdam rugby friends. I spotted a particularly beautiful small girl who was about my height and remarked to Kev that I was going to ask her for a dance. 'You're wasting your time there, Henry, she is a lesbian,' he responded in a hushed tone. 'What is a lesbian?' I asked innocently, thinking this might be a continental thing or something to do with race. Kev immediately responded, 'She likes girls better than fellows.' 'You mean she is a kind of female homosexual,' I asked, putting it into terms that I could understand. 'You've got it in one,' responded Kev.

This story may sound incredulous by today's understandings, but it is true. At 24 years of age, I knew all about nuclear physics, the workings of atoms, the theory of flight, but I knew little about the human mind and body.

· · ·

Crescent College was a great school, but as we had to get the 5.00 pm bus back to Killaloe every day, we missed out on the rest of college life, including the great sporting tradition of the Crescent. But this deprivation was more than made up by the great life we had in Killaloe, with swimming in the Shannon at Burn's Shore and the Two-Mile-Gate, fishing on Lough Derg, climbing Cragg Hill, exploring the Ballyvalley Woods, playing hurling against boys from neighbouring streets, snaring rabbits, going to PF Ryan's cinema (or the 'pictures' as we called them), and making model airplanes with Jim Ryan.

Of course, we thought that Limerick, being a city, was a very sophisticated place. It was only when our Limerick classmates came to visit us in Killaloe and marvelled at the fantastic facilities we had for all these pursuits that we realised that we were privileged to be living in such a unique place.

. . .

I remember the summer of 1951 when I was 13. We were at our usual 11.00 am Sunday Mass in Killaloe and I was being as attentive as I could be, although my back was on fire from the previous day sunbathing at the Two-Mile-Gate. The next thing I remember was waking up on the floor of the church porch. I had fainted from sunstroke. From then on, my mother tried to encourage us to wear a hat – but we regarded this as not very manly.

I went back to the Two-Mile-Gate over 30 years later in 1983 with Davida, and our children Maeve (10) and Breffni (8), spending a week holidaying on the Shannon. I was then the Director of Personnel of AnCO, the industrial Training Authority. We anchored our hired Emerald Star cruiser off the beach and rowed ashore. It was a marvellous holiday. A further 30 years later, our son Breffni was back at Two-Mile-Gate with his daughter Bonnie in the brilliant summer of 2013.

With my wife Davida and children Maeve and Breffni off Two-Mile-Gate in 1983 – our hired Emerald Star cruiser is in the background

Our son Breffni at Two-Mile-Gate with his daughter Bonnie in the brilliant summer of 2013

Later that year, on Christmas Day 2013, a total of 102 swimmers braved the ice cold waters at Two-Mile-Gate in a family fun swim. Watched by over 300 spectators, to the sound of Christmas music and hot drinks supplied by the Killaloe Coast Guard mobile catering wagon, they raised €7,640 for a local charity. This is an annual event, initiated as a solo swim at the Pier Head in 1989 by Christy McGrath, originally from Bridge Street and a nephew of my Killaloe boyhood friend, John McGrath.

. . .

In 2005 we had a 50th reunion of the Crescent College Leaving Certificate Class of 1955. Although I actually did my Leaving Cert at Presentation College Cork (more about that later) this had been my class for four years. Out of the Crescent class of 28 students, three were deceased, four were abroad (Chicago, Florida, South Africa and Australia), nine were in Limerick, seven were in Dublin, three were in Galway, and the whereabouts of two was unknown. Probably reflecting the absence of a university in Limerick at the time, very few had gone to third level. Because we had been so dispersed, I had only met three out of the 28 in the intervening 50 years.

The reunion was in the Ballyneety Golf Club, outside Limerick, and was organised by Leonard O'Brien and attended by 14 past-pupils. Tom Fitzgerald had travelled the longest distance – from Chicago. We were amazed at how well we all looked and how little we had changed. One year after the reunion, one of the attendees, Marcus McInerney, passed away. He had retired from a very important position in the European Commission. The obituary which appeared in *The Irish Times* in July 2006 revealed his adventurous side:

> His delight in new and especially outdoor experiences, when he could feel the wind on his cheeks, led him to sail, to fish, to fly planes and go ballooning. On one wild and windy night in Belgium, he was observed skating on a forbidden lake in the Tervuren Park, using a golf umbrella as a source of rapid propulsion across the ice.

The next runion lunch was our 55th in Limerick. Having heard from around the table of all the medical conditions we were enjoying, Noel Sweeney, who would have been known in the class for his humorous approach, made the following comment in his speech: 'Gentlemen, the only thing I can say about old age, is that it doesn't last long.' Noel passed away before our next annual lunch, organised by me in Dublin in 2011. We have had further reunion lunches in Galway in 2012, in Limerick in 2013, and the 2014 reunion is planned for Killaloe.

In November 2009 there was a 150th reunion dinner in Dublin to recognise 150 years of the Jesuits in Limerick, from 1859 to 2009. In the book *The Crescent*, edited by Tony White and published to recognise the contribution of the Crescent and its alumni, a total of 250 past pupils are cited for their 'exceptional contribution to society' over that 150 years. Not surprisingly, famous people are identified with the year they left the college in brackets, such as Canon John Hayes (1904) the founder of Muintir na Tire in 1937; Donogh O'Malley (1937) who was a reforming Minister for Education in 1965-68 and who introduced 'free education' to secondary schools; Terry Wogan (1954) broadcaster, knight, and probably the best known Irishman in Britain; John Murray (1955) who was appointed as Chief Justice in 2004; Desmond O'Malley (1957) who was founder and leader of the political party, the Progressive Democrats; and Bill Whelan (1968) *Riverdance* co-creator and composer.

My brother Bill and I also get a mention:

In the world of media there has long been an old Crescent presence in *The Irish Times* ... with Bill Murdoch (1954).

And in my case:

> Over the years a small number of Crescent alumni have been to the fore in Irish public administration.... Henry Murdoch (1954) was for many years Assistant Director General of both AnCO and its successor, FAS, and is the author of *Murdoch's Dictionary of Irish Law*.

Based on the contribution which thousands of Crescent past-pupils have made to society over those 150 years in social, professional, religious, commercial, sporting and voluntary activity, maybe Fr McLaughlin was correct when he said to my mother, 'A Jesuit education will give you a character which will maintain you for life.'

4

The Catholic Church in Action – The Dark and Humorous Side

*'You will go to Hell' – Fr Michael Casey condemn-
ing me when my fingers touched the chalice (1950)*

In the 1950s the Roman Catholic Church had a huge influence over the lives of all the people in the Republic of Ireland. Sir Edward Carson had earlier predicted that Home Rule
in Ireland would mean Rome Rule. His prediction was partly
correct. While we did not get Home Rule for the island of Ireland of 32 counties, we got the Irish Free State of 26 counties.
And the Catholic Church largely controlled the schools and
the hospitals in those counties. There was even recognition in
the 1937 Constitution of Ireland of the 'special position' of the
Catholic Church. This provision was removed by referendum
of the people in 1972 as part of the process to achieve peace in
Northern Ireland.

Most of the priests of the Catholic Church in Ireland were
decent, honest and holy men who preached the doctrine that
they had been taught in the seminary. They believed that the
Catholic faith was the only 'true faith' and they went in their

St Flannan's Roman Catholic Church, Killaloe, in the early 1950s – the trees were removed during renovation works in the late 1950s (CCL)

thousands as missionaries abroad to preach that faith. But there were a few bad apples who abused the dominant position in which they were placed.

In 1950, when I was twelve years of age, I travelled into Crescent College in Limerick every morning with my brother Bill in the post office mail van. Bill was now in third year. We sat in the back of the van with the mail bags and the parcels. It was a good deal for the driver and a good deal for my parents, who were paying less than the bus fare. But by today's standards it was not very safe.

This arrangement lasted less than a year because some busybody complained to the post office, the driver was reprimanded and we had to get the 8.00 am bus from then on to Limerick. The journey of some 12 miles (19 kilometres) took nearly an hour as the bus would stop to collect passengers en route and also diverted off route into the villages along the way, for example, to O'Brien's Bridge, Bridgetown and Clonlara. The buses were very old fashioned until we got a brilliant bus which had a heating system in it, which when it worked gave a waft of warm diesel-smelling air, but at least it was warm.

I was an altar boy in Killaloe in 1950 and assisted at 7.00 am Mass every morning. I would get up at 6.45 am, have a quick wash, and fly up the street in time to don my surplice. After Mass, I would fly down the street, down my breakfast with speed, and catch the 8.00 am bus, parked at the Anchor Bar, into Limerick.

I loved reciting the Latin, which I had learned off by heart. *Ad Deum qui laetificat juventutem meam* – 'To God, who giveth joy to my youth.' *Et introibo ad altara Dei* – 'and I will go to the altar of God.' *Sicut erat in principio, et nunc, et simper, et in saecula saeculorum. Amen* – 'as it was in the beginning, is now, and ever shall be, world without end. Amen.' I loved ringing the bell at the consecration, pouring the water and wine into the chal-

Interior of the Catholic Church in the 1950s (CCL)

ice, and holding the spatula under the chin of persons who were receiving Holy Communion. I also loved the one shilling (€0.06) which I received at Christmas from Canon Molloy, a kindly old man, and the shilling I got at the occasional funeral.

When we went to confession, we always would seek out the Canon because he gave the least penance. When you told him your sins, which were usually that you told a lie or disobeyed your parents, he had a tendency to respond: 'Never mind my child, shure I would have done the same myself. Now say three Hail Marys.' Once when I was sitting in a queue with other children lining up for confession, I bragged to those around me: 'I'm going to tell the Canon that I murdered my mother last night, and see if he says that he would have done the same himself.' Of course, once inside the confessional, my courage dissipated, and I never learned what his response would have been.

Canon Molloy was a kind old man. He was known locally as 'Molloy' even though his official name, according to local historian Sean Kierse, was 'O'Molloy', and this is the name on the headstone of his grave in the Catholic church grounds in Killaloe. However we knew him as 'Molloy' and that is the name he was identified with in the local newspapers at the time. He was a native of Birr and had been ordained in Maynooth in

1905. He was appointed parish priest of Killaloe in 1941, was made an Archdeacon in 1956. He died on 21 January 1958 aged 80 years.

In those days, our life was surrounded by religion. My mother's brother Fr Laurence was a priest in Cong, she had two sisters who were nuns, and my mother's nephew Jim Tarpey was a Jesuit priest. And the Catholic Church was seen as all powerful and involved in everything. In sporting events, the ball would be thrown in by a priest. Official openings would be performed by a priest. And everything was blessed by a priest. I even had the canoe which I built when I was 15 blessed before I exposed it to the Killaloe Canal to see if it would float.

Mrs and Mr Prendergast with my sister Hilary in 1952

On occasions I just could not understand the inconsistencies in the teachings of the Catholic Church. There were very few Protestant families in Killaloe out of a population of 900. They were all very decent people – the Stokes, the Bensons and the Prendergasts. The Prendergasts lived on New Street and they were great friends of my mother and father in the 1950s.

Mr Prendergast was a retired banker and a great fisherman. He had a row boat similar to the one my father had, and he had it moored near the Pier Head, from where the Killaloe Coast Guard now operates. He was known as 'Prenney' and his wife was known as 'Mrs Prenney'.

We all knew, as Catholics, that if we lived a good life, we would go to Heaven, and if we lived a bad life, we would go to Hell. But then, we also had Confession. When I was about 14 years of age, I remember asking the local curate Fr Michael Casey, who was a young priest, 'If I live a very bad life, but on my deathbed am truly sorry and get Confession, will I go to Heaven?' I was told that yes, I would. I then asked in relation to Mr Prendergast: 'If Mr Prendergast lives a very good life, will he go to Heaven?' No, I was told, he would go to Hell. When I asked why this could be so, I was told it was because we Catholics had the only true religion. It didn't make sense to me, but we were expected to believe it.

·   ·   ·

My father's best friend in Killaloe was Howard Benson, the Protestant owner of the Benson Box Factory, by far the largest employer in Killaloe. They went fishing together regularly. When Howard's father William Benson died in May 1950, the funeral took place in St Flannan's Cathedral in Killaloe. My father stood outside the cathedral with a huge crowd of Catholic well-wishers, while the funeral service went on inside with a small number of mourners. The Catholics could not enter the Protestant church without committing a mortal sin, and yet these same Protestants would attend a funeral Mass in the Catholic church.

My father was very annoyed that he could not participate fully with his friend during a time of his friend's grief, particularly as the Murdoch roots were in Presbyterianism. But he should not have been surprised because the Catholic rule regarding attending Protestant services had been publicly demonstrated only a year before at the State funeral of Douglas Hyde, the first President of Ireland, who died on 12 July 1949. The nation was subjected to seeing the whole Catholic cabinet, except Minister Noel Browne, remaining outside St Patrick's Cathedral in Dublin, while the funeral service of Hyde, a Protestant, took place within the cathedral. The cabinet subsequently joined the cortege when the coffin left the cathedral. Even former Taoiseach Eamonn de Valera, then leader of the opposition, did not attend the funeral, but was represented by Erskine Childers, who was to be a future President, and who was a Protestant. This to me was the dark side of Catholicism.

·   ·   ·

Howard Benson had established the Benson Box in 1938 (the year I was born). He was then a 22-year-old English-born entrepreneur from Leicester. He chose Killaloe over Youghal, which was also recommended, because it was centrally located and near to his markets, it was near Limerick port for the import of cardboard from Holland, and as he was a keen fisherman, it was near good fishing grounds!

Old photo of Benson Box factory from the back (CCL)

Benson Box vans with drivers William D'arcy and William Gissane (CCL)

He started making boxes in the old Band Hall, on the 'new line' (now the premises of John Phelan of Harry Brann, auctioneers), while the present factory in Newtown was being constructed. The employment provided by Benson was greatly welcomed, because Ireland was in a depressed state, and Killaloe probably even more so, with its tourism fishing industry adversely affected by the Ardnacrusha Hydroelectric scheme.

At its peak in the 1950s and 1960s, the Benson Box factory employed 145 persons, which was a huge proportion of the population of Killaloe of about 900 people. Their products then were mainly boxes for shoe and hosiery factories throughout Ireland.

As kids in Killaloe in the 1950s, we were proud of the Benson Box logo and the distinctive Benson Box green vans which traversed the country delivering its products. And they were always good for a 'free' lift to Limerick or beyond, for us impoverished kids! And then as an adult, when I joined Aer Lingus in 1962 at the age of 24 as an aircraft development engineer, I will always remember walking in Dublin's O'Connell Street, seeing a Benson Box van, and being immediately proud that Killaloe was having an impact on the capital of my country. It also made me homesick for Killaloe.

My father met Howard Benson in the Lakeside Hotel in 1949 when looking for accommodation for us in Killaloe. They became fishing companions and lifelong friends. They fished mainly for salmon and trout at the Newport and Mulcair rivers and at Plassey and Castleconnell.

Howard Benson was a fine man. In many respects he reminded me of my own grandfather, William Murdoch, from Dingle in County Kerry, who was a Presbyterian from County Down. It probably was their common strong Protestant work ethic and high moral standards, which they both demonstrated in practice in their lives and in their business dealings. I am told that when the Benson Box factory was in trouble during difficult business cycles, the last option Howard exercised was making a worker redundant.

Howard Benson married Peggy (Margaret) Parsonage in 1940. They had a daughter Kathleen, but Peggy tragically died in childbirth in 1946 at the tender age of 26. Harold married Dora Clarke in 1947 and they

Howard Benson (1916–2009), founder in 1938 of Benson Box (photo courtesy of Roy Benson)

enjoyed 62 happy years together, with their children Roy, Sheila, Dorothy and Joan, and of course Kathleen.

Howard Benson died on 1 October 2009 aged 93. My father had died four years earlier in October 1995 aged 91. Howard was laid to rest at St Flannan's Cathedral, Killaloe, where he had served as a choir member, churchwarden, vestry member, treasurer and member of the Diocesan Council. The Cathedral was full to the back door with Catholics and Protestants alike, and an overflow outside. No Catholic mortal sins anymore. The *Limerick Leader* reported his death with the caption, 'A Gentleman of great humility and strength who ensured that countless young men and women from Killaloe and Ballina were spared the "scourge" of emigration, passed to his eternal reward recently.'

Howard's son Roy took over the reins at Benson Box in 1975 after qualifying as an accountant. The company employed 45 persons at that time. Roy's son Keith joined the company in 2008 having also trained in accounting. The company has had to diversify over the years into new markets with the demise of footwear manufacture in Ireland, and currently employs 20 persons.

. . .

My mother said the Rosary every evening in the sitting room after our evening meal and my kneeling brothers Bill, Laurence and I responded. My sister at this time was in boarding school in Dublin. My mother had difficulty in keeping us kids pious during the Rosary, because we would get up to all kinds of antics which often lead to uncontrolled laughter. But, by today's standards, we were a very religious family.

There was a strict rule in our house against the use of bad language. It just was not tolerated. My brother Bill, who had a mischievous streak, would regularly seek out words in the dictionary which were respectable in their own right, but similar to words which were not respectable. Bill found that the word 'chit' meant a young impudent child, so he would regularly, in front of my mother, say to Laurence or me, 'You are only a little chit'. I remember him irreverently calling across to my friend Jim Ryan on the far side of the Main Street in Killaloe, 'Hey, urine'. When challenged by Jim to explain himself, he said that all he had shouted was, 'Hey, you Ryan'.

On another occasion we were having our evening meal in the kitchen in Aillebaun House, the only warm room in the whole house as it had a range. My father mentioned Jack Crowe, who had a substantial drapery business in the town. Laurence, who would have been only about nine at the time, said knowledgeably, 'Daddy, Mr Crowe is only an old fucker'. He certainly was not old and also was not the latter. We were all gobsmacked. I had never heard Laurence use bad language before or since. There had to be an explanation and there was. My mother immediately turned on Laurence and said angrily, 'Where did you hear that expression?' Laurence innocently and openly responded 'Mammy, I heard you and Daddy talking about Mr Crowe last night, and Daddy said that Mr Crowe was only an old fucker'. There was no answer to that! But that word was never again used in our household.

In fact, my father got on very well with Jack Crowe who would have been a substantial customer at the bank. And Bill, Laurence and I were very friendly with his son Jim, who was about our age, and whom I met in 2013, for the first time in some 50 years, during his trip to Ireland and Killaloe from his home in New Zealand.

Jack Crowe was a real entrepreneur. Apart from being a retailer, he established the Killaloe Weaving Company which produced scarves and stoles which were exhibited at international fashion fairs. The initial production was carried out in 1955 in an upstairs room over Crowe's shop on Main Street. The production later moved on to the Band Hall on the Limerick Road. In a fashion article on Easter bonnets in *The Irish Times* on 5 April 1966 by celebrity Terry Keane (later to be a mistress to Taoiseach Charles Haughey), she refers to 'jaunty caps in white leather, beanies, mini-style boaters and trilbies in gossamer-weight Killaloe tweed'. The weaving company also supplied the high fashion stores in New York, such as Lord & Taylors and Bloomingdales.

A regular visitor to the weaving company when it was in Church Street was Bishop 'John Joe' Rafferty, Auxiliary Bishop of Perth in Australia. The Bishop had been born in Killaloe in 1912, ordained as a priest in 1936, emigrated to Australia, served as a priest in Perth, and was appointed an Auxiliary Bishop in 1955. He died at the young age of 49 in 1962 and is buried in the church grounds of St Flannan's in Killaloe, on the left-hand side, behind the headstone of the common grave of the five boys who drowned in the canal in Killaloe in December 1931.

Jack Crowe was married twice. His first wife Lil (née Holmes) died after their son John was born. He subsequently married Marie (née McKeogh) and had five more children, Jim, Michael, Betty, Paddy and Amelia. They all lived in the distinctive 'Big House' on the Main Street, now the home of rugby legend Keith Wood. The house was originally a military barracks before becoming the home of Killaloe-born Surgeon General John O'Nial. He died in 1919 and the house was acquired by Jack Crowe.

The Crowe family is now widely dispersed with Jim in New Zealand, Betty in Guensey, Paddy in Inis Oírr, and Amelia in Kells. The eldest son, John, died in a tragic accident during our time in Killaloe in the 1950s, and Michael died in 2011. Jack Crowe died on 14 November 1982 and his wife Marie died on 30 November 1993. They are both buried in the cemetery of the Catholic church in Ballina.

Betty Crowe became a chiropodist and practised for some years in Cork and Dublin. She married Tony Dundon from Portlaoise and after some years in Johannesburg they resettled in Oldcastle in County Meath. They subsequently went to Southhampton, bought the Sunnydene Hotel in Guernsey and are still running it. Amelia, the youngest in the Crowe family, lives in Kells, County Meath, where she was the Heritage Officer for the County Council, before they abolished the post, and now works for the Council in a managerial role.

Paddy Crowe lives on Inis Oírr (meaning 'east island') which is the smallest and most eastern of the three Aran Islands in Galway Bay, with a population of some 300. Paddy is the manager of the Co-operative on the island and in December 2013 was the recipient, on behalf of the islanders, of a Liveable Communities gold medal award in Xiamen, China. He has three daughters. Sinead is a primary teacher on Inis Oírr, Roisin has just qualified with a law degree from University of Limerick, and Sorcha is in her final year in UCC studying Nutritional Science.

. . .

On one morning in 1951, when I was 13, I had rushed down from the Church at 7.45 am after serving at Mass. I must have been in some distress because my mother asked me what was wrong with me. I told her that I was going to Hell. 'Don't be foolish,' she said, 'what put that stupid idea into your mind?' I told her that I had been serving Mass as usual, with the young curate Fr Michael Casey saying the Mass, and when I was pouring the wine into the chalice at the right-hand side of the altar, I accidentally touched the chalice with my fingers. Fr Casey had said angrily to me, 'I will see you in the Sacristy'.

I told her that in the Sacristy after Mass, Fr Casey had said to me: 'You touched the sacred chalice with your hand. You will go to Hell. Only an ordained priest can touch the sacred chalice. It is a mortal sin. You will go to Hell.' I could see that my mother was furious. I told her that I was not going to assist at Mass any more. 'You will serve at Mass tomorrow morning, as usual,' said my mother. 'You are not going to Hell. You just leave Fr Casey to me. Now, off to the bus with you.'

Next morning, I ran up to the church, as usual, to be greeted by an apologetic Fr Casey in the Sacristy. He told me that what he had said to me yesterday morning was all wrong, that my touching of the chalice was accidental, and of course was not a sin, and that there was no question of my going to Hell. I was relieved. Later, my mother told me that she had visited Fr Casey and had told him that what he had said to me was wrong and that if he did not apologise to me, she would report him to the Bishop and have him removed. She said that far from saying I was going to Hell, he should have realised that I was an angel, getting up every morning at 6.45 am to serve Mass, when other boys were sleeping in their beds.

Well, I was certainly not an angel but I was blessed with having an articulate and courageous mother, prepared and able to take on the might of the Catholic Church to protect her son. And I never blamed Fr Casey – he was a victim of his training as a priest at the time, where everything was black and white. I was to learn later that there is an awful lot of grey in life, and that jiving to Elvis Presley actually was not a sin.

Fr Michael Casey was one of three curates in Killaloe in the 1950s. He was a native of Ennis and followed the then traditional route to the priesthood – St Flannan's College, Ennis and then Maynooth. He was ordained on 17 March 1933. He left Killaloe shortly afterward his encounter with my mother and in 1961 was appointed parish priest of Kyle and Knock. He died in 1998.

.   .   .

The reading from the altar of the Easter and Christmas 'dues' (financial contributions to the Catholic Church) created no problem for my father, who had a good job in the bank in Killaloe – that is, not until the bank strike of 1950. The reading of the dues was a very formal affair. At the end of Mass, the priest would name every street alphabetically, listing the parishioners along the street by head of household, and stating how much they had contributed. It was a 'name and shame' job. As ours was the first house on the Canal Bank, we figured early. 'Canal Bank: A J Murdoch (my father) – £1-15s (€2.25); Peter Lacy (the local painter and decorator who had taught me to swim) – 2s 6d (€0.16); Mr X – silence – which meant that he had contributed nothing, which wasn't surprising since we all believed that he was an atheist, although he could have been a Catholic who objected to this method of public extortion!

The dues provided a certain antediluvian confirmation of the position of one's family in the local society, even in this small village of 900 souls. The local doctor would contribute the highest at £3 (€3.85), followed closely by the bank manager at £2-10s (€3.22), and successful shopkeepers at £1-10s (€1.92). Local publicans, of which there were many, were surprisingly as low as 10s (€0.64). Tradesmen gave 2s 6d (€0.16). My father's contribution was usually a respectable £1-15s (€2.25).

All very cosy and accepted at the time – even by those whose name was followed by silence, as they likely would not be present in any event. Until the national bank strike of December 1950 which left my father with no income for seven weeks. There was no strike pay in those days. The usual conversation at our meal times at that time was about money and how would we survive. The Christmas dues were payable right in the middle of the strike.

'We just cannot pay,' my father said. My mother agreed but asked, 'Will you be able to put up with the silence when the priest reads out your name?'

'Of course,' he replied, 'won't everyone know we're on strike.' Well, he was not that confident when we took our place at 11.00 am Mass on the first Sunday of January 1951. I could see the tension on his face as the priest came to 'Canal Bank'.

'Canal Bank: A J Murdoch,' said the priest, pausing for a moment, and then said, '£3'. This was nearly double what he had paid on the previous occasion. My father was relieved but at a price. After Mass he said with some admiration, 'the Church should be in banking – in effect, they have given me a loan which I will have to repay with interest, as they had upped the ante by 70 per cent from £1 15s to £3.' And they had, because when the strike was over the following month, my father paid the £3 and at the next dues also paid £3. And the local doctor Dr Mary Courtney, increased her contribution to £4 to stay on top of the pile.

. . .

I have not been particularly religious all my life but I was glad to have been brought up as a Catholic. I think it is important that everyone is brought up with an established religion, what-ever it is, because most religions have the same basic tenets and they provide good building blocks for development into adulthood. What I do not like is the absolute certainty of some religions. We certainly had it in the 1950s in the Catholic Church. The mantra that the Catholic Church had the only true religion is now virtually gone.

But it is as strong as ever in our daughter Maeve's new re-ligion. When I asked her future husband Ahmed, before they were married, what religion their children would be brought up in, he said, 'Muslim, of course.' When I asked why, he re-plied, 'Because we have the true religion.' Muslims really be-lieve that theirs is the true religion. But in the 1950s, many Catholics believed the same about their religion and had no difficulty in justifying the *ne temere* rule which required the children of a 'mixed' marriage (as it was then called) of a Cath-olic to a Protestant, to be brought up as Catholics. The rule was sometimes interpreted as also requiring the non-Catholic to attend instruction in the Catholic faith in the hope of con-verting the 'non-believer'! The imposition of the *ne temere* rule was deeply, and rightly, resented by the other faiths in Ireland at the time. Good riddance to it.

. . .

The Latin Mass, or Tridentine Mass as it is properly called, was replaced by the current Mass around 1970 after the Sec-ond Vatican Council. I missed the Latin Mass but I could un-derstand the need for the change. In the Tridentine Mass the priest stands with his back to the congregation and prays in Latin, a language which is understood by very few of the billion Catholics in the world. The current Mass requires the priest to face the congregation and to speak in the local language. The current Mass is much more consumer friendly and more egali-tarian. However the breaking of the traditional 1,500 year old Mass was resisted by a number of Catholic groups across the world. The strength of feeling was recognised by Pope Benedict XVI in 2007, when he authorised a wider use of the traditional Mass.

The change from Latin to English had an amusing and unplanned effect on me. At a point in the Latin Mass before the Communion, the literal translation was 'Lord, I am not worthy that thou shouldst enter under my roof, say but the word, and my soul shall be healed.' (*Domine, non sum dignus, ut intres sub tectum meum* ... etc). In the current Mass, this has been changed to the simpler 'Lord, I am not worthy to receive you. Only say the word and I shall be healed.' The first time I heard this in 1970, I irreverently, thought that the last sentence should be, 'Only say the word and I shall be well-healed!'

This irreverence did not prevent me from later becoming chairman of a hospital operated under the trust of the Catholic Sisters of Mercy, or in losing my shirt in bank shares in the 2008 banking crisis!

. . .

In 1951, I overheard my uncle Laurence telling my mother on one of his frequent visits to us in Killaloe, 'Maureen O'Hara is not a patch on Etta Vaughan.' Fr Laurence Lyons, my mother's brother, was the Catholic curate in Cong, County Mayo, during the shooting of the film *The Quiet Man* in 1951. Fr Laurence had a small unacknowledged influence on this film. He served as a priest in Cong from 1946 to 1966.

Fr Laurence loved two things in life – God and fishing. There was fantastic fishing in and around Cong. He also fished with my father in Kilkee and in Killaloe. These were his holiday destinations every year, when we lived there. Sometimes, I wonder if he

My uncle Fr Laurence Lyons (1946)

put fishing a little ahead of God. We always looked forward to his visits. Not only would he bring one of those huge circular tins of sweets, but more importantly he gave us penniless children a whole half-crown (2s 6d (€0.16)) each. That was a lot of money in those days. His visits were good for my father, who was also an avid fisherman. He took great pleasure in bringing Fr Laurence salmon fishing to the Mulcaire River at nearby Newport and Annacotty when we lived in Killaloe.

Film director John Ford, unidentified priest, John Wayne,
our uncle Fr Laurence Lyons, and Lord Killanin, on the set of
The Quiet Man (1951) (Courtesy of Connacht Tribune)

We were fascinated as young children to hear Fr Laurence tell us about the filming of *The Quiet Man* which had totally enveloped Cong in 1951. We were always asking him whether John Wayne was as tall, strong and brave as he appeared in western films. The story of the film concerned Sean Thornton (John Wayne), an Irish-American from Pittsburg returning to Ireland to reclaim his family's farm. He ends up falling in love with and marrying the fiery Mary Kate Danaher (Maureen O'Hara), sister of the bullying, loud-mouthed local squire 'Red' Will Danaher (Victor McLaglen). Danaher refused to allow his sister the full dowry to which she was entitled. Sean was willing to let the matter rest, but Mary Kate wanted to obtain her dowry at all costs. She believed that Sean's reluctance to fight for it was a result of cowardice. The truth, known only to one other person in the village, was that Sean was a professional boxer in the United States under the name of 'Trooper Thorn', and retired after accidentally killing an opponent in the ring.

The story was set on the Isle of Innisfree, an island in Lough Gill in County Sligo. Many scenes for the film were actually shot in and around the village of Cong, and in the grounds of Ashford Castle, now a luxury hotel.

Fr Laurence told us that Etta Vaughan was the understudy to Maureen O'Hara. As many scenes had to be rehearsed repeatedly, Etta was worked very hard, according to him, and then Maureen had only to appear once or twice and do her stuff. 'With all that make-up and lipstick, Maureen looked like a fallen woman, instead of a lovely Connemara girl,' he said in his priestly way. Etta Vaughan, according to him, should have had the star role. I think he was partly influenced by the fact that Maureen O'Hara was a Catholic and yet also a divorcee.

Etta Vaughan was a young lady from Moycullen near Galway. She was five years older than Maureen O'Hara but very like her in build and looks. According to Des MacHale in his excellent book *Picture the Quiet Man* (2004), Etta had come over to Ashford Castle for afternoon tea to see the movie stars at close quarters. She

Maureen O'Hara and her stand-in Etta Vaughan (1951). (Courtesy of Connacht Tribune)

was spotted by an assistant director. When he saw this lovely, slim and red-haired lady, whose height and figure were very similar to Maureen O'Hara's, he offered her the job of stand-in and double on the spot. He was surprised that she had to get her mammy's permission. She was paid £50 (€64) per week, which was a huge amount of money, more than the annual university fees at the time. According to MacHale, apart from being the stand-in, she appeared as Maureen's double in at least three scenes, including the pony trap ride by Kylemore Abbey. Etta subsequently got married to Bernard O'Sullivan, settled down in Galway, and at age 87 in 2002 was knocked down by a

A scene from The Quiet Man *(1951)*

car when crossing a street in Galway city and sadly died shortly afterwards.

As regards Fr Laurence's unacknowledged influence on the film, he told us that the now famous fishing scene on the river involving the Catholic priest Fr Peter Lonergan (played by Ward Bond) was prompted by him. This was the scene where Maureen O'Hara embarrassingly tells Fr Lonergan in the Irish language that she would not let her husband share her bed on their wedding night and that he had to sleep in a *mála codlata* (sleeping bag). To which Fr Lonergan responded angrily: 'Woman, Ireland may be a small country. God help us. But here a married man sleeps in a bed, and not a bag.' And then he hooks a big fish which drags him into the water. Fr Laurence explained to us nephews: 'I was fishing at that spot and had just hooked a fish when the director, John Ford, passed by with his entourage. He liked the scene and introduced it into the film with the bit of Gaelic added on.'

The Quiet Man Cottage Museum in Cong is well worth a visit. The ground floor is designed as an exact replica of 'White-o-Morn' cottage. Great effort has been made to ensure that all the furnishings, artefacts and costumes are authentic reproductions. The four poster bed, tables and chairs, treasured by Mary Kate Danaher, the thatched roof, the emerald green half-door and whitewashed front are all there. The proprietor of the museum, Gerry Collins, who served as an altar boy to Fr Laurence for many years in Cong, remembers him as a 'lovely gentleman and very kind'.

He told me that Fr Laurence had another influence on the film. Fr Laurence, who was a 'clerical consultant' to the film, was responsible for coaching American actor Ward Bond on how to be like an Irish priest – Fr Peter Lonergan in the film. Ward Bond (1903–1960) had a rugged appearance and easy-going charm, probably more suited to the many western films he had already appeared in. He would be regularly seen in Cong with his hands in his pockets. 'Well, Ward, the first thing I have to tell you is that an Irish priest would never be seen with his hands in his pockets,' counselled Fr Laurence. Quick as a flash, Ward responded, 'I suppose that is because Irish priests have their hands in other people's pockets!'. I am sure this story has been told many times in Cong.

In his book, MacHale tells the story of Ward Bond strolling around Ashford Castle in his clerical garb, when he met a visiting priest who asked him what parish he was from. Ward told him that he was from the parish of Hollywood and that he was very good friends of Fr Bing Crosby and Fr Spencer Tracy. The visiting priest, who was not a cinema-goer, said that he knew a lot of priests in America but that he didn't know them!

MacHale is the acknowledged authority on *The Quiet Man* and has written four books about the film. In his latest ebook, *Ripples in the Quiet Man* (2013), he identifies 125 errors in the finished film, for example,continuity and costume errors, editing inconsistencies, and the like, which he calls 'ripples', although his admiration for the film continues unabated.

Fr Laurence Lyons remained as a curate all his life. Frequently he was offered promotion as a parish priest elsewhere, but he declined because the fishing would not be as good as in Cong! Whenever I visit his grave at the back of the church in Cong, I am reminded of a kindly and saintly man whose interest in fishing had a small influence on a famous and successful Irish-American film. That success was recognised recently by the decision that the film be added to America's National Film Registry in 2013, meaning that the original copy will be preserved at the Library of Congress.

I have a soft spot for *The Quiet Man* because of the links with my uncle and with the author of the short story, Maurice Walsh, upon which the film is based. Maurice was born in County Kerry in 1879 and died in 1964. He wrote 20 novels and numerous short stories. He had his first novel, *The Key above the Door,* published in 1923. His Quiet Man story, appeared in the Saturday Evening Post in 1933, and was bought by film director John Ford for $10. He had another novel, *Trouble in the Glen*, turned into a film in 1954. His son, also Maurice, was an excellent captain of Dun Laoghaire Golf Club in 1949, and a most courteous president of the club from 1983 to 1985 during my membership there. I played golf with him on many occasions. He was very proud, and rightly so, of his literary father. His sons, Daire and Ross, continue the golf tradition of the Walsh family as members, as do Daire's two sons, Maurice and Mark Walsh.

I was fortunate also to meet Lord Killanin (1914–1999) a number of times. Apart from his huge influence on the Olympic Games, he had a big influence on the Irish film industry, which became a strategic focus for my role in FÁS in the 1990s.

Maureen O'Hara (1920–) has had strong links with Killaloe. She married airline pilot Charles F. Blair Jnr. in 1968 and he frequently landed flying boats on Lough Derg in the 1970s. Captain Blair, a former US airforce pilot and owner of Antilles Air Boats at St Thomas, based the 42-seater flying boat, the *Southern Cross*, at Killaloe for the summers of 1976 and 1977. The arrival of the flying boat to Killaloe was greeted by the *Ne-*

nagh Guardian of 31 July 1976 with the headline: 'Maureen O'Hara attracts the crowds at Killaloe':

> Hundreds of people congregated at Cormacruisers Marina at the weekend, as the flying boat carrying well known film star, Maureen O'Hara, and piloted by her equally renowned husband, Capt Charles Blair, surfaced on the Shannon in the vicinity of the Marina harbour.
>
> Bill McCormack, the popular owner of Cormacruisers was quickly alongside the flying boat to ferry the party ashore at the marina. Capt Blair and his wife are seeking permission from the Irish Government to start a summer airboat service in the West of Ireland, plying from Bantry to Foynes, Foynes to Lough Derg, to the Aran Islands, Galway and Ashford Castle on Lough Corrib.
>
> During his re-fueling period at Killaloe, which lasted from about 2.30 to 8pm, Capt Blair made a survey of the marina extensive shoreline and seemed to be very happy with what he found. Should he decide to have a landing stage erected at the marina, it would prove a big boost to the influx of visitors to the area.

Well, Captain Blair got his licence and soon was carrying locals from Killaloe/Ballina and hundreds of tourists on sightseeing flights to the south and west coasts, mainly to the Aran Islands and Glengarriff. At a fare of £15 (€19), passengers were treated to the novelty of two bars on board. Captain Blair regarded the Shannon at Killaloe as the perfect landing spot for flying boats.

Captain Blair was quite a character. His motto was, 'The sky is full of new frontiers'. On 22 June 1942 he took off from Foynes, County Limerick for the USA in a VS44 flying boat. His flight plan included the usual refuelling stop at Newfoundland, but approaching Newfoundland he decided to continue to New York without stopping. He landed at New York with just 95 gallons of fuel in the tank. After a flight of 25 hours and 40 minutes, this was to be the first non-stop commercial flight from Europe to New York. On 2 September 1978, Captain Blair

*Captain Blair's Shorts Sandringham VP- LVE in Killaloe in 1977
(Reproduced by kind permission of photographer Steve Williams)*

was killed with three others when the engines failed in a Grumman Goose near to his airline base. On his death, Maureen O'Hara took over the running of her husband's airline, the first female owner of an airline in the world.

The *Southern Cross* landed for the last time at Killaloe in September 1980 after a transatlantic flight. This great flying boat remained in the care of Cormacruisers in Killaloe until her final take-off from Killaloe on 9 February 1981, heading for the Solent near Southampton where she is preserved in a transport museum.

Maureen is a patron of the excellent Flying Boats Museum in Foynes, County Limerick, which she officially opened on 8 July 1989. It is housed in Aras Ide, which was the terminal building during Foyne's six years at the centre of transatlantic transport. Brian Cullen from Killaloe is the current chairman of the museum. It is well worth a visit. In September 1989 in a promotion of its airline, Ryanair landed a flying boat called *Spirit of Foynes* on the waters of Killaloe in a sponsorship deal involving the museum, which unfortunately did not come to fruition. It was a Shorts Sandringham airplane in the Ryanair livery.

The Lakeside Hotel in Killaloe has acknowledged Maureen O'Hara's and her husband's influence by having an 'O'Hara Bar' in the hotel and by calling their restaurant 'The Blair Suite', which was officially opened in 1987 by Maureen.

Recently Mountshannon, near Killaloe, has been designated as a base for sea planes by the Irish Aviation Authority. In July 2013, Harbour Flights commenced operations from the Lakeside Jetty in Mountshannon, offering tours by sea planes of Lough Derg, the Burren, the Cliffs of Moher and St John's Castle Limerick. (See www.harbourflights.com.)

Maureen O'Hara cutting the tape at the opening of 'The Blair Suite', in the Lakeside Hotel Killaloe in 1987, in the presence of Danny (left) and Jerry McKeogh (far right) owners of the hotel, and Christopher Byrnes (hotel manager)

And I touched John Wayne's (1907–1979) yacht in Los Angeles in 1968. I was on the yacht of Bob Nordskog, owner of the Nordskog company that made the galleys (kitchens) for the Aer Lingus Boeing airplanes. We passed John Wayne's yacht. I earnestly asked him to go astern so that I could touch the possession of one of my childhood heroes, and I did.

· · ·

My uncle Fr Laurence died on 15 July 1966 after three years of poor health. He is last listed in the Cong parish records of performing baptisms, which was the role of curates like him, on 5 May 1963. During his final illness, he still said Mass in his house whenever he was able to, with an altar set out near the window, and Gerry Collins of the Quiet Man Cottage Museum was his altar boy on these occasions. Gerry was delighted to get time off from school. Fr Laurence was a kindly and saintly man.

There was blue bloody murder over his will. His assets amounted to £1,000 (€1,282) which was a fair amount of money at the time, as it represented about a year's salary in a good job. He left it equally between my mother and my spinster auntie Eileen. But there was a problem. Archbishop Walsh, in charge of the diocese which included Cong, sent a bill to the solicitor handling Fr Laurence's estate, for £680 (€872) for the repair of the house in which my uncle had resided. He cited Provincial Statute 158 of the Catholic Church, under which the occupier of a parochial house, on vacating it, had to make good the damage to the house from his private resources. Fr Laurence had obviously vacated the house permanently on his death, and the Archbishop wanted his slice of the action. My mother's legacy would have been reduced from £500 to £160.

Most Catholics at that time would have bowed under the direction of an Archbishop. But Archbishop Walsh did not reckon on the resilience and tenacity of my mother. She was quite emphatic in her correspondence. The Church had failed to maintain the parochial house during Fr Laurence's occupation. The Church might have a claim under canon law but not under civil law. She was willing to make a gift to the Archbishop of £100, but not for repairs and her offer was without prejudice and was final. If necessary, she was willing for the civil courts to decide the issue.

That was it. The Archbishop, faced with such clarity, accepted the £100 from my mother as a gift, and withdrew his claim for repairs. Her brother, Fr Laurence, would have been proud of her. And I am proud of her, reading her correspondence, with copies of her handwriting faithfully preserved by the use of carbon paper.

During Fr Laurence's time in Cong, the three church areas of Cong, Cross and Neale were served by three priests. Now, in 2014, Fr Paddy Gilligan, who lives in Fr Laurence's old house, is the sole priest for the parish. Fr Gilligan was in the same class in school at St Gerard's in Castlebar as Des MacHale, the eminent writer about *The Quiet Man* movie. Ireland is certainly a small place.

5

MY MOTHER THE ENTREPRENEUR

'It put me off eggs forever' (1951)

My mother was an innovative, entrepreneurial and hard-working woman. She managed the household finances as well as our education and upbringing. My father thought he was in charge as head of the household, but in reality the only major decisions he made would have been those on banking matters within the walls of the Provincial Bank on Royal Parade. And he was happy to let his wife have this role as she was totally competent in it. This allowed him time to concentrate on his fishing and fly-making.

People in Killaloe thought we were rich. We were, in the sense that our dad had a good, permanent and pensionable job, and we ate well and were well clothed, but there was no discretionary money at the end of the month. The outgoings in 1951 were considerable. My sister Hilary was in an expensive boarding school (Cabra) in Dublin, my brother Bill (then known as Billy) and I were in an expensive day school (Crescent College) in Limerick, and Laurence would be joining us there in a couple of years.

Mother with glass cloches, for growing tomatoes, which she made herself (1951)

My mother, similar to other mothers at that time, was a great knitter. All our sweaters (or as we called them 'jumpers' or 'pullovers'), gloves and scarfs were knit by her, and holes in socks were darned, and the worn elbows of a jacket was quickly covered by a leather patch in the shape of a rugby ball. And she was a dab hand at embroidery and crochet work, which skills she used into old age. She created the crochet flowers for my bride's hair at our wedding in 1972. These crochet flowers were to be worn subsequently by our daughter Maeve at her First Communion in 1980.

But my mother was different from other mothers because, despite being busy looking after four young children, she was always searching around for ways to increase the income coming into the household or to reduce the outgoings. So her first project was to produce as much food as possible. We had an extensive garden in the front of Aillebaun House with its magnificent views of Killaloe bridge. But she was not interested in the view. Her interest was to extract the maximum from every square inch of the land. In a short period of time, she had the whole area cultivated. So we became self-sufficient in general vegetables – potatoes, carrots, cabbage, beetroot, parsnips, and a whole variety of lettuces. When particular species were in season, we had them in abundance. For example, for a number of weeks every year we would get fed up of having rhubarb tart every day.

But my mother's greatest achievement was her production of tomatoes and strawberries. The tomatoes were produced under glass cloches, like tents, which my mother made herself. There wasn't plastic sheeting available at the time. And then there were the strawberries, delicious fat juicy strawberries, and these were the money makers. She made contact with a number of firms in Limerick (for example, Liptons and Cruises Hotel) who gave her £1 (€1.28) for a large punnet. My deal with my mother was that I would bring a

Strawberries in season – me with brothers Bill and Laurence with a punnet (1952)

punnet into Limerick on my bicycle (24 miles, 39 kilometres return) for one shilling (€0.06). And I couldn't get enough of the work.

The next project on my mother's list was our egg-laying hens. With the front garden totally cultivated and a small back yard, there wasn't space for free-ranging hens, so my mother came up with the idea of hens in cages. She read up about this method, got plans on how to build and operate the cages, got the materials from Speights in Limerick, and built the cages herself, with some help from us boys. Soon we would have a two-storey block of hen cages in our back yard, four hens on each storey.

The hens had their own individual cage, standing on netting wire which was on a small slope. The hen's poo would go through the netting wire to a waste tray below, while any egg that was laid would roll down the inclined netting wire to a retrieval box outside the cage. As a kid I used to look at this happening, marvelling at the efficiency of it all. I soon learned why the eggs did not break when they rolled down and hit the wood of the retrieval box. The egg shell immediately after laying was warm and flexible and would bounce off the wood. The shell only became brittle some time after contact with the air.

I don't know how cruel the system was, but the hens seemed to be happy. They were well fed and had the company of their colleagues in the adjoining cages. And when they became unproductive they were killed humanely. My mother taught me how to do this with a quick pull of the hen's neck. It was as easy as killing a fish, with which we were already familiar. And then the hen became the Sunday roast. All very efficient. And we didn't mind the extra chore of having to clean out the cages. But the process had a lasting effect on me – it put me off eggs for ever, the only food I don't eat to this day.

The only project my mother got up to which was not successful was the production of mushrooms. As usual, she read everything about mushroom production. You needed plenty of indoor space – we had plenty of that in dilapidated Aillebaun House – and a special large growing box. I helped my mother in building the box. It was sheeted in asbestos for insulation. I sawed those asbestos sheets and must have ingested some asbestos dust, which was not known then as being carcinogenic. It hasn't done me any harm, yet. However, the project was not a success as the mushrooms were small and production rates were poor, and there was no saving on buying mushrooms in a shop.

My mother was brilliant at doing crosswords and used to enter the crossword competitions in the Sunday newspapers. One Sunday in 1953 she was the only person in the *Sunday Press* competition with all the answers correct and won the huge sum of £300 (€385). We all got a bonus in our weekly pocket money. The only problem was that my mother's name and address were published in the newspaper as the winner and of course there was a big emphasis on the size of the prize to encourage more contestants who paid an entry fee of about two shillings (€0.13). In the next few weeks she received hundreds of 'begging' letters from all over Ireland. Some of the letters were probably genuine but my mother thought that a lot were from chancers – particularly the ones who said that they would pray for her if she would send them a few 'bob'. Some even enclosed what they claimed were 'relics' from well-known saints.

.   .   .

My mother was not the only entrepreneur in the Killaloe area. Another entrepreneur was J. B. (Barney) O'Driscoll, in the nearby village of Portroe, when in 1923 he revitalised the 'Killaloe' slate quarries. I met Barney in 1951 when I was 13 years of age. He was a larger-than-life individual who not only re-opened the slate quarries but also brought industries and employment to this part of north Tipperary.

The slate quarries had employed 400 men in the 1770s. In his *A Topographical Dictionary of Ireland* in 1837, Samuel Lewis said that the quarries were producing 100,000 tons of slates annually. William Bassett, in his *Directory for County Clare (1875–76)*, said that the 'extensive' quarries were providing employment for a large number of people and, under the 'energetic management of the present superintendent, Captain Hickie', were making rapid progress. It may seem strange that these unique blue-grey slates, quarried and processed near a County Tipperary village, should use the name of a County Clare town. But then Killaloe was a well-known name, already famous for its scenery and particularly for its fishing. It was a good marketing ploy.

Slates were initially delivered by horse and cart, by canal boat from Garrykennedy Pier to Limerick for export, by the canal system from Shannon Harbour to the Midlands and Dublin, and by rail from Nenagh from about 1863. However in 1913, the Killaloe Slate Company Ltd was in deep trouble when a landslip had covered a large area of free veins of slate and the company had suffered heavy financial losses, according to *The Irish Times,* 31 March 1914. The quarries were closed by 1917.

By this time, Barney O'Driscoll was politically active with Sinn Féin and the Volunteers in the fight for Irish freedom. He was a native of Union Hall in West Cork and an experienced quarry man. He was imprisoned in 1918 in Cork for 'inciting to crime'. A police sergeant named Malone reported to his superiors about a meeting of Sinn Féin in Skibbereen on 30 March 1918 at which Michael Collins had stated that 'the words of advice which Barney O'Driscoll gave them (Volunteers) ... were the words of advice he would also give them' and 'if anything happens to Barney O'Driscoll, I hope every Volunteer will know what to do'. This was a clear message of reprisal action. Michael Collins was Director of Intelligence for the IRA and later was the Commander-in-Chief of the National Army of the Irish Free State. He was killed in an ambush at Béal na Bláth, County Cork, on 22 August 1922.

Barney O'Driscoll was also interned in Ballykinlar Jail in County Down for his political activities. It was here that he met the McDonnell brothers who told him about the rich slate quarries lying idle near Portroe. They urged him to investigate the quarries when he regained his freedom. He subsequently did so and in 1923 he bought the quarries from the then owners – the Smithwick family. The purchase had to be organised by his Protestant solicitor in Cork because the Smithwicks would not sell the quarries to a Catholic.

KILLALOE SLATE QUARRY CO. LTD.

Slate and Slab Manufacturers

Directors: J. B. O'DRISCOLL, M. Inst. B.E.; W. WOOD WOLFE; A. F. DOYLE; F. O'DRISCOLL

Telephone
3 PORTROE

NENAGH
CO. TIPPERARY
Glasgow Office—33 North Frederick Street

Telegrams
SLATES PORTROE

YOUR REF

OUR REF

The letterhead of Barney O'Driscoll's slate company

The McDonnell brothers had a sister Mary. She became Barney's bride in 1925 and they had three children – Fin, Mary and Noel. Barney set out to modernise the quarries, installing an electric generator until power came from the Ardnacrusha hydroelectric scheme in 1931, an air compressor for drilling the stone, and diamond saws for cutting. Killaloe slates became very popular in Holland, Scotland and England, and were used to roof the power house at Ardnacrusha, the GPO and the Four

Courts in Dublin. In the 1930s the quarries were employing over 200 men.

By the 1950s the quarries were beginning a slow decline, as asbestos slates and tiles were cheaper than natural slate. Then, on 5 August 1956, the final blow came with a massive landslide which covered land and machinery, luckily while the workers were on holidays. Barney made the difficult decision to close the quarries after 33 years under his leadership. However in 2014, slates are back in production again from Portroe, under the name 'Killoran slates'. (See www.killoranslate.ie.)

Apart from his quarry business, Barney was a great entrepreneur and an avid promoter of industrial development in Ireland. He was friendly with many German industrialists, and even met Herman Göring, Hitler's Minister for the Interior, in Berlin many times. He was instrumental in setting up the 'Barlite' plastic factory in 1934 and the 'Tubex' factory near Portroe in 1938, making aluminium tubes mainly for toothpaste. This was where I met Barney in 1951.

As a 13-year-old kid, I was fascinated at how the tubes were made with the cap installed at one end and the other end being open, to be filled by the toothpaste manufacturer to whom the tubes were shipped. Unfortunately, both factories are now closed. Tubex was sold in 1978 to a German company. The plant in Portroe closed in 2003 with the loss of 55 jobs, while its sister plant in Nenagh making plastic tubes, which opened in 1997, closed in 2006 with the loss of 28 jobs, citing the rising cost of plastics, labour and energy. Dr Cornelius Grupp, the head of German company Tubex Holdings GmbH, is the owner of Clarisford House in Killaloe, or the Bishop's Palace as we knew it in the 1950s.

Barney O'Driscoll also established (with the UK Midland Metal Spinning Company, Wolverhampton), the Irish Aluminium Company in Nenagh in 1934 which produced cookware under the 'Castle Brand', featuring Nenagh Castle in its logo. During the Second World War, aluminium was hard to source and the factory struggled to survive. Most of the workforce were taken to England to help the war effort. The remaining workforce had to cut turf to drive the furnace because it was the only fuel available.

Barney O'Driscoll at his wedding to Mary McDonnell in 1925 (courtesy of their granddaughter Barbara O'Driscoll)

Barney O'Driscoll was also a great believer in the ancient Irish sport of 'road bowling' which consisted of throwing a 'bowl' – an 18 cm iron or steel cannon ball weighing 0.8kgs along a country road. The competitor who takes the least throws to complete the course wins. The sport is popular in Armagh and in Cork, where they still talk about Bill Bennet 'lofting' the viaduct on the Cork to Bandon road. Barney often described bowling as 'poor man's golf' but a game which, even if played poorly, was very enjoyable if you were properly matched with your opponent. He accepted that the game could be regarded as a bit anti-social, as it required the closure of a road, but this should not cause a problem if it were a secondary or tertiary road on a Sunday afternoon. As far as he was concerned, this was a small price to be paid to support a game played by Cuchullain.

Barney's wife Mary died in 1961 and Barney died a few months later in a tragic motor accident. His car was in collision with a horse and cart on the road from the quarries to Portroe. The shaft of the cart went through the windscreen and into his forehead. He initially survived the crash but later succumbed to his injuries. He and Mary are interred in Lisboney cemetery, a mile outside Nenagh on the Dublin road. Barney's positive impact on North Tipperary was immense.

• • •

The Minogues, William and Christina (nee Costello) had a butcher's shop on Church Street in Killaloe which was opened on 1 November 1919. They were our butchers. My mother wanted to cure a lambskin and asked William if he could give her one. He explained to her that it was a very difficult process and queried whether she was up to it, removing all the flesh and salting it meticulously. He told her that she would have to wait a while, until the lamb's hair growth was sufficient. When she came to collect the skin, and inquired about the cost, he told her that if she was going to undertake the task of curing the skin, he would undertake the task of charging her nothing!

The Minogues had three children, Chris, James and Margaret. There was great excitement in Killaloe in 1951 when Mr Minogue's Irish Sweepstake's ticket drew the horse 'Royal Tan' in the Grand National that year. The Sweepstakes, which had been established as the Irish Free State Hospitals Sweepstakes in 1930 to provide funds for hospitals, were hugely popular. They sold tickets throughout Ireland, but also to the emigrant Irish in the USA and the UK.

There was considerable speculation in Killaloe, before the Grand National in 1951, as to whether Mr Minogue would sell his ticket or a share in it. At that time there were plenty of investors, usually bookmakers, who would pay, say 25 per cent of the potential prize for a winning horse. If the horse won, they would quadruple their investment. If the horse came third, they would get their money back, and if the horse fell or was not placed, they would lose their money. For the ticket holder it provided certainty of money in the bank, irrespective of what happened at the race.

Everyone in Killaloe knew that 'Royal Tan' was a seven-year-old gelding and a great horse but not the favourite. Mr Minogue's daughter Chris has told me that her father was approached by a bookmaker who indicated that he would like to buy a half share in his ticket. She was a teenager at the time. She thinks that her father was interested but the bookmaker did not follow through with his offer. The bookmaker must have been gutted when 'Royal Tan' came second in the race on 7 April 1951.

On that day, everyone in Killaloe was glued to the wireless to hear the commentary on the race at the Aintree Racecourse. We heard the commentator telling us that there was a crowd of 250,000 persons watching the race near Liverpool. There was no television then. We had huge questions. Would 'Royal Tan' complete the race? Would Mr Minogue become a millionaire? Imagine a millionaire in our population of 900 in Killaloe!

There were 36 starters in the race, but after the first round of the course, 32 horses had fallen or were withdrawn. There were now only four horses in the race in the second round, and one of that four was 'Royal Tan'. The tension and excitement was unbelievable. Another horse fell. There now were only three horses in the race, and one was 'Royal Tan'. These three horses were the only ones to finish the course, but all competing horses returned safely to the stables. The winner was 'Nickel Coin' – a 40/1 odds outsider – a mare, and in the long history of the Grand National, the most recent mare of the only 13 mares which have won the race. Second in the race was 'Royal Tan' – our Killaloe hero. And third was a horse called 'Dennistown'.

We were all so thrilled. Mr Minogue's horse had come second in the race and the prize money was £20,000 (about €625,000 in today's money) which he shared with Jim Farrell from Portroe who owned half of the ticket. That was an awful lot of money in those days. Not quite a millionaire but nearly. I never found out what Mr Minogue did with the money. I am sure it was initially deposited in the Provincial Bank in Killaloe where my father was the cashier and teller. Anytime I asked my father about this, even in his 92nd year, he gave me a lecture on banking confidentiality.

And I was unable to get any clues from Mr Minogue's behaviour, because before the Grand National that year, Mr Minogue was a Killaloe butcher driving a Morris Minor car and after the Grand National, he was a Killaloe butcher driving the same Morris Minor car.

Another beneficiary in Killaloe of the Minogue win was Mr P. F. Ryan, the cinema, shop and petrol station owner on Royal Parade, who had sold the winning Sweepstake ticket. For many years afterwards, he was heard to proclaim, 'Royal Tan from Royal Parade'. Three years later, 'Royal Tan', now a ten-year-old gelding and trained by Vincent O'Brien, was the winner of the Grand National in 1954, but we did not have a Sweepstakes ticket winner in Killaloe. However, *The Irish Times* on 21 March 1969 noted that Sweepstakes ticket CBC40007 (c/o P. F. Ryan, Royal Parade, Killaloe) on the Lincoln race had won a residual prize of £801, slightly smaller than the Minogue's massive win.

Although giving the public appearance of a charity, with nurses in uniform drawing the winning tickets from a rotating drum, supervised by uniformed gardaí, the Irish Sweepstakes was actually run by a for-profit company which delivered handsome dividends to its shareholders. The company went into voluntary liquidation in 1987 having failed to win the licence to run the new Irish National Lottery, which was won in 1986 by An Post.

William Minogue died on 13 June 1966, aged 76, and his wife Christina died on 6 October 2000, aged 93. Their daughter Chris continued to run the butcher's shop until 1999 when she closed it and retired.

William Minogue's brother Jimmy was a taxi driver and had a shop at The Green in Killaloe. He was married to Helena McCarthy and they had four children, three of whom entered religious life – Joseph (Conrad) who was ordained in 1951, Therese (Sr Francesca) who was professed in 1954, and Helen (Sr Theodore) who also was professed in 1954. Mary was the only one not to enter religious life. She became a teacher. Fr Joseph was killed in a motor accident in 1972.

· · ·

In the summer of 1951, I kept a short dairy for just seven weeks, from 21 June to 30 July 1951. All the diary entries were made contemporaneously, so they give a sample of what we kids did in Killaloe, as seen through the eyes of a 13-year-old. At the time Hilary was 17, Bill 15 and Laurence was 11. While it was only two years since we arrived in Killaloe, the diary entries demonstrate how quickly we had been integrated into the community. Also, they show how much we were involved in sport – hurling, cricket, horse-riding, fishing and particularly cycling, where we appeared to cycle to a place without any particular reason. It was as if the bicycle gave us a great feeling of freedom and we wanted to exercise that freedom.

Bill in centre at Laurence's and my confirmation day in 1951

And we had no problem about cycling the round trip of 24 miles (38.6 kilometres) to and from Limerick, just to see a film, or the 'pictures' or the 'flix' as we called them then. And there were wet days, breaking the myth that all the days of our childhood were sunny ones.

We had our dinner in the middle of the day, and the food quality (and probably quantity) rose when there was a visitor, like cousin Fr Jim Tarpey SJ. We hadn't a telephone in the house, so phoning meant using the public coin-operated telephone up near the post office. The diary entries also show the amount of hurling matches we had between streets in Killaloe, for example, our Canal Bank versus New Street.

The entry for 24 June 1951 discloses that our dad attempted to buy a copy of a British tabloid newspaper, *The Sunday People*, at Gleeson's newspaper shop. Obviously Una Gleeson didn't think a respectable bank official should be buying such trash, because I record that dad was angry when Una Gleeson

told him, 'we don't get it and anyway they were all sold out!'
There are other entries about negotiating an increase in our
weekly 'pocket money' (Bill 2s 6d; €0.11), exam results, riding horses up Tountinna mountain and losing them for two
hours and arriving home by nearly midnight. And there was
the commission paid for delivering, by bicycle, our mother's
strawberries for sale in Limerick and no shortage of transport-
ers. I didn't get a look-in on this income stream while Bill and
Hillary were at home for the summer, but I came into my own
in later years when they were off the pitch. We certainly had an
active childhood with never a dull moment.

. . .

My sister Hilary was very interested in horses in her teenage
years and regularly rode the horses of Michael Quigley, who
lived out on the Ogonnello road. She had excellent horseman-
ship skills. I didn't have a clue. I was never able to co-ordinate
my movements with that of the horse, so when the horse's back
was rearing up, my backside was moving down, which wasn't
very pleasant for the horse – and certainly not pleasant for me.

I cannot remember any money passing, so Michael must
have been glad to have someone to exercise his horses.

My sister Hilary with Michael Quigley's horses 1953

Michael Quigley's son Jack, who I met in 2012, inspired my books on Killaloe (see the Preface). This book is dedicated to him. He was a highly respected member of the community and was honoured in December 2012 when he was asked to switch on the Christmas lights in Ballina. Jack's daughter Mary is married to Mike Durack and lives at The Fountain, Ballina, and his son Michael is a postman in Killaloe.

Jack passed away on 17 July 2013 in his 93rd year, and his wife Nellie had died on 12 February 1989. Jack's father Michael, who let us ride his horses, died on 18 March 1962, and his wife Nora died on 8 December 1951. They are all laid to rest in a combined grave at the beautifully managed graveyard at Our Lady and St Lua's Church in Ballina. Whenever I can, I pay my respects to their memory by visiting this graveyard.

Michael Quigley (top) in 1953, taken on my Baby Brownie camera. His son Jack (below) in 2012 (courtesy of Charlie McGeever, photographer, Ballina

As kids in Killaloe in the 1950s, we played a terrible trick on our teenage sister Hilary, using her love of horses. On New Street at the entrance to the Aillebaun Walk was the house of Alex Hogan. It had a walled garden with a fantastic orchard, abundant with the best of plumbs, pears and apples. It held a magnetic attraction for us young fellows – my two brothers Bill and Laurence and Gussie Henchy. We would scale the back wall and try to grab as much fruit as we could before an angry Mr Hogan would chase us back over the

DR. MADELEINE MCCARTHY & ASSOCIATES

Harbour Health

RESULTS

Your results should be back in the surgery within ....days of your test being taken. Please ring the mobile number below to speak with Jackie (Practice Nurse) **between 2.00-2.30pm Mon-Friday.** Texts will not be answered.

If the phone is busy please do not ring the main surgery number, just try again. The nurse will advise you what the plan is, including if the results are normal. Unfortunately time does not allow any further discussion. If you wish to discuss the results in more detail please make a follow up appointment with the doctor.

We now have an environmental 'green' policy and would encourage patients **not to request a printout.** As a disincentive we are introducing a charge for a paper printout.

TEL: (085) 1166120

When the phone is not on (if Jackie is on leave or not available) please ring between 2-3.00 pm to find out if your results are back.

wall. We didn't regard this 'rawking' (as we called it) as theft – we were just helping ourselves to the fruits of nature.

However we needed a new strategy when one day, having clambered over the wall, we were met by an obviously frustrated Mr Hogan brandishing a shotgun. We hightailed it over the wall like lightning and held a council of war. We came up with a terrific scheme – if we could get our sister Hilary to call on Mr Hogan, we could be rawking the fruit out the back while she was talking to him at the front door. But how could we get her to call on him without divulging our plan?

Knowing her passion for horses, we told her that Mr Hogan had recently acquired a piebald pony and was looking for someone to exercise it, and that she should call on him. And the plan worked but only once, as Hilary smelled a rat when Mr Hogan told her that he hadn't got a pony at all. That was the end of our rawking. From all the western movies we saw in PF Ryan's cinema down on Royal Parade, we knew the power of the shotgun! Hogan's house and walled garden is now a small select housing estate. Every time I pass it, I am reminded of our rawking days.

As kids, we did not know that in 1952 one of the horses in the Irish Army team was called 'Killaloe'. *The Irish Times* of 6 November 1952 reported that Lt Col D Corry of the Irish Army team was eliminated at the New York National Horse show when his horse 'Killaloe' knocked an obstacle.

.   .   .

I have no doubt but that our mother's entrepreneurship came from her father who we never met. As kids we had only one set of grandparents alive – our dad's parents in Dingle, County Kerry. Our mother's father, James Lyons from Ballyhaunis in County Mayo, died in 1932 before any of us were born. And his wife Kate died in 1915 at the young age of 50, when our mother was only 13. They had 15 children, our mother being the youngest, and even though one was a priest, two were nuns, and one never married, the rest produced 45 children providing us with loads of first cousins, most of whom we never met.

When Kate died, teenager Greta moved in with her elder brother John Lyons, who was a dispensary doctor in Kilkelly, County Mayo, and his kindly wife Mae (nee Higgins). It was not unusual in those years of large families to have older children rear younger children.

James Lyons (1852–1932), my maternal grandfather who I never met

James Lyons was born in 1852 in Ballyhaunis around the time of the Famine.

He was a very small man in stature but he was an entrepreneur with great energy. He quickly built up a substantial business in Ballyhaunis. Not only was he a general merchant, but he had a commercial hotel, a seven day liquor licence and was an undertaker as well. He placed an advertisement in the *Western People* newspaper in 1894 when he was 42 years of age proclaiming his new hearse business:

A Want Supplied. JAMES LYONS, the proprietor of this old-established Hotel, feels pleasure in announcing that he has added to his already extensive posting establishment a HEARSE and an additional NEW CARRIAGE. Both vehicles are of superior description, built in the most modern style by eminent Dublin builders. Mr Lyons desires particularly to announce to the people of Ballyhaunis and neighbourhood, who have had in the past to go to neighbouring towns for Hearse accommodation, that he is now in a position to supply from his establishment in Ballyhaunis a Hearse and Mourning Carriage. Funeral contracts undertaken and punctually carried out. Terms strictly moderate.

James used his relative wealth to ensure that all his children were well educated. But there was trouble in the family because his children took up different positions on the Treaty with Britain in 1922. This was not unusual in Irish families at the time. The trouble got worse when one of the family, our mother's brother Jimmy, joined the Irish Free State Army as an officer. However, happily, the funeral of their father James in 1932 brought the family together again and old wounds were healed. James got a great send-off with the funeral Mass being celebrated by his son (our uncle Fr Laurence from Cong) and 40 priests – yes 40!

The obituary in the *Western People* was fulsome in its praise of him in the flowery language of the times:

> In the passing away of Mr James Lyons, Ballyhaunis has lost one of its outstanding and most honourable landmarks. Born close on 79 years ago in the town of Ballyhaunis, he came of a stock which for many generations had been very closely identified with the public and commercial life of Ballyhaunis and the county, of which it is the centre. For close on 60 years he himself has been in business in Ballyhaunis, and with an industry and an integrity of character for which there must be few parallels, he had all his undertakings crowned with success. In the sphere of life which he adopted he was brought into contact with countless people, and it is but the bare truth to say that everyone who ever came to know him, knew him as a man industrious beyond the ordinary, honest and just in all his dealings. ... He died on February 13th, full of years, and with his life's work done, and well done.

There is one mystery about my grandfather James's business which I have been unable to solve. In a photograph of his shop front taken about 1900, there is a carved message. 'Only the finest lagnours supplied'.

What are lagnours? I have consulted widely with language and history experts and with local historians. I have had many possible explanations, including one that lagnours means wines. There is no doubt but that my grandfather supplied wines and that he would have had the finest wines. The other is that lagnours were a type of leather leggings worn by farm-

*My maternal grandfather outside his shop on
Main Street, Ballyhaunis (1900)*

ers which were strapped around their trousers to protect them
from dirt. Both explanations are plausible but they are certainly not conclusive. Perhaps I will get the definitive answer some
day.

While I never met my Mayo grandfather, I certainly knew a
lot about him and his entrepreneurial spirit which my mother
inherited and which we, his grandchildren, also inherited. Because we moved around so much as kids, apart from Killaloe,
it has been difficult for us to identify ourselves with a definitive
county. So it not surprising that in more recent years I have
been adopted as a stray by Mayo, no doubt influenced by my
mother and grandfather. I am a member of that fine organisation Muintir Mhaigh Eo, and in the 1990s I had the honour to
serve as captain and subsequently as president of the Mayo
Golf Society in Dublin.

.   .   .

My paternal Kerry grandfather, William Murdoch, was also a
businessman but very different. He must have cut an unusual
figure as he walked up Green Street in the County Kerry town
of Dingle in 1904. He was a tall, erect, imposing figure of a

man – what you would expect of a northern Presbyterian, born as he had been in 1880 in Loughbrickland, County Down. But what was this Presbyterian businessman doing in Catholic Dingle – well, he was a Catholic also, or was he?

At the turn of the century our grandfather had come south to be apprenticed to the retail trade in a big general merchants in Tralee called Latchfords. There he was to meet my grandmother, Honoria Noreen Tracy (1885–1956), a Catholic from Cappoquin, County Waterford. As was the norm at the time, he converted to Catholicism, or did he? He died aged 84 in May 1964 and is buried in a family plot in the old Rahenyhoid cemetery. Some years later I asked a local Dingle man if he knew my grandfather. 'The Presbyterian,' said he, 'of course I knew him. A fine cut of a man was your grandfather and a decent man.'

I suppose the description of my grandfather as 'The Presbyterian' was understandable. While he regularly attended Mass and all his children were brought up as Catholics, he stood out as different in many ways. The general store which he had established on Green Street (now Lisbeth Mulcahy's weavers shop) was the traditional one, with a counter on each side as you entered the front door. But unlike all the other stores, it did not have a pub at the back of the shop, reflecting his approach to temperance and moderation. Also, he had that northern

With parents and Dingle grandparents (1942) – Bill, Laurence, Hilary and me

My granddad's hardware and grocery store with a road frontage of 45 feet, five bedrooms, and side entrance to a large yard, out-offices and garden on Green Street, Dingle

Presbyterian approach to diligent hard work, honesty and principles, such as keeping your word and paying your taxes.

He particularly preached tolerance – 'respecting differences' as he would put it, whether in religion or politics. At the risk of offending all Dingle people, I venture to guess that these would not have been the prevailing characteristics of the local population at that time! While the local population might have regarded my grandfather as still a Presbyterian, not so his relations in Loughbrickland. When they heard that he had taken the Roman shilling, he was immediately cut off, to the extent that he learned of his own father's death months after the funeral had taken place.

While my grandfather preached tolerance and respecting differences during the 60 years he lived in Dingle, I wonder what he would think of the conversion of our Catholic daughter Maeve to Islam following her marriage to a Muslim, and the marriage of our Catholic son Breffni to a Quaker. Would he enquire, 'Have you gone too far in respecting differences?' I am convinced that if he had met Maeve's husband Ahmed Al-Dam and Breffni's wife Becci Haughton, and our brilliant grandchildren (Amira, Nabil, Malik, Tamara, Daisy, Luke and Bonnie), he would emphatically applaud how his son Archie (my father) had brought us all up to respect differences.

I had a special relationship with my grandfather William. I was 10 years of age in 1948 when he visited us in Kilkee. He saw the work we kids were doing at the time with fret saws

Granddad's business letterhead (1959)

and plywood. We got the plywood from the large tea chests in which tea was delivered to local grocery shops. I made a pipe stand and posted it to him in Dingle. He was delighted with it and to encourage me further, he wrote to me saying that he would fund 50 per cent of the material costs of any project I undertook, provided it was something which would be useful, which he had approved beforehand with a budget of the costs involved, and provided I gave some form of proof of completion of the project.

The incentive certainly worked because over the next few years I made a lot of things from wood, particularly when we came to Killaloe and got involved with Jim Ryan in making model airplanes. And in 1952, now 14 years of age, I sent my grandfather details of my biggest project ever, complete with costings and timeframe. I was going to build a 14 foot (4.3 metres) canoe or kayak, complete with paddles. The structure was going to be wood and marine plywood, using rust-proof brass screws throughout, the hull would be planked, and to finish it off it would be covered with rubberised canvass, similar to the covering on curraghs, but this was a new product which had come on the market recently.

I got the plans for the canoe in a book which I borrowed from the library in Killaloe. The cost of the materials was £12 (€15.38) which was a lot of money at the time, but granddad quickly approved the project. I got all the wood materials from

*With Bill and Laurence before the launch of
my home-made canoe (1953)*

Speights in Limerick and the McGraths in Bridge Street collected them and delivered them, free of charge, on their lorry.
I had to get the rubberised canvas and special glue from England. I then spent the whole of that winter and the following
spring building the canoe in a large room in the dilapidated
part of our Aillebaun House, having checked beforehand that I
would be able to get it out the window when completed.

At times I wondered if I had taken on too much, particularly
in fitting the planks on the hull frame. They had to be individu-
ally steamed using an electric kettle and bent into shape. But
eventually, in May 1953, the project was complete and ready to
be launched. I was fairly confident that it would float but I took
the precaution of getting our local curate, Fr Michael Casey, to
bless the canoe. Then my brothers Bill and Laurence helped
me carry the canoe the short distance down to the Killaloe canal where, just opposite the house where the Grimes lived, we
launched the canoe and it did float.

The Killaloe correspondent for the *Clare Champion*, Tommy Grimes, had this to say the following week:

*The canoe floats on the Killaloe Canal – the Lakeside Hotel
is in the background, behind the trees (1953)*

Paddling his own canoe. Henry Murdoch (15) of Aillebaun
House, Killaloe, spent his spare time from last Christmas
building a canoe, and a right good job he made of it (writes
our Killaloe correspondent). Henry was a proud boy last
weekend as he paddled around the Shannon in his craft.
The boat would do credit to any master craftsman. Henry
is a son of Mr A Murdoch, accountant, Provincial Bank
and Mrs Murdoch, and is at present a student at the Crescent College, Limerick.

I got great enjoyment over the years from that canoe, as did
my siblings. Sr May Doyle, sister of my old pal Sam Doyle, has
told me that she often stood on the Aillebaun, feasting on the
beauty of the lake and the hillocks of Clare and seeing my sister
Hilary paddling my canoe up and down the canal. She com-
mented, 'We envied her as it was the first canoe we ever saw in
Killaloe.'

Some years later I endeavoured to convert it into a sailing
canoe by adding a Scandinavian tiller, two lifting side keels,
and a mast and sails, but it was a failure as it kept capsizing
with the slightest puff of wind. I don't know whether this was

The unsuccessful conversion to a sailing canoe (1955)

a design fault or the fact that at that time I had not sailed a boat before. Either scenario or both is a possibility.

. . .

Peter Lacy, who lived just below us, on Canal Bank was the local painter and decorator. But he was more than that. He was the person who taught most boys and girls in Killaloe and Ballina, over many decades, how to swim. And amazingly, he could not swim himself. He taught me how to swim at the Pier Head, using the local river reeds under my arms as a floatation device. My elder brother Bill and my younger brother Laurence had both learned to swim in the sea at Kilkee, but I was obviously a slow learner in that department.

Most people do not believe me when I tell them that I, and countless other young people in Killaloe, were taught how to swim by a man who could not swim himself. I was beginning to doubt my own memory. I am glad however to read in Phil Edmonds recent book *Reconnecting with the Soul of Ireland* (2009) that he confirms that Peter Lacy could not swim himself. Phil would be about 13 years younger than me and undoubtedly Peter's technique had got more sophisticated by then. Gone were the reeds and in came the harness. 'He would place a harness around us and with a rope would haul us up as he gave us instructions how to swim,' recounts Phil. He then describes how they would be allowed to 'go off the rope' when Peter judged them ready to swim without support.

There is a plaque at the Pier Head which recognises the contribution made by Peter Lacy. It states: 'Erected by the members of St Lua's swimming club to the fond memory of Peter Lacy, founder member of the club, who dedicated much of his life to teaching boys and girls how to swim'. Peter founded the club in 1936. By 1959 the club had 149 members – not bad from the combined total population of Killaloe/Ballina at the time of 1,100. Peter was elected as President of the club in 1981. He is referred to in the *Nenagh Guardian* of 14 February 1981 as the 'Mayor of Killaloe'. He made an enormous contribution to Killaloe/Ballina throughout his life. He died on 30 August 1986, aged 75, and the headstone on his grave in the Killaloe Cemetery was erected by members of the club.

•   •   •

Just upstream from the lockkeeper's house (now the Killaloe Library), the annual St Lua's Swimming Gala took place every summer. It was organised by Peter Lacy. It consisted of races in the canal for all ages, usually over 50 yards (45.7 metres) or 100 yards (91.4 metres). My brother Laurence was a great swimmer and won many prizes at these annual galas. These included the Boys under 16 in August 1954, the Captain Bramwell Perpetual Memorial Cup in 1955 and 1956, and the 50 yard freestyle in 1957 and 1959.

My brother Laurence in 1956 with his cups for swimming

The Swimming Gala always attracted a large crowd, who got great enjoyment from the slippery pole competition. This was a long three-metre heavily greased pole which was placed horizontally out over the canal, near the walkway which currently brings you down to the canal wall. The object was to reach the end of the pole without falling into the canal. The person who walked or slid the furthest without falling was the winner. However, most contestants fell off, into the canal water, after a metre or so. This was because, apart from the grease, the further out you got, the more the pole would bend and get 'bouncy'.

It is a wonder that no one ever got hurt, because it was quite possible to hit your chin off the pole on your descent into the water. I suspect that slippery pole competitions would not be allowed today, on health and safety grounds.

Laurence was great at fishing as well as swimming. One day in early 1956, when he was 15 years old, he was on his own on Lough Derg trolling for trout in our dad's rowing boat. He hooked a small trout which immediately, and very unusually, started splashing on the surface. Laurence spotted a pike's tail breaking surface near the trout. He was using a long line with a nylon leader of just six pounds (2.7 kilogrammes) breaking strain, tied to a one inch (2.5 centimetres) home-made bait with a tiny treble hook, both of which could be easily broken by a small pike. He was not using the wire 'trace' that you would normally use for pike fishing. Laurence stopped reeling in and let the pike take the trout. He let it run with the trout for a moment, cautiously struck the rod and crossed his fingers! He hooked the pike! Then, wherever the pike went, Laurence followed in the boat as he could apply only gentle pressure on the fish. After about 20 minutes of very careful play he had the pike on the surface beside the boat and managed to lift it manually on board without a fishing net or gaff. The little hook was in the lower lip of the pike and was half straightened! Our scales in Aillebaun House were too small to weight the pike, so it was weighed in Crotty's shop four days later and came in at 29.5 pounds (13.4 kilogrammes). You may think that this is a 'fishy' story, but it is true.

· · ·

There is no doubt but that our mother's entrepreneurship rubbed off on my brother Bill and, to a lesser extent, on me. Bill spent his whole working life in the private sector and was a real entrepreneur, taking real risks. I was less so, well able to take risks, but from the comfort of the permanent and pensionable protection of the public sector. Even in the mid-1980s, when I was managing director of Cleanaway Ireland, a waste management firm in the private sector, I was on a 'career break' from the public sector. And even when I was made redundant, practised at the Bar in 1986 and set up Topaz Publications in 1988 to publish my book *Murdoch's Dictionary of Irish Law*, there was a potential financial penalty for failure, but I had the assurance of a job back in the public sector. And when, in 2000, with Lendac Data Systems, we launched the internet version of the dictionary, a one-stop shop for Irish and European law with over one million hyperlinks to legal sources, I was on a public sector pension. There was risk in all these innovations, but it was minimised as much as possible.

On the other hand, at one stage in his career, Bill left a permanent and pensionable position with *The Irish Times* to fill a gap in the market – a monthly business magazine which would have in-depth analyses of business stories. That was real risk taking, with the potential for huge losses or gains, and no assured route back to *The Irish Times*. Bill was the founding editor of *Irish Business* magazine in 1975, and was subsequently appointed as Business Editor of *The Irish Times* in 1978.

6

Killaloe Professor Number One – Jim Ryan

'We don't have a 12 volt battery; let's try the elec-
tricity' – Jim Ryan, Professor Number One, to me
Professor Number Two, before the explosion (1952)

Jim Ryan was one of the most remarkable persons I have ever met. In the short time that our paths crossed in my formative years in Killaloe, he was probably the one person, other than my parents, who had the greatest, and most positive, influence on my life. When we came to Killaloe in 1949 when I was 11 years old, the Ryan family became friendly with ours. They owned a sweet and newspaper shop just up the road from us on Main Street/Church Street, at the intersection with Bridge Street – now 'Kincora House'.

Except for Carmel, the Ryan children were all adults and much older than us Murdochs. Jim Ryan was three time my age. Born in 1918, Jim was only 14 years younger than my parents and was 20 years older than me. His brother Sean was a concert tenor and occasionally came home to Killaloe. He had a beautiful voice and sang at Christmas Mass – 'Panis Angelicus' (The Bread of Angels). His other brother, Brendan, had a job in the duty free airport at Shannon and his sister, Maureen, was married to Danny Collins, who also worked in Shannon. Carmel was the baby of the family.

Jim Ryan in Canada in 1995

The Ryans were a very musical family and everyone was expected to do a turn at their musical afternoons. They taught me to sing the musical hall song of 1900 – 'Burlington Bertie from Bow' – which I reluctantly and badly performed. I can still remember it now:

> I'm Burlington Bertie. I rise at ten-thirty and saunter along like a toff. I walk down the Strand with my gloves on my hand. Then I walk down again with them off. I'm all airs and graces, correct easy paces. So long without food so long, I've forgot where my face is. I'm Bert, Bert, I haven't a shirt. But my people are well off you know. Nearly everyone knows me from Smith to Lord Rosebr'y, I'm Burlington Bertie from Bow.

My brothers Bill and Laurence, our friend Gussie Henchy and I spent a considerable amount of time in Jim's company. He had served in the Royal Air Force (RAF) and was an expert on airplanes.

Sean Ryan as Burlington Bertie (CCL)

He had studied veterinary science, though was not a qualified vet, but he knew a lot about animals. To us he was a very knowledgeable and hugely entertaining. He introduced us to practical things like making model airplanes that flew – free flying ones, hand controlled ones by wires, and we even built a radio controlled one. The engines we used were either jets, fired by a special tablet of combustible material, or fuel powered engines with propellers.

We made up the fuel ourselves, getting the basic materials from Bennet's Chemist shop (now Collins) on Main Street. Starting the propeller engines by physically twirling the propeller was a feat in itself. When the engine fired into operation, you had to extract your hand rapidly or else your fingers could be taken off. Jim was the founder of the Kincora Model Flying Club and we four were its members. We even put on an exhibition of all our airplanes in the community hall (now Whelans's supermarket on Church Street) in Killaloe for An Tóstal in 1953 and 1954. An Tóstal was a Government initiative in which all villages and towns were encouraged to host some events at a designated time to encourage tourism. It was a similar initiative to that of The Gathering in 2013.

The founder members of the Kincora Model Airplane Club at Aillebaun House in 1953: Gussie Henchy, Jim Ryan, myself, and my brothers Laurence and Bill

The Irish Tourist Board in 1952 explained that *tóstal* meant pageant, muster, array or display, and that in English the explanatory wording 'Ireland at Home' would be used. 'It is intended that the whole country will, for the period of three weeks, be at home to Irish exiles and friends from everywhere' the Board was quoted in *The Irish Times* on 8 April 1952. A national organiser was appointed, Major-General Hugo MacNeill, and he explained that the intention was to lengthen our short tourism season which was concentrated in the months of June, July and August.

The initiative was a great success throughout the country. Dublin was spruced up, with flower baskets on lamp standards and festoon lighting on the arches of the Liffey River bridges. There was a Tóstal flag and a tie, and some wondered if the festival would lead to a special dress code for An Tóstal. An

Oige opened a new youth hostel, the first in Connaught, at Lettermullen, Connemara as its contribution to the initiative.

But the 'at home' initiative was not without its controversy. It was criticised by one *Irish Times* reader who wrote that he lived with his wife and six children in a labourer's cottage, without sanitation or light, and had to use his garden as a dump.

'What's this about An Tóstal. There are many of us here in Ireland who would be ashamed to show our 'exiled' relatives the conditions under which we have to live' – 18 October 1952.

And Aer Lingus was criticised for having a poster promoting An Tóstal printed in England. An Aer Lingus spokesperson explained that they had to get the printing done in England due to a printers' strike in Ireland in July 1952, according to *The Irish Times* of 8 November 1952.

Killaloe took to the initiative with enthusiasm. In his book *History of Smith O'Brien GAA Club* (1991), local historian Sean Kierse recounts that:

> ... the Killaloe Tóstal Committee was elected from representatives of all organisations in the district. The festival was opened on Easter Sunday at The Green by Canon Molloy. This was followed by a parade to the Ballina sportsfield where two hurling matches were played. That evening the Tóstal Queen was crowned at a dance in the Kincora Hall. Other events that took place during the following two weeks included fishing competitions, children's sports, old-time waltz competitions, ceili dances, a model aircraft exhibition, and a fancy dress display.

The *Nenagh Guardian* on 25 April 1953 captured well the enthusiasm for An Tóstal in Killaloe:

> Last Sunday was childrens' day at Killaloe. Hundreds of happy children paraded the town from the Bridge to the Sportsfield, where they all took part in a most enjoyable afternoon's sport. The procession was headed by a band of musicians and the route was lined with crowds of people. At the end of the sports the children returned to the bridge where open air dancing was held.' Notable prize winners

included Deirdre McKeogh (under 11) and Pat Brooks (under 16).

There followed a concert to mark the anniversary of the Battle of Clontarf (1014) which was opened by an adult choir under the direction of local national school teacher Nora Lynch, with a rendition of 'Remember the Glories of Brian the Brave'. Under the heading, 'The spirit of Kincora lives in Killaloe', the *Limerick Leader* reported on 2 May 1953:

> Then a group of tiny dancers from the Collin's School Ballina, appeared in a scene representing the Fort of Kincora. Killaloe Boys' National School rendered a selection of Moore's melodies, and Miss Josephine Hogan sang an old Killaloe folk song 'I love the boys'. Mr Peter Lacy brought the house down with a spirited rendering of 'Brian na Banba'.

Our model aircraft exhibition was officially opened by our parish priest Canon Molloy on 16 April 1953 and we got great publicity in the local press. The *Nenagh Guardian* reported on 25 April 1953:

> MODEL FLYING CLUB: Very Rev Canon Molloy PP VF, President of the Kincora Model Flying Club, opened the display of model planes and gliders held by the club in connection with the An Tóstal celebrations. He paid tribute to Mr J J Ryan, the club founder, and to the boys for their taking up such a healthy and interesting hobby. The exhibition was very well supported and a large number of new members were enrolled.

We held another exhibition the following year in 1954 with some of our classmates from Crescent College Limerick participating. This is what the *Nenagh Guardian* reported on 1 May 1954:

> The Exhibition of Model Airplanes staged by the Kincora Model Flying Club in connection with An Tóstal was an outstanding event in the local programme and one that deserved much more support than was given to it. A much admired exhibit was the radio controlled model displayed

Killaloe Model Plane Exhibition

With Cathedral in background, my brother Laurence,
John Doherty, Canon Molloy, me, Jim Ryan, Gussie Henchy,
my brother Bill on the right (1953)

by Mr W E Modin, Pan American Airways, Shannon Airport. Mr Jim Ryan, Club Instructor, showed a night flying diesel model complete with full lighting equipment. Other exhibitors were the brothers Larry, Harry and Billy Murdoch and Gussie Henchy, Killaloe, with Des Croucher, Fergus Byrne and Harry Hayes of Limerick.

So all five members of the club got a mention in the newspaper, even though they called me 'Harry'. Des Croucher was a classmate of Bill's at Crescent College and Fergus Byrne and Harry Hayes were my classmates there. We gave Canon Molloy all the gate receipts and he gave us each a shilling (€0.06) for our troubles. I don't know if he gave Jim Ryan anything!

An Tóstal celebrations continued in Killaloe for a number of years even after they had ceased in other towns. In May 1955, Joe McKeogh Jnr of Inchamore, Ballina, was elected King of Kincora at a dance at the Kincora Hall. Miss Olive Mills (10) was crowned as An Tóstal Queen in 1956 at a *ceilli mhor* at the Killaloe boys' national school. And in opening the 1956 An Tóstal ceremonies on the Green, now Archdeacon Molloy said that he was proud 'to stand on the historic spot where the Royal

In 1954 with our airplanes at Aillebaun House and old railway house in background; at back, Des Croucher, our dad, Bill Murdoch; sitting down,Hilary Murdoch, our mother, Maurice Power; at front, Gussie Henchy, me and brother Laurence

Palace of Brian Boru once stood and from where the great king ruled our country so wisely and so well'. In the children's fancy dress parade that took place later, with more than 30 children taking part, winners included Gussie Henchy and Pat Mulcahy as 'The Smith O'Brien hurling team 1888-1956' and Dick Edmonds as 'Coarse Angler'.

Forty-six years later in 2002, An Post issued four stamps to commemorate the declaration of Brian Boru as High King of Ireland, each depicting a different event in the life of Brian. The design is by Finbarr O'Connor.

Postage stamp issued in 2002 to commemorate the 1000th anniversary of the declaration of Brian Boru as High King of Ireland (reproduced by kind permission of An Post).

• • •

We got the parts for our airplanes from London, from the then famous department store known as Gamages. A

96

friend of my parents, Olive Stokes, who was married to a Shannon businessman Jack Lynch, went to London often with her husband, and she would always bring us back an airplane kit. Olive's father Arthur Stokes had been manager of the Provincial Bank (later AIB) before our family arrived in Killaloe in 1949.

The Lynchs lived in a beautiful house on Lough Derg off the Ogonnelloe Road, just past the present University of Limerick Activity Centre. I met their son Stephen Lynch by chance in Reddan's Pub in October 2013 while researching this book. Ireland is a small place and Killaloe is even smaller! Olive died on 12 May 1977 and Jack died on 11 September 2001. They are both laid to rest at St Flannan's Cathedral.

We flew our airplanes in local fields and bogs, always attracting a crowd. It was all so exciting, tinged on the odd occasion with great grief. The first flight of a newly constructed airplane was always nerve-racking. With a free flying airplane, we would first check if it would glide properly, without the engine running. We would then make the appropriate adjustment, including one to the rudder to ensure that it would fly in a fairly large circle, away from buildings and trees but not too far away to be retrieved subsequently. We would then start the engine and send her on her way.

Flying our airplanes in a local bog near Birdhill in 1954:
my brother Laurence and Bill, Jim Ryan, myself,
Gussie Henchy and local children

It was a wonder to watch one's own handiwork fly away up into the sky, climbing all the time until the fuel ran out after about five minutes, and then to see her gradually descending in a gentle glide and landing in a field, hopefully not too far away. On the odd occasion, after takeoff the airplane would go into a stall and nosedive into the ground with the engine screaming, and be concertinaed into an unrecognisable heap of balsa wood. A month's work destroyed! Luckily this was only on the odd occasion.

Our exploits did not go unnoticed. After a day flying our airplanes near Castleconnell, the following article entitled 'Killaloe takes to the air. Enthusiastic Young Fliers' appeared in the *Nenagh Guardian* of 28 March 1953:

> Killaloe folk are accustomed to the throb of the big airliners majestically over Kincora along the airways east from Shannon Airport. Air operations around Killaloe are not however confined to the big fellows of sub-stratosphere build. Did you happen along the Limerick – Nenagh road on Sunday evening last, you might have seen, near Castleconnell, quite a few Killaloe youths standing around a varied collection of miniature airplanes. If you stopped to ask what it was all about, you would have learned that Killaloe Model Airplane Club had just concluded a very successful day's air operations.
>
> You would have heard that the enthusiastic young airmen had 'started flying that morning after first Mass' in Killaloe, and had followed the fortunes of their home built craft over hill and dale, almost to Bunratty. You would have been told of the performance of the 'big powered one', the large model which is the pride of the club. It, according to one potential birdman (who is at present around 10 years old), got to 'an altitude of 300 feet, or maybe yards, and flew nearly a mile at a time.
>
> And you would have noticed that all these little lads, though maybe a bit tired from their cross-country aeroplane chasing, were quite happy in the recollection of a day's excellent sport, and bubbling over with ideas regard-

ing the future flying of the little planes they so carefully shepherded back to base on Sunday evening.

It would seem that Killaloe's very young folk are getting their very young feet set on the floor of the yet Young Air Age we live in. That is all to the good. One learned that the driving force behind Killaloe's Model Aeroplane Club is Mr James Ryan, Church Street, Killaloe, whose keen interest in aeronautics is mainly responsible for giving Killaloe's Model Aeroplane Club its wings.

·   ·   ·

I spent a lot of time in Jim's company, more than the others. I called him 'Professor Number One' and he called me 'Professor Number Two'. He had a den where he carried out all his model-making and experiments above the archway of the Ryan house.

Jim cut a large round hole in the floor through to the archway, creating a trapdoor. When I arrived at the archway, I would announce my presence by pressing a bell and speaking into an intercom wired system he had set up: 'Professor Number Two calling Professor Number One. Permission to enter?' If Jim was in his den, he would answer: 'Professor Number Two. Permission granted.' He would then lift the trapdoor and a ladder would descend. It was all James Bond stuff, years before James Bond came on the scene.

Ryans' home is now 'Kincora House'

I had no difficulty with science at secondary school because many of the chemistry experiments I had already carried out with Jim. He just loved doing experiments. He had a book of chemical experiments which he generally followed exactly.

One such experiment was a basic one of showing how you could coat a metal object with copper by using an electric current and a copper sulphate solution. We had the metal object, a key, we had the copper sulphate solution and a tub to contain it. But we did not have the recommended 12 volt battery.

'Let's try the electricity,' said Jim, when I queried if we could use the house electricity. He connected the key in the tub with wire to the light fitting in the ceiling. He must have realised that there was some risk involved because we both went out of the room while Jim turned on the light switch using a brush handle through the nearly closed door. There was a load explosion, the main electric fuse for the house was blown, the copper sulphate solution was all over the ceiling and the walls, and the poor key was a sorry shadow of its former self. I do not know how Jim explained this to his mother, but I tailed it rapidly down the trapdoor, out the archway and down home.

In today's times of political correctness, the friendship of a 32-year-old man with a 12-year-old boy would be frowned upon. I am glad I was brought up in a time when there was no such jumping to judgment, because I would not have learned as much as I did about science and technology, and what people would now call 'thinking outside the box'. There was something else about Jim Ryan or 'James Joseph Aloysius Ignatius Archibald Zinclaire Hugh Ryan' as he would sometimes humorously call himself. He made up stories, mostly about the little people in the forest, and in telling these stories, which would be rich in characters, he would intertwine his detailed knowledge of trees and flowers and fauna. He often would say to me that as long as you can think, you should never be bored because your mind can create whatever world you want it to.

With Jim's influence, I suppose it is no wonder that ten years later I joined Aer Lingus as an aircraft development engineer in 1962, and was licensed to approve modifications to Boeing, Fokker and BAC airplanes. I subsequently spent two years at the Boeing Airplane Company in Seattle in the late 1960s and spent the last three years of my ten years with Aer Lingus as the Aircraft Leasing Manager, a job which was filled by Tony

Ryan when I left in 1972. Tony Ryan went on to create GPA and Ryanair.

I was not surprised to hear that Jim Ryan, Professor Number One, used his veterinary skills to carve out a great career for himself in Canada because I saw those skills displayed in practice. He had a great love for animals and they for him – which we saw when he befriended the wild animals when Duffy's Circus came to Killaloe every year.

Jim Ryan with circus wild bear at Killaloe, 1953

We also saw that skill with our cat Smokey. She had been poorly for some time and was rapidly getting worse. My mother asked me to get Jim to have a look at her. Jim sent me up to Bennet's Chemists for some ether and cotton wool. He laid out Smokey on a pile of newspapers on our scullery table, applied the cotton wool laced with ether over her nose, opened his surgical case and his array of instruments, and cut Smokey open. I could only half watch. Jim seemed to know exactly what he was doing. He cut some parts out of Smokey and then sewed her up. I watched Smokey nervously. She gradually woke up, rolled over, stretched herself, jumped off the table, snuggled up to the warm range, and lived happily for the next two years.

Jim was not just building model airplanes and doing experiments with us. He had to earn a living. In 1954 he built a garage and petrol station on the 'New Line', the road approaching Killaloe from Limerick on the County Clare side. It wasn't surprising that the station had as a theme the little people of his stories. So there were large scale concrete mushrooms, toadstools and leprechauns, all suitably painted.

One large mushroom had fairies inside, each carrying a placard with a marketing statement, for example, 'We mend

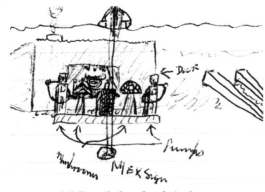

My childhood sketch of Jim's garage

punctures like lightening', and, 'Have you changed your oil recently?' The *Limerick Weekly Echo* in December 1954 ran an article about Jim's garage with the heading 'Killaloe Man's Novel garage – with Leprechauns'. Jim was into innovative marketing before his time!

Then Jim's interest in model airplane and experiments suddenly ceased. The Bennet's Chemists, next door to the Ryan's shop, had some spare space in their premises so they decided to open a ladies hairdressing salon. They recruited a hairdresser called Elsie Cregan from County Tipperary. She was a 19-year-old beauty and it wasn't long before Jim was smitten. They got married and in 1958, when I was an engineering student in University College Cork, they emigrated to Canada. That was the end of Professor Number One and Professor Number Two but not an end to the memories.

· · ·

I lost touch with Jim and Elsie for the next 40 years. In 1996, I happened to be attending the opening of a new sewerage works in Ballina, across the river from Killaloe. I was an Assistant Director General of FÁS – the training and employment authority at the time. I had some spare time that morning, so I decided to take a stroll up the Main Street in Killaloe. I passed two ladies outside Minogue's butchers and said 'Good Morning'. They nodded in acknowledgement. I thought they were Chris Minogue, daughter of the butcher, and Patricia Brooks, a lady that I remembered as a beautiful girl from my teenage years, who had worked in the Benson Box factory, but I wasn't sure. I went up the street, passing Ryan's old house and the memories of my childhood came flooding back. I came down the street, again passing the two ladies.

Chris Minogue asked, 'Are you one of the Murdochs?' When I said that I was, she said, 'Say nothing, I want you to meet my mother.' She brought me into the butchers and called out, 'Mammy, come out here, there's a man who wants to meet you'. Mrs Minogue came out and greeted me. 'Do you know who he is?' asked her daughter. 'He is one of the Murdochs – Bill or Henry,' she said.

Well, we got chatting about the past. They told me that Sean Ryan, the tenor, was now retired and was living in our old house, Aillebaun House. And they told me that my old pal Jim Ryan was very ill. His young sister Carmel, who worked in the tourist office, would be able to give me details. I met Carmel and she updated me. She suggested I talk with her sister Maureen who then lived in Royal Parade as she had all the contact details. I got all the details from Maureen including the number of the telephone beside Jim's bed in a hospital in Toronto. She said he was making a good recovery, and that he would love to hear from me.

So I telephoned Jim that night when I got back to Dublin. It was a slightly croaky voice that answered me. I said to him, 'Professor Number One. This is Professor Number Two. How are you?' He didn't appear to hear me, so I repeated it, a little louder this time. He responded, 'Professor Number Two from Killaloe – Henry Murdoch?' he enquired, nearly disbelievingly. After all it was nearly 40 years since we last spoke.

We had a great chat. I know he really appreciated my call. So next day, I sent him a get-well card, a few photos from the old days in Killaloe, and a copy of my book *Murdoch's Dictionary of Irish Law*, which I suitably inscribed, and a long letter telling him about my family and all the things which had happened in the previous 40 years.

Rather than send me a long letter when he was discharged from hospital, Jim sent me photos of his family and his home, all numbered, and an audio tape to explain them, with his favourite music playing in the background. In the tape he told me about the time he and Elsie emigrated to Canada, how times were tough at the start, how he had got a job as a technician in a laboratory in the University of Toronto dealing with rabies in animals, and how he had got a contract to provide a rabies testing and an isolation station from the local government and had held the contract for 34 years.

He told me about the birth of his five children – Jamie, Sean, Paul, Cora and Gráinne – what they were doing, who they had married, and about his seven grandchildren, with two more on the way. He particularly referred to his latest grandchild Erik, who was the son of his daughter Cora, who he said 'was the delight of my life and the apple of my eye'. He told me that they had put their lovely house 'Tara' in Stouffville, Ontario, on the market as they needed a smaller house. And he was looking forward to the next stage of his life, now that he had beaten the cancer of the bladder.

Jim's house in Stouffville, Ontario, Canada (1996)

Jim and Elsie with their children and grandchildren – Erik is at the bottom right

Unfortunately, about seven months later Jim passed away in 1997, aged 79. I was so sad. Professor Number One was finally gone. But he would be delighted that now in 2014 his grandchild Erik – the delight of his life and the apple of his eye – is studying for a degree in Communications at Dublin City University and is a frequent visitor to his relations in Killaloe.

• • •

Following Jim Ryan's death in 1997, I lost touch with his family for the next nearly 10 years. In December 2007, I was doing a spring-clean and came across the photos and audio tape which Jim had sent me. The cassette tape brought a lump in my throat when I played it. It needed to be preserved in a more permanent form. The cassette player needed to play it was no longer being sold. I was heavily into making DVDs from all kinds of media at the time, so I decided to make a DVD of Jim's photos, using his voice as the commentary, and his tenor brother Sean's song 'The Lake Near Killaloe' which I had on a vinyl record, as background music.

His family loved the DVD.

> I have just finished watching the incredible DVD you so kindly sent to me. It brought tears and laughter to me.

And:

> I can't say enough how wonderful it is …. it brought tears to my eyes … Mom came in just after it started and sat down and watched … she really loved it as well and told me that it was really the first recording of dad's voice that she had listened to since he died.

Jim's wife Elsie telephoned me some days later to thank me for the DVD. She passed away on 1 December 2009. I am glad I made the DVD and made contact with Jim's family. I think that Professor Number One would be pleased with his Professor Number Two.

· · ·

There is some controversy in Killaloe as to who composed the song 'The Lake Near Killaloe'. I always thought it was composed by Sean Ryan as he told us he had written it. It is a beautiful song with terrific lyrics and is wonderfully sung by Sean Ryan. The chorus of the song went:

> Oh, I long to row my boat away
> And dream my love of you

And watch the sun beams turn to gold
The Lake near Killaloe.

Jim Crowe, who lived on Main Street and now lives in New Zealand, and who visited me in Dublin in 2013, said that Sean and I, in a rather drunken state, sang the song together in a row boat, which he, Jim, rowed across the Shannon River in 1959, to bring us home from a night out in the Lakeside Hotel.

Sean Ryan at the height of his career in the 1950s (CCL)

Sean and his wife Joan lived in our old Aillebaun House when my parents left Killaloe in 1961. Sean died on 7 June 2003, leaving a daughter Marianna. His wife Joan had died before him on 12 March 1978. At Sean's funeral, the recording of 'Ave Maria' which he had sung at the dedication of the Catholic church in Killaloe in 1958, was played.

Reference was also made by the officiating priest in his eulogy to Sean's song 'The Lake Near Killaloe', when a lady in the church rose to object, saying that the song was written by her father and that Sean Ryan had only sung it. Most people in Killaloe that I have talked to since have said that the intervention at Sean's funeral was inappropriate, and that anyway, whoever had written it, Sean Ryan had sung the song beautifully.

Sean's brother, Brendan Ryan, died a week later on 15 June 2003, aged 77, leaving his wife Rose, and daughters Mary Rose, Marguerite and sons Brendan and James. He was a talented pianist and a life-long member of the Killaloe Parish Choir. He was a kind gentleman. His sister Maureen had four children with Danny Collins – Brendan, Annemarie, Kay and Carmel. Maureen died on 14 December 2009 and Danny passed away in December 2012.

Professor Number One's sister Carmel is the last member of the Ryan family of that generation who has survived. She lives in Aillebaun House.

7

THE TRANSFER WHICH DID
NOT TAKE PLACE

*'I will be sacked by the bank for disobeying an in-
struction' – My father's response when my mother
rebelled against another transfer (1954)*

Mick Cleary and his wife had a small newspaper shop on
Bridge Street. Mick had a rowing boat, similar to that
which my father had, with a small Seagull outboard engine,
moored at the canal wall beside the current Library and Visitors' Centre. Mick was a great fisherman and often fished
with my father on Lough Derg. Mick was so keen on fishing
that he used to insist on his dinner being brought up to him
on a Wednesday at Crowe's shop, where he worked, so that
he would waste no time in getting out fishing when the shop
closed for the half-day. That was when we all had our dinner
in the middle of the day! Mick was a regular winner of the Perpetual Cup which my father put up in 1962 for the largest trout
caught in Lough Derg. I still have the Cavan Anglers' Perpetual
Cup for the heaviest trout which my father won in 1936. This
prompted him to put up a cup when he was leaving Killaloe, in

*Our family at Aillebaun House in 1952 with Cragg Hill
and the Lakeside Hotel in background.*

recognition of the pleasure he got from angling on Lough Derg
over the previous 12 years.

My father was very embarrassed by an incident with Mick
Cleary in 1953 for which I was responsible. I was then 15-years-
old and a fifth year student in Crescent College in Limerick.
A fellow student in the college, Jackie Gleeson, whose father
had an electrical business on O'Connell Street in Limerick, was
an authorised agent for a Dublin-based charity football pools.
This particular football pool required the participants to select eight matches in the following Saturday's English soccer
league matches which they believed would result in a draw.
The best forecast won the first prize of £100 (€128) – a lot of
money at the time, being about two years' fees at university.

Jackie Gleeson asked me to be his agent in Killaloe. I accepted enthusiastically as it would give me an income of one
shilling (€0.06) a week throughout the winter. The deal was
that I had to get 12 participants every week in Killaloe, each
paying one shilling, giving an income per week of twelve shillings (€0.64). I would give Michael eleven shillings in cash every Wednesday, keeping one shilling commission for myself,
and he would take his commission of one shilling, and submit

ten shillings to the charitable pools headquarters in Dublin with the forecast forms by Friday, before the Saturday matches.

My father was nervous about my involvement as he knew I would be targeting the local traders, who would all have been customers of his Provincial Bank, the only bank in the area. He was concerned that those approached by me would feel 'pressurised' to be participants in the pools because I was his son. But he and my mother wanted to support this demonstration of an entrepreneurial spirit and to support the charity, so I got the go-ahead.

Everything went fine for about four months. Every week I got 12 participants, submitted their draw forecasts to Jackie Gleeson and eleven shillings in cash every Wednesday, pocketed my own shilling commission, and I shared the excitement every Saturday with my customers as they and I checked their scores against the results announced on the radio, or the 'wireless' as we called it.

That was until one Saturday evening when Mick Cleary came over to our Aillebaun House and told us that he thought he had correctly forecasted eight draws and would be eligible for the first prize. I checked my records and he was right. We were all excited. Even my father was excited. I thought that the news of getting a winner in Killaloe in a national football pool would spread like wildfire, and instead of 12 participants per week, I could get the whole 900 population involved, make a lot of money for the charity, and particularly make a lot of money for 15-year-old me!

It was not to be. When I got into Crescent College on Monday morning, I immediately sought out Jackie Gleeson, told him that I had a participant in Killaloe who had correctly selected eight drawn matches, and that we were all going to be rich. That was when he told me the devastating news that he had forgotten to send on the forms and the money to Dublin the previous Wednesday, and that he would give me back the money I had collected for that week. You can imagine the consternation this caused back in Killaloe. My father and mother were devastated and hugely embarrassed. I just didn't know how to handle it, except to ensure that everyone knew that I had acted properly and had passed on the forms and the money. The most composed person of all was Mick Cleary. He took the news with a great calmness, 'if it wasn't to be, it wasn't to be.'

That was the end of my involvement in promoting football pools in Killaloe and my one shilling a week commission. To this day, I do not know if the failure of Jackie Gleeson to submit the forms and money to Dublin on that occasion was an isolated incident or otherwise. I will give him the benefit of the doubt as he is now deceased. Also, I do not know if my father and Mick Cleary came to some form of arrangement. In later years I often asked my dad, but he was reluctant to talk about it. I know that his whole moral being would have been to make sure that that wrong was put right and that Mick Cleary was not out-of-pocket. But I also know that he did not have any funds to pay Mick. All my dad divulged to me was that Mick told him that he did not blame me, and that he (Mick) would not have on his conscience anything which might prevent us Murdoch children going to university.

This leads me to believe that my father offered money in compensation to Mick Cleary and that he refused to accept it. I believe that it is likely that my father, who was a brilliant fly and lure maker (for catching trout), gave Mick Cleary some of his best flies and lures in compensation. It is a logical conclusion, but also one which recognises Mick's generosity and the fact that he and my father remained close friends while my father remained in Killaloe.

The Murdoch Perpetual Challenge Cup was my dad's present to his angler friends when he left Killaloe in 1961. The *Nenagh Guardian* reported on 22 September 1962 that the Killaloe–Ballina Anglers' Association had decided that the cup would be awarded outright to the person who won it three years in succession or five years in all. There was stiff competition for the cup over the years, with between 12 and 15 boats taking part every year, and the heaviest trout being about 3 pounds, 10 ounces (1.64 kilogrammes) in 1968.

The cup was won by Joe McMahon and Jimmy Kelly in 1962. Mick Cleary won in 1969 with a trout weighing 2 pounds, 7.25 ounces (1.11 kilogrammes). The last record I have is for September 1970 when Joe Kissane and John McCarthy of Cross Roads, Killaloe, won with a trout weighing 2 pounds, 12 ounces (1.25 kilogrammes). What happened to the cup since then is unknown as the records of the Anglers' Association were stolen in recent times. My dad was delighted that his memory lived on in Killaloe after his departure.

The Clearys had a large family of seven – Noreen, Kay, Carmel, Liam and Michael and two infant daughters Rita and Bernadette. Mick died on 26 February 1975, aged 66, and his wife Margaret (Peggy) died on 25 October 1994, aged 76. They are buried in Ballina cemetery with their infant daughters. Liam still lives in Bridge Street.

· · ·

I had never seen my father look so worried as on that day in May 1954. He had just seen my mother off to the Dublin train at Birdhill, County Tipperary, some three miles from Killaloe.

I was 16 years of age. My mother had donned her finery for her Dublin trip. Out had come the fur coat. I can still smell the moth balls. She had a determined look on her face and that's what worried my father. A few days earlier he had received a letter from the General Manager of the Provincial Bank of Ireland. It said simply: 'Dear Murdoch' (officials of the bank were addressed by their surname) – 'Please report

Birdhill Railway Station in 2014

for duty as the cashier/teller at the bank's branch in Colooney, County Sligo on (a date a fortnight away). Yours sincerely etc.'

'We are not moving,' my mother declared.

My father was aghast – a bank official did not disobey an instruction. 'We have to go,' he said.

'I'm going to Dublin,' said my mother 'to see the General Manager.' My father was even more aghast at this.

We all awaited her return from Dublin with trepidation. What did she say to the General Manager and how did he respond? She told us that she had been met with great respect and given a cup of tea and a scone. She said that she told the General Manager that when she met and married my father in Killarney, the first thing the bank did was to transfer him to far away Cavan, then to Carrick-on-Shannon, years later to Kilkee and then to Killaloe. All in 21 years. Our education had been terribly interrupted and just as we were coming up to university age, we were being transferred even further from a university town.

'I told him that we would accept a transfer to any university town where the Provincial Bank had offices – Dublin, Cork, Galway, Belfast or even London, but otherwise we were not moving from Killaloe.'

What was his response, we enquired?

She said that he seemed genuinely taken aback and just sought confirmation. 'You are saying that you will not transfer except to a university town?'

'Yes,' was my mother's emphatic response, reminding him that she was a university graduate and didn't see why her children should have obstacles put in their way to getting a similar education.

My father's reaction was instantaneous. 'I will be sacked by the bank for disobeying an instruction.'

There was an anxious wait over the next few days. Eventually a letter arrived from the General Manager to my father. It simply said 'Dear Murdoch. I refer to my meeting with Mrs Murdoch on Tuesday last. Your transfer to Colooney is hereby cancelled. You will remain in Killaloe. Yours sincerely etc.'

That was it. No transfer to Colooney. No transfer to a university town. Remain in Killaloe. We kids were delighted and very proud of our mother. Years later, when I asked her how did she have the courage, as the wife of an unremarkable lowly bank official, to take on the General Manager of a big bank, she said that she reminded herself that the man sitting opposite her probably didn't even have his Leaving Cert, whereas she had an honours B.Comm degree and an H.Dip in Ed. from University College Dublin!

.   .   .

My father had a Standard 10 car. But it was up on blocks all during the war, as there was no petrol available. It was a beautiful looking car, with a running board on each side, a cooling water temperature gauge on the bonnet, and windscreen wipers that you could operate manually, in case the electric motor was not working.

It also had front-opening back doors, which were very fashionable at the time. In Killaloe we had a large open-fronted garage at the back of Aillebaun House, just off Crotty's yard and that is where our car remained on blocks until about 1954, when my father sold it to two English men for £20 (€26), which was a

My father's car –
a Standard 10 in 1945

lot of money then – my university fees a year later were £50 (€64).

.   .   .

Killaloe had a thriving eel fishery in the 1800s. There were numerous eel fisheries above and below the bridge. A major one was located at a weir upstream from the existing bridge, near the old railway station, and just below the Lakeside Hotel.

Looking downstream at old weir with Canal Bank at right.

savages. We found it hard to believe that the French, who we knew from our cinema-going to be a sophisticated people, regarded the Killaloe eels as a delicacy. But then, there was a certain consistency with the French, because didn't they also eat horse meat!

•   •   •

Killaloe was a brilliant place to live in. With a population of only 900, everyone was thrown together. Our best pals were the sons of local people, such as the sons of postman Grimes, of shopkeeper Crowe, of haulier McGrath, and of garda sergeant Doyle. There was no class distinction amongst us kids, although we believed that our father was a chip above the block. You could just sense that there was a pecking order and that a bank official was held in high regard. This was probably confirmed in our home where our mother emphasised that we were a cut above the rest! She would sometimes snobbishly refer to persons who were not at our level, about their tendency to 'revert to type'. This was the 1950s.

My father's job in the bank as 'cashier and teller' was a simple one. Essentially, he took in and gave out cash every day and had to balance the transactions at the end of each day. That was when the 'Dublin letter' had to be sent out with the day's statistics. The manager was the person who approved loans and overdrafts. If the cash did not balance and it was negative, my father would go back in the evening to try to find the error. If he couldn't find it, he would have to put in his own cash to make the books balance. Otherwise it would be a black mark and there would likely be a visit from a dreaded 'inspector', as the internal audit officials were then called. My father sometimes worked till midnight to try to balance the books.

Naturally my father believed that his job was a very important and onerous one. He was not amused one day when I told him of my conversation with Tommy Grimes, the local postman, who lived near us on Canal Bank.

'How is June getting on in New York,' I enquired, referring to his 19-year-old daughter who was the elder sister of my hurling and football friend Tony Grimes.

'She is getting on fine, Henry. She has a job in a bank in Manhattan,' he replied.

'Is she the porter?' I enquired as, to my knowledge, there were only four jobs in a bank – porter, clerk, cashier, and manager. While all the porters in the banks in Ireland were males, I knew from the movies that Americans were very progressive and women often did men's jobs. There were even cowgirls in the cowboy films.

'No, no, she is a cashier. She has the same job as your dad. She takes in cash and cheques and has to balance the books every day, just like your dad,' he said proudly. And he was right as I found out some years later on a visit to the USA. There were 19-year-olds doing my dad's job. My 50-year-old father was not impressed!

• • •

Another great friend was John (known to us as 'Sam') Doyle who was son of the local garda sergeant who lived opposite the boys' national school in New Street. Sergeant John Doyle was a traditional policeman, upholding the law in a quiet, un-confrontational way, and was married to May Glynn. They had three children, John ('Sam'), Seamus, who became a Carmelite Priest in 1964; and May, who trained as a primary teacher and became a Presentation Sister in 1962.

Sam, who was a little older than me, was my brother Bill's best friend initially until Bill went off to sea as a radio officer, and then Sam and I became great pals. His sister May believes that John got his 'Sam' name from Bill as he was always known within their family as John.

Bill and Sam were always up to mischief. At one stage they were banned by P.F. Ryan who ran the local cinema on Royal Parade, because they caused a near riot in the cinema one night by releasing itching powder from the balcony onto the unsuspecting clients in the stalls below.

You had to have a good memory watching a film in that cinema. There were two projectors and they would be switched from one to the other, because a feature film might come in eight reels. P.F. was reputed to drink a bottle of whiskey every day and he frequently would get the reels mixed up, so you might get the last reel showing first. Of course getting 'The End' after 15 minutes would lead to loud guffaws and roars from the patrons, which would only lead to panic by P.F., and you might get reel four then. P.F. had a public address system. Sometimes he would inadvertently leave it switched on. So in the middle of a western cowboy film set in the Rockies, we would be entertained by P.F. shouting to his young son Raymond, 'Where the fuck is the next reel?'

There was a story going the rounds in Killaloe about Sergeant Doyle in the 1950s which I have not been able to verify. A new Superintendent had been appointed in Limerick who sent out a message that he wanted closing times in pubs in his district to be rigourously enforced and that he, personally, would be making unannounced visits to towns and villages to check on how this was being implemented. One night, Sergeant Doyle got a tipoff from one of his garda friends in Limerick that the Superintendent was on his way out to Killaloe. So up on his bike Sergeant Doyle gets and knocks on the door of every pub in Killaloe in a pre-arranged signal. Of course, when the Superintendent arrived in Killaloe, he found all the pubs closed and Killaloe all quiet and peaceful. He complimented Sergeant Doyle and told him that as he was doing such a good job, there would be no need for any further inspections. It is a nice story and it could be true.

John (Sam) Doyle with his mother May, sister May and brother Seamus outside their house in Killaloe in the 1950s

Sam Doyle went on to follow his father's footsteps to become a garda himself. He was a great character. He was tall and handsome and had a great sense of fun. And he had a car, the original Volkswagen Beetle. When I returned penniless to Killaloe in the summer holidays from university in Cork and Sam was home from Dublin visiting his parents and relatively wealthy, we would regularly make the 60 mile (96 kilometres) drive in his Beetle down to dances in the seaside resort of Ballybunnion.

We danced or jived to the bands of the day, 'The Clipper Carltons' and 'The Dickies', often to 3.00 and 4.00 am and then we had the drive back to Killaloe. But we were young. 'Henry, women love airline pilots,' Sam said to me one such night. 'So tonight, we are Pan American pilots, over-nighting in Shannon Airport. I am a Captain and you are my co-pilot.' Well, 6 foot (1.83 metres) Sam looked the part, but 5 feet 3 inch (1.60 metres) me and still growing did not. The fact that I can remember the chat line we were to take, but cannot remember the outturn, must mean that it was unsuccessful!

Sam served in the gardaí in Dublin, subsequently went on to get married and had three children. The *Nenagh Guardian*

*My friend John (Sam) Doyle
in the late 1950s*

recorded on 9 January 1960 the congratulations from Peter Lacy, secretary of the St Lua Swimming Club in Killaloe, to Garda John Doyle for his rescue from the River Liffey of a drowning man. Sam died suddenly in 1996 and is buried in Shanganagh Cemetery in County Dublin. My brother Bill attended his funeral. I was abroad at the time and always regret that I could not be there. Sam was a great guy.

Sergeant Doyle died on 14 June 1970 and his wife May on 2 November 1997, aged 90. Their son Fr Seamus was killed in a car accident in Zimbabwe in 2004. Their daughter May is a Presentation sister in Shantalla, Galway and still very active in her early 70s, teaching English to non-nationals and helping out with adult literacy.

· · ·

In the early 1950s, my dad's boss at the Provincial Bank was Mr Doherty, the manager. The Dohertys had a son, John, who was a great pal of my brother Bill, and older than me. One day I was over in the bank house when I was 13 years of age and John offered me a chocolate sweet from a fancy packet, which was labelled, 'New chocolate coated laxative sweets'. I thought they were delicious and asked John if I could have another. Three sweets later, I didn't have to ask anyone what 'laxative' meant, as a particular part of my body went into overdrive!

While the relationship between my mother and Mrs Doherty, as the boss's wife, was cordial, there was always a certain tension and rivalry between them, with my mother thinking that her husband should have had Mr Doherty's job. That rivalry extended to us children. On one occasion when my mother was over in the bank house for afternoon tea, Mrs Doherty announced with great pride that her son John had secured a clerical job in a major Dublin insurance company. My mother responded with greater pride that her son Henry (me) would be going to University College Cork to study electrical engineering for four years. To which Mrs Doherty responded in a put-down: 'I'm not surprised, shure isn't he very good at fixing the chain on his bike. I have seen him do it.'

However, when my mother broke her leg in a car accident in Cork in 1955, the Dohertys were very supportive and arranged for my father to be transferred temporarily to the Provincial Bank in Cork. (See Chapter 8, Our Parents' Unselfish Decision.)

· · ·

After the cancellation of the transfer to Coolooney, my father and mother remained on happily in Killaloe for the next seven years to 1961, making 12 years in total in Killaloe. In the late 1950s, when Mr Doherty retired as manager in Killaloe, my father was very disappointed that he did not get promotion to the vacancy. Mr Fitzgerald from another branch was appointed. Dad thought he was being punished for refusing the transfer to Coolooney. However, in 1961, he was offered promotion as manager of the Provincial Bank in Abbeyfeale, County Limerick. Killaloe had been their longest posting. He retired from the bank six years later in 1967, after serving 46 years. He had entered the bank in Kanturk, County Cork at age 17 in 1921.

The *Nenagh Guardian* reported on 11 November 1961:

> BANK APPOINTMENT: Mr James (Dick to his Nenagh friends) Hanlon has been appointed to fill the position of Accountant in the Provincial Bank, Killaloe, recently vacated by the transfer on promotion of Mr A J Murdoch to be Manager of the Abbeyfeale branch. Mr Hanlon, who was transferred from Dingle, is a keen angler and the location of his new post is likely to provide him plenty of sport in this respect.

Ireland is a small place, our dad from Dingle being replaced by a man from Dingle !

Although our dad was happy to retire on a manager's pension after only six years at that level, he and my mother really missed Killaloe, the Shannon and Lough Derg, and particularly their friends. They would have retired to Killaloe if we, their children, had been scattered all over the place, but by 1967 we were now all in Dublin, so they bought a house in Dalkey, County Dublin for £2,750 (€3,525) which they got from the bank by taking a reduced annual pension of one-tenth of that amount. As my father lived in retirement for 29 years, to the fine old age of 92, in effect he repaid the bank £7,975 for that £2,750!

. . .

At one stage when my parents were living in Abbeyfeale in 1967, I was working for Aer Lingus in Seattle USA, at the Boeing Company, during the construction of the first Boeing 737 for Aer Lingus.

My secretary and me putting the last touches to the first Aer Lingus Boeing 737 airplane EI-ASA in Seattle in 1969 in a PR stunt

The Provincial Bank was directly across the street from the post office. The telephonist sat behind a window, the lower half of which was blanked out with brown paper, so that she could not be seen from the street. When she was not busy, she would stand up and could be seen taking in everything that was happening on the main street.

I was at a reception in Seattle one evening and was getting bored listening to two Air Force generals praising the US telephone system. Of course they were right. It took a year in Ireland at that time to get a telephone and you could get any colour as long as it was black! In Seattle you could get connected in 24 hours with a multitude of colours on offer. One of the

Generals turned to me and said, 'That's service. I bet you don't get service like that in Ireland.' National pride prevented me agreeing with them.

'Well,' I said, 'I telephoned my parents in Abbeyfeale in Ireland yesterday. I got through to the international operator in White Plains, New York. In seconds I could hear her talking to the 'Dublin Exchange' and seconds later, I could hear the Abbeyfeale operator responding, Abbeyfeale' pronounced 'abbeyfail' in a lovely rich Kerry/Limerick accent. The White Plains operator asked to be connected to 'Abbeyfeale 15'. Abbeyfeale had only 20 telephones at the time.

'Connecting you – tis ringin',' the Abbeyfeale operator responded. And after a few moments. 'I'm sorry – there's no answer.' The White Plains operator then asked me 'Seattle caller, did you hear that?'

'Yes I did, thanks very much,' I responded.

Immediately, the Abbeyfeale operator interrupted, 'Is that you Henry?'

'Yes it is. How are you?'

'Grand and how are you? Well Henry, your Mammy and Daddy have gone to the pictures. I saw them walking up the street with their hat and coat on. They should be back about 11 o'clock. It's a long picture – *My Fair Lady* – with Julie Andrews. I'll tell them you rang.'

Turning to the two Air Force generals, I said, 'Now that's service. I bet you can't beat that in the States with all your coloured telephones!' They had no answer to that.

8

OUR PARENTS' UNSELFISH DECISION

*'Elderly woman knocked down by car' ... 'the
cheek of them' – My mother responding to Cork
newspaper headline (1955)*

When my brother Bill and I came back from a cycling tour of County Kerry in 1954, my parents made a brave and unselfish decision. My mother would move to a flat in Cork with her three teenage sons for a year and my father would stay in Killaloe. We were at a crossroads in our education. My sister Hilary was okay. She was pursuing her nurse education in Charing Cross Hospital in London. She wanted to be a doctor but my parents could not afford to put her through medical school. Bill had just done his Leaving Certificate exam in Crescent College Limerick and had passed every subject except Irish, so he could not be admitted to university under the rules at that time. But that was not relevant because he wanted to become a radio officer and the best course available was in Cork. It was the Radio Telegraphy Institute at Carrig House in Tivoli, run by P. J. O'Regan. The course was one academic year, and it had a terrific record. All graduates got immediate employment as radio officers. Carrig House is now the location of the Silver Springs Hotel in Cork.

I also wanted to be a doctor but my mother had decided that I would be an engineer because I was very good at mathematics and science subjects, and one of my parent's best friends from their time in Killarney was Jimmy Lawlor, who was then the Chief Engineer in the Ardnacrusha Hydroelectric Power Station only a few miles away. They could see me as an engineer in the ESB – a good permanent and pensionable job. And the degree programme was only four years compared to the six years for medicine.

My mother was determined that there was going to be a doctor in her family to emulate her siblings but Laurence was to be the one. He was the youngest and they would be just about able to afford it, as I would be already graduated as an engineer, half way through Laurence's studies.

But there was a problem. To get into an engineering degree programme you needed a good mark in honours mathematics in the Leaving Certificate, and Crescent College Limerick told my mother that there was not going to be an honours maths class in 1954–55 as the class was not good enough. I think that the real reason was that that they did not have a person who could teach honours maths.

But there was a brilliant honours maths teacher in Presentation College (called 'Pres' and pronounced 'Prez') in Cork, named Freddie Holland. So my mother came up with the solution. She would move to Cork for a year with her three sons. She would rent rooms in a house, Bill (18) could do his one year course to become a radio officer, I (then 16) could do my Leaving Certificate year and get my honours maths and qualify for entrance to engineering at the university, and

Crest of Presentation College Cork – Viriliter age, *meaning 'act manly'*

Laurence (14) would continue his secondary education in a different school but just for one year.

My parents just did not have enough money for an alternative solution. After a year Bill would be off earning at sea, I would be in university in Cork studying engineering and Laurence could finish his secondary education in preparation to enter medical school. It made sense, but it was very disruptive for my parents. We kids made the transition without too much difficulty. We had a flat at 6 College View, Western Road, in Cork, the second floor of a house occupied by the owner Mrs Ryan and her daughter Mollie. It was called a flat but we were really sharing a house. It was within five minutes walk of Pres, which was handy for Laurence and myself, but not very convenient for Bill and his radio telegraphy college in Tivoli. But he managed. There were 15 in his class, mostly from Cork.

I was sorry to leave all my schoolmates in Crescent College Limerick and to start again making new friends in Pres. Cork had a reputation of being very 'clannish', but Laurence and I had no difficulty. I suppose we were unique at the time in Pres. We were attending a day school but, unlike our fellow pupils, our home was not in Cork but Killaloe.

Presentation College at its old location on the Western Road, Cork
(Photo courtesy of Sean O'Connell)

The other major change was the fact that, unlike Crescent College, there was no physical punishment of pupils in Pres. I remember being scolded by a Presentation Brother in Pres and being reminded of the sacrifice which my parents were making for my education. I thought that the next thing would be the leather strap, or maybe they used a cane in Cork, or maybe they had a more sadistic form of punishment like the public schools in Britain – down the trousers and a few belts on a bare bottom! But no, it was a simply verbal reminder: 'Henry, don't let your parents down. They are sacrificing a lot for you.' Much more powerful than the leather strap of the Jesuits.

Another difficulty in that change of school was in relation to loyalty. Pres played rugby against Crescent in the Mardyke. I had a Pres scarf around my neck of about six months' vintage, but my heart (of four years' vintage) was with Crescent. I ended up applauding both sides. To the credit of my fellow pupils of both Crescent and Pres, they made me tremendously welcome at the 50th reunion of the 1955 Leaving Certificate class in 2005 in Limerick and in Cork, as if I had been with them forever and had never left them. Thanks, fellas.

There was another difficulty in my transition to Pres. My maths. I thought that I was good at maths. I was good by Crescent standards, but that was 'pass' maths. The sixth year class I had joined had already been doing honours maths for a year. After about a week at Pres, our maths teacher, the legendary Freddie Holland, took me aside and he said, 'you don't know what is going on, do you?' He had already told the class that everyone in his class always got honours.

I had never done calculus and the class was well into it. So I did not have a clue and I was well behind. 'I want you to stay on after school for 20 minutes every day,' he said, and I was willing to oblige. So every day until Christmas 1954, Freddie Holland gave me a grind in maths for free, and by Christmas he said, 'OK Henry, you are now up to the standard of the class.'

I got honours in the Christmas test that year in honours maths and I also got honours in the Leaving Certificate in 1955, thanks to Freddie Holland.

. . .

It was all very hard on my father. He was living on his own in Killaloe, cooking and fending for himself. It was a huge sacrifice. Initially there were rumours in Killaloe that there were difficulties in their marriage and that was why we were in Cork. My father told me years later that he even had a visit from a local curate, who told him that he should make peace with his wife because their separation was giving a very bad example to the people of Killaloe. It is just as well he didn't tell my mother, because she would have gone straight to the bishop to have the priest removed.

Marian Shrine in Killaloe in 2014

But when we all arrived back in Killaloe for the Christmas holidays in 1954, the rumours dissipated rapidly. It was great to be back with our dad and to see the New Year being introduced with bands on the street and people all following behind. And then there was the unveiling of the Marian Year Shrine near the Pier Head, which was built by the people of Killaloe. My old friend Jim Ryan had contributed all the sand and gravel needed in its construction and my father had contributed 10 shillings (€0.64).

The shrine was blessed on 9 January 1955 by the Most Rev Dr Rogers, Bishop of Killaloe, who had a very cultured accent with a slight American twang. And our local Canon Molloy was his usual elderly forgetful self. He said that he hoped that everyone who passed the shrine would say a little pray, 'a Hail Mary or a ..., or a ......'. Fr Dwyer beside him had to whisper in his ear as a result of which Canon Molloy said, 'yes, yes, that's right, say Mary pray for us, Mary pray for us.'

We loved being back in Killaloe, listening to Radio Luxembourg and AFN. The song 'Mr Sandman' was number one in the American charts. And then there were all those books to read. My favourite authors were P. G. Woodhouse, Edgar Wallace and Erle Stanley Gardner. We had a great library in Killaloe. But we were also very lazy, often not getting up until after midday after reading in bed until the early hours. We were then quickly out of bed when we would hear our mother coming up the stairs with a wet cold facecloth!

Our home, Aillebaun House, was a big, rambling old house. Half of it was not habitable. My mother used that part for growing mushrooms and we used it for our sports, for example, table tennis and building model airplanes, and my canoe. It was the coldest and dampest house I have ever been in. In my bedroom you could observe drops of water on the walls making a race to the floor. Reading a book in bed required a routine of one hand outside the bedclothes and the other inside, with a switch of hands every five minutes before numbness had set in. We did not have the luxury of a bedside light for reading, only the ceiling light, so I rigged up a string and pulley system so that I could turn off the wall mounted switch at the door by a dextrous pull of the string, without having to leave the warmth of the bed.

There was trouble in the bank again. Dad was working restricted hours in accordance with directions from his union, the Irish Bank Officials Association (IBOA). But there was hope because the Minister for Finance had asked the banks to enter arbitration to sort out the dispute. And then the holidays were over and we had to return to Cork in January 1955.

· · ·

If everything had worked to plan we would have had an un-eventful year in Cork. We would have come back to live with dad in Killaloe at the holidays in July 1955, Bill would have got his qualification as a radio officer, I would have got my Leaving Certificate with honour maths, and Laurence would have advanced another year in his secondary education. All that happened, but there was an intervening event.

My mother was knocked down by a car at Gaol Cross in Cork, near where we lived on Western Road, on 13 January 1955. We had come back to Cork only two days previously from Killaloe. Professor Lucy Duggan, who was a college friend of my mother, met us at the train in Cork and brought us in her Morris Minor car to our flat in Western Road. Lucy, who was later to become my 'Cork mother', was Professor of Education in University College Cork.

My mother was crossing the road at Gaol Cross when a car came from nowhere and knocked her down. She was brought to the nearby Bons Secours Hospital in an ambulance. I heard about it when I came home from school and was told by Mrs Ryan. I ran up to the hospital. My mother already had an operation. She looked terrible. She had broken her leg in five places, had broken three ribs and had an ugly gash in her head.

We thought that she was going to die but the surgeon said that, provided no complications set in, she would be okay. Lucy was brilliant. She contacted my dad in Killaloe and he came immediately on the train. And Mrs Ryan was wonderful, cooking meals for us hungry teenagers.

There followed a difficult six months for us all. My dad applied for a temporary posting to the Provincial Bank in Cork, on the South Mall opposite the City Hall, and it was granted, even though relationships in the bank were at breaking point. He had just received a letter from the directors (sent to all employees) stating that if he did not stop working restricted hours and comply with their directions, he would be summarily dismissed and lose his pension rights. The IBOA instructed its members to ask for a copy of their written contract of employment, in the full knowledge that they did not have one. Dad was replaced in the bank in Killaloe by Dick Coldhurst from Crosshaven, County Cork, who stayed in a B&B above Reddan's pub at the top of Main Street in Killaloe. The whole of Killaloe knew about our mother's accident.

Life went on. We followed the international rugby. The international between France and Ireland took place on 22 January 1955. I wrote in my diary at the time, 'Kyle played great. Tony O'Reilly, 18-year-old, played terrific but was heavily marked by four Frenchmen.' The 26-year old French hypnotist,

Mother in crutches after the car accident in 1955

Paul Goldin, was performing in the Opera House. Bill got to see him and thought he was terrific. I queued for hours but couldn't get in.

We all quickly came to realise how much we depended on our mother. Dad was a terrible cook and we youngsters were worse. The flat was always in a state of disarray. It was very hard on our dad who was also doing a full day's work at the bank, which unlike Killaloe was a very busy city branch. And it didn't help that we were highly critical of his cooking and the wanton way in which he would spend money on groceries, as we saw it. Things got so bad that we would wash only our own delph and argue on communal things like pots. It was inevitable that we needed a maid. Kitty started on 14 February 1955 at five shillings (now €0.20) per day, including her meals, for five days a week, excluding Tuesdays and Sundays.

She was great. She kept everything tidy and clean and was a great cook.

My mother was to spend nearly four months in hospital. She made a remarkable recovery. But I thought that she would blow a fuse on the day after the accident when she read the heading in the *Evening Echo*: 'Elderly woman knocked down by car.' The article went on, 'An elderly lady, Mrs Margaret Elizabeth Murdoch of ... is at present in the Bons Secours Hospital suffering from a fractured leg and facial injuries. They are the result of an accident etc.'

My mother who was then 53 years of age, but only admitted to being 49 (so that she could be younger than my father) was beside herself with anger. 'How dare they call me elderly, the cheek of them.' I tried to placate her by saying that they hadn't just called her a 'woman', they had correctly called her a 'lady'. But it was of no avail. But it diverted her attention away from her pain. She had plaster on her leg from 6 inches (1.5 centimetres) above her knee to the butt of her toes.

Her sister, our Auntie Sal, who was a doctor, came down from County Galway to visit. The only trouble was that she stayed with us and so Laurence and I had to share a bed. Even a broom down the middle of the bed didn't stop the fights. And her brother Uncle Laurence, who was priest, came down from Cong to see her. We were glad that he stayed in the Imperial Hotel. And three ladies, Mrs Joan Brislane and Mrs 'Prenney' Prendergast (two Protestant ladies), and Mrs Nora Lynch (the national school teacher), came all the 75 miles from Killaloe to visit our mother.

My old pal Jim Ryan wrote to me from Killaloe expressing sympathy for my mother's accident and ending: 'Keep the old flag flying and a stiff upper lip. God bless you. Don't forget to let me know if I can help in any way. Your old friend, Jim.' I have that letter to this day. Dad's boss in the bank in Cork, Mr Tierney, was very good to dad and to us, and regularly visited my mother. He also suggested a good solicitor. And grandfather from Dingle sent us a large parcel of food and goodies.

The big advantage of all these visitors was the sympathy they had for us poor teenagers without a mother, which resulted in significant amounts of money being given to us. We were never so flush with cash. But dad had a huge financial problem. Lucy Duggan had told him what Professor Kylie's fees would be – several hundred pounds. That was an awful lot of money in those days. And then there were the hospital bills and the medicines and dressings. It could ruin us unless we won an action against the driver of the car and his insurance company.

Dad was very critical of the garda investigation of the accident. They had not even tested the brakes of the car. Dad became a detective. He located the conductor of the bus and the sweet van which were stopped near the scene of the accident and got statements from them. Although 'Murphy' was a relatively common name in Cork, it was extraordinary that all the main parties or witnesses to the accident had the surname 'Murphy' – the driver of the car, an independent witness, the conductor of the bus, the driver of the sweet van and, would you believe it, the solicitor acting for my mother.

Well, our mother got better. She was on crutches for a few weeks after being discharged from hospital. Bill qualified as a radio officer and went off to sea with the British merchant navy, I got my Leaving Certificate with honour maths and got ready to go to University College Cork, and Laurence advanced another year in his secondary education and became a boarder in Rockwell College. We left Cork in July 1955 and returned to Killaloe. It was great to be back even if the house was still as damp as ever.

The insurance company made a settlement with my mother. I have no record of what it amounted to, but knowing my mother with her sharpness and tenacity, you can be sure it was a generous settlement. I know that my parents had no difficulty in paying my university fees the following October, or Laurence's fees at Rockwell College, which would have been quite expensive, and which had not been in my mother's original plan.

. . .

In 2005 we had a 50th reunion in Cork of the Presentation Leaving Certificate Class of 1955. Out of the 35 students, eight were deceased, 18 were still living in Cork, six in Dublin, and one each in Athlone, Mullingar and Birmingham, and the whereabouts of one person was unknown. An amazing 17 out of the class got honours in mathematics and most went on to university in Cork. One subsequently became a consultant paediatric surgeon and one got a Ph.D. in mathematics. In the intervening 50 years, I had met eight persons out of the 35.

The reunion was organised by Noel Horgan and Jim Fitzgibbon. It was attended by 20 of our class and was preceded by a golf competition in Monkstown Golf Club, organised by Liam Coughlan, and a pre-dinner reception in the Rochestown Park Hotel. Dr Sean Corkery travelled the longest distance, from Birmingham.

. . .

Bill in uniform as a radio officer in 1955

When Bill became a qualified radio officer in 1955, he was awarded a City & Guilds certificate in radio telegraphy, which was recognised throughout the world.

Some 45 years later, in 2000, I was invited to join the governing Council in London of the City & Guilds Institute where Prince Philip had been President since 1951. I was to meet him every year for the next eleven years. Strange how things come around to close the loop.

I have been unable to discover any links of the British royal family with Killaloe. There is a passing reference by William Bulfin in his book *Rambles in Eirinn* (1902) in which he wrote: 'I believe someone belonging to the royal family of England passed up the Shannon a few years ago, and said that Killaloe was quite a picturesque place.' Also Princess Margaret and her husband Anthony Armstrong-Jones passed through Killaloe on Saturday 31 December 1960 on their way to Birr Castle to spend a seven-day private visit to their friend, the Earl of Rosse. The royal couple were greeted next day at a service at St Brendan's Church in Birr, by the Dean of Killaloe, Edwin Owen. They got a great welcome. *The Irish Times* on 31 December 1960 quoted a local chemist, Mr William Butler, as saying that he would like to meet Mr Armstong-Jones again as he had given him tips about photography many years ago. 'He had his first studio over my shop,' he said.

Prince Philip, President of City & Guilds until 2011

Fast forward to Tuesday, 10 May 2011, and I was sitting opposite Prince Philip at lunch in the Ritz Hotel in London. He was flanked by the Chairman of City & Guilds, Michael Howell, and by the Director General, Chris Jones. 'Prince Philip, I just want to tell you, that when you and Queen Elizabeth come to Ireland next week, you will get a great welcome.'

The lunch was to celebrate the recipients of awards from Prince Philip followed a brilliant ceremony earlier in Buckingham Palace. The main award was the Prince Philip Medal which he had established in 1962 to honour persons who had travelled the City & Guilds qualifications path and had made most of their individual talents and abilities. The 2011 winner, who had started his life as a plumbing apprentice and was now a board member of SummitSkills, was at the lunch with his wife.

Of course, I had broken all kinds of protocol in addressing the Prince as I did, because, as my mother always told me as a young boy, 'you should not speak until you are spoken to!' But

I had got to know Prince Philip over ten years of these presentation ceremonies and I knew and appreciated his approach to his role and his often impish wit. That wit had often got him into trouble but I always found it refreshing, while not always necessarily 'politically correct'. I remember when he was reported as saying, 'If you see a man opening a car door for a woman, it means one of two things: it's either a new woman or a new car.' Or when speaking to a driving instructor in Oban, Scotland, he asked, 'How do you keep the natives off the booze long enough to get them through the test?'

Prince Philip looked a little startled at first at my unscheduled few words about his impending visit to Ireland. My intervention was made in the silence following a formal thank you by the chairman Michael Howell for the Prince's 60 years of service as President. Prince Philip responded and interestingly remarked how the new UK government following the Second World War wanted to reform everything, including less reliance on craft apprenticeships, and here was the new UK coalition government in 2011 rightly putting a huge emphasis on rejuvenating apprenticeship training.

Back to my few words: 'Prince Philip, I just want to tell you, that when you and Queen Elizabeth come to Ireland next week, you will get a great welcome.' With a broad smile on his face and a discernible glint in his eye, he immediately responded, 'But will I get back?' The lunch table erupted in laughter at the immediacy of his response and the humorous way in which it was said. And while I also laughed and immediately responded, 'Of course you will get back', there was a nervousness in my laugh.

Because I, like most Irish people, wanted Queen Elizabeth and Prince Philip to get a great welcome and take us out of our gloom and doom. We also feared that, despite the best efforts of our security organisations, there might be an incident which would shame us all. When Prince Philip asked, 'But will I get back', I immediately thought of Mullaghmore and Classiebawn Castle, County Sligo and 27 August 1979 when the great grandson of Queen Victoria, Lord Louis Mountbatten and three other innocent persons were blown to pieces in his boat *Shadow V*. I had a personal link with that place because 20 years later I bought the yacht *Curlew* at Mullaghmore from the owner of Classiebawn Castle, Hugh Tunney, the first Irish owner of the castle since the lands were confiscated from the O'Connor Sligo in the seventeenth century. Mountbatten came into ownership of Classiebawn Castle in 1922 and for many years spent the month of August there on peaceful holidays with his family.

The persons at the Ritz lunch would not have been as aware of this, or of the historical significance of the Queen's visit as we were in Ireland, so I continued: 'As you are aware, Prince Philip, this is the first visit of a UK reigning monarch to the area now known as the Republic of Ireland in 100 years. The last visit was in 1911.' There was a discernible gasp at the lunch table at this historical gem.

Quick as a flash, Prince Philip responded proudly: 'A monarch may not have been over to Ireland in those 100 years but I have; in fact, I have been there twice on the invitation of your President Mary McAleese to her award ceremony, which is modelled on my Duke of Edinburgh Awards. I can't remember the name.' I interjected, 'The Gaisce Awards,' and he said, 'That's it.'

The visit of Queen Elizabeth and Prince Philip to Ireland a week later was a huge success. The Queen acknowledged the difficult past between our two nations, our shared values and our potential for the future by working together as equals. She got a very warm welcome everywhere she went, but particularly, and perhaps surprisingly, in 'republican' Cork, exemplified by the iconic photograph taken of her on 20

Queen Elizabeth at the English Market in Cork, laughing with fishmonger Pat O'Connell, in 2011. (Photo courtesy of Valerie O'Sullivan)

May 2011 in the English Market, laughing with fishmonger Pat O'Connell, when he told her that in Cork the fish was called a 'mother-in-law' fish. Pat recounted his meeting with the Queen in his book *The Fishmonger* (2013).

Well, Prince Philip did get back! He stepped down as President of City & Guilds on reaching his 90th birthday on 10 June 2011, and his daughter, Princess Anne, has taken over that role. And a right good job she is making of it. I had the honour of attending a ceremony in Buckingham Palace on 29 April 2014, at which Princess Anne presented a number of awards, including her father's medal to Len Conway, the principal of the Building Crafts College, Stratford, East London. It was a fantastic ceremony in a building steeped in history.

The award recipients, and we guests, met beforehand for a reception on the ship *HQS Wellington* which is moored on the Thames at the Embankment in London. Built in 1934, it saw active service during World War II and is now providing active service as the Livery Hall of the Honorary Company of Master Mariners. How appropriate for mariners to have

HRH Princess Anne, President of City & Guilds in the Picture Gallery, Buckingham Palace in April 2014, with Chris Jones (Director General) and Richard Sermon (Vice Chairman)

HQS Wellington at anchor on the Thames

a 'floating' meeting place to run their affairs. In its nautical museum, the ship has a number of model ships on display, including one of itself and, intriguingly, one of a 600 foot (183 metres) vessel called the *MV County Clare*, built in 1970 by Austin & Pickersgill Ltd, Sunderland, for the Saturn Shipping Co Ltd in London. I have been unable to find out what is the connection with County Clare.

Following the maritime reception, we were transported from the *HQS Wellington* to the palace. As I walked across the loose pebble square into the palace, I thought about all the famous people who had traversed the same path, and wondered what my parents would have thought of their Killaloe son walking into the bastion of the British establishment.

Fiona Burford, who organised the ceremony for City & Guilds, amusingly told us beforehand in the ballroom of the palace, that the correct way to address the Princess was to call her M'am, pronounced as in 'ham' and not as in 'John'.

You have to hand it to the royal family in the way that they perform their public duties, as exemplified by Queen Elizabeth standing with Prince Philip for a whole hour, greeting guests at Dublin Castle in 2011. Princess Anne was the same, having a good few congratulatory words with each award recipient, and then spending an hour in the Picture Gallery afterwards, greeting their family members and guests.

That Picture Gallery, where we had a champagne reception following the award presentation, was an eye opener. It is a 47 metre-long room, designed in the 1820s as an appropriate setting for the royal collection of paintings. It has the most impressive collection of paintings I have ever seen, including great artists such as Titian, Rembrandt, Rubens, Van Dyck and Claude. A City & Guilds councillor told me that he was in the room a year ago with an American visitor, who asked where he could see the originals of the paintings, not realising that these were the originals!

9

Going to University from Killaloe

'You have him beaten – keep leading with a straight left arm' – My boxing trainer Michael Long at City Hall, Cork (1956)

My first year engineering class in University College Cork (UCC) in 1955 had about 50 students – all bright young men from all over Munster, but mostly from Cork. And we were all men. We all had honours mathematics in our Leaving Certificate, so we had to be bright! Because of this, we regarded ourselves as walking geniuses and had a certain disdain for those ordinary mortals at university doing mundane subjects such as arts and commerce. In Irish universities we 'studied' or 'did' subjects. I was later to learn that at UK universities they 'read' their subjects, for example, 'I am reading engineering at Oxford'. I often wondered, how could you 'read' a subject!

We had a certain degree of respect for those doing technical subjects at UCC, such as science and medicine. The 'meds', as we called them, were well motivated individuals who were not terribly intelligent, but intelligent enough not to kill their patients. If they only had our intelligence, and honours maths,

Crest of University College Cork

they would be brilliant. One thing we could not fathom, however, was why nearly all the 'med' students had parents who were medical doctors. I don't think there was anyone in our engineering class whose father was an engineer.

We engineers were actually two groups in one – civil engineers and electrical engineers. We did the same course for two years and then we split, one more year for civil engineering and two more for electrical engineering. UCC had a great reputation for civil engineering since its establishment in 1845 as one of three Queen's Colleges in Ireland. UCC introduced electrical engineering as a speciality in the 1950s and consequently had no reputation in it. We were the second class. This would not be good for the graduates, but UCC did a clever thing. Professor Teago had just retired from Liverpool University. He was the author of the definitive books at the time on electrical generators, the type the ESB would use, and where we were hoping to find employment. UCC invited him to Cork to oversee the new electrical engineering faculty.

It was a clever move because all we graduates had to do was to put on our curriculum vitae (we didn't call our 'applications for jobs' such a sophisticated phrase then) that we were students of Professor Teago and the job was in the bag, at least in the UK. He was a fantastic character. He was born on 11 November 1886 so he was already 71 years of age when we met him for the first time in our third year class in 1957. He had a butterfly collar which really set him aside as different and of another generation. But he was very kind and we all loved him because he was our passport to jobs. And he was determined that we would do well.

Professor Teago had been educated at Armstrong College, Newcastle-upon-Tyne and Durham University. Between 1926 and 1952 he was Robert Rankin Professor of Electrical Machinery and Electrical Engineering Electrotechnics at the University of Liverpool. He became a Professor Emeritus in 1952 at Liverpool on his retirement. He was subsequently awarded an honorary doctorate by the National University of Ireland for his work in Cork.

He died on 4 October 1964 when we, his Cork students, were in our mid-twenties. He was a great man and really helped us on our way. The fact that out of our electrical engineering class of 16, the top two graduate students, Kevin O'Brien and Declan O'Riordan, went on to head their Masters class in the top university in the world at that time, the California Institute of Technology (Cal Tech) is a testament to Professor Teago.

Professor Teago taught me a lesson. He always commenced his lectures exactly at 9.00 am in the Electrical Engineering Building. I used to arrive at about five minutes past nine on my 50 cc moped, screeching to a stop on the gravel in front of the new building, and would slip into a seat just inside the door. I thought he never noticed. Then

Kevin O'Brien and Declan O'Riordan at our BE graduate golden jubilee celebration in 2009

one morning, I arrived early and was in my seat just inside the door when Professor Teago arrived. He walked up to the lectern, looked down at me and said innocently, 'Mr Murdoch, have you been here all night?'

. . .

When I enrolled as an undergraduate student in UCC in 1955 there were 1,300 students at the university. In 2013, there were some 20,000 students. My best friends in 1955 were not only in my own faculty but other faculties as well, in medicine, agricultural science, science and arts. Which was good – across faculty friendships. Not easy in an expanded university.

Our class in engineering was an eclectic group of 50 students. I quickly became a friend of Sean O'Connell, whose father was a monumental sculptor. I played tennis with Sean and even though he left the engineering class after a year to study architecture at a local design college, he and I have remained life-long friends.

Sean and Elaine O'Connell's wedding in 1961, with bridesmaid Annette Parfrey (now Gurr).

I was best man at his wedding in 1961 to Elaine, was godfather to their first child Ita, visited them when they and I lived in England, holidayed together with my children Maeve and Breffni and their children Ita, Maeve, Nessa, and Kensa, attended their childrens' weddings, and holidayed with their and our grandchildren. I have also pocketed a substantial number of one Euro bets from Sean in golf over the years, including in Dooks Golf Club in Glenbeigh, County Kerry where he and Elaine are members.

Another student in that 1955 engineering class who remained only for one year was the legendry Mick O'Connell from Valentia Island in County Kerry, now rightly regarded as one of the greatest Gaelic footballers of all time. It is rumoured that when he quit the class to go back to the island in 1956, the President of UCC, Dr Atkins, travelled to Valentia to try to persuade him to return, but to no avail. Mick and I shared one thing in UCC: we were both from a small community, and now studying in a city, he from Valentia Island and me from Killaloe. I found Mick to be a shy and unassuming individual and a bit ill-at-ease in this urban environment.

I wasn't surprised that the island man returned to the island. Mick was a different man on the football field. Gone was the shyness. He was at ease with the ball. He was a brilliant footballer, winning four all-Irelands for Kerry. At the presentation to Mick of

Our 1955 classmate, famous footballer Mick O'Connell

the Degree of Doctors of Law, *honoris causa*, in University College Galway in June 2004, the President of UCG said that high fielding of the ball was the outstanding feature of Gaelic football at the time and that Mick was its greatest ever exponent.

I was not ill-at-ease in UCC because I had a transition year at Presentation College in Cork. But I certainly was not an extrovert. I was reasonably confident in my intellectual ability. I could turn to my Leaving Certificate results, after all, but I was less confident in my social ability. At 17 years of age I was the youngest in the class, but I was also at about 5 foot 1 inch (1.55 metres), not only the smallest person in the class, but the smallest student in the university at the time. And I was particularly conscious of this fact.

I had joined the university branch of the local defence force (FCA). People used to call the FCA the Free Clothing Association because you were supplied with a fine big overcoat, which made a great eiderdown on the bed, and a fine pair of sturdy boots. All the students who joined with me got their overcoat and uniform within a week. I had to wait for two months for mine, while a special order was sent up to Dublin for a uniform to fit me.

In the summer of 1956, Sean O'Connell and I went to the Army camp in Templemore for a two-week training session. It was tough but we learned a lot – doing route marches, firing bazookas and real rifles, throwing neutered grenades and guarding ammunition huts which had no ammunition in them.

Privates Barrett, Lynch, Murdoch (me) and Harrington in 1955

The sergeant in charge of us was a regular full-time soldier who thought we university students were privileged 'softies'. We were certainly privileged but we would dispute being 'softies'. After about three days at the camp, I had a terrible problem with the 303 rifles which had been issued to us. Every morning we had a drill out on the square and every time my rifle hit my shoulder it hurt my collar bone. The engineer in me came up with a brilliant solution. I rolled up a pair of socks in the way my mother showed me, and placed them inside my tunic, to protect my collar bone. It worked brilliantly but for the intervention of the sergeant. I was not aware that every time the rifle hit my shoulder (and the socks) it bounced.

'Private Murdoch, one step forward, at the double,' he yelled at me. I stepped forward from the line, the sergeant opened the buttons of my tunic, and took out my pair of socks, saying with glee, 'Now, look what we have here.' His view that we were softies had been proved. As punishment, I spent the rest of that day whitewashing the side of one of the barrack buildings.

．　．　．

My small stature did not let me escape the wrath of the army sergeant but it was to be my saviour in university. There was a very active boxing club in the university at the time and coming up to Christmas 1955 there was going to be an inter-faculty boxing competition. There was only one entry for the flyweight competition (maximum 8 stone 7 ounces (51.14 kilogrammes)) and it was a Chinese student in the medical faculty. There was terrific rivalry between the engineering and medical faculties in UCC. I was approached as I was the only one in the engineering faculty who would make the weight.

'Will you box for the engineering faculty'? I was asked. I felt honoured to be singled out, but I protested, 'But, I have never boxed before'.

'Don't worry about that – we'll get you trained.' I agreed. For the next four weeks I was trained by Michael Long, a well-known boxing trainer. Apart from getting very fit, he showed me how to punch, how to side-step, and how to protect myself. He emphasised the straight left hand for punching, with the right hand and elbow protecting my body. I drew confidence from his statement to me, 'Henry, most of the boxers you will meet will be taller than you, and will present a bigger target.'

My boxing career was about to begin in a ring erected in the Rest (the Restaurant building) in UCC in December 1955. That was no problem. To the delight of my engineering colleagues, I dispatched the Chinese medical student with relative ease for a points victory over three three-minute rounds, using the techniques recently learned from Michael Long. I was now a hero in my class. The footballer Mick O'Connell wasn't even getting a look in. I was now hovering between being an introvert and an extrovert. The message of my boxing success got to Killaloe – probably through my parents. When I returned for Christmas in 1955, there was some amazement expressed to me, for example, 'we didn't know you were a boxer'.

. . .

But there was more to come in my second bout early in 1956, this time in the salubrious surroundings of the City Hall in Cork at the inter-varsity boxing championships, called the Irish Junior Universities' Boxing Championships for the Morrow Cup. I was in the big time now before a large audience, boxing for my university in the college colours, a red singlet and white shorts. All the Irish universities were represented from Northern Ireland and from the Republic.

Beating taller David Allen of Queen's University Belfast in Cork in 1956

UCC won the Morrow Cup for the first time, with three points to spare over our nearest rival Queen's University Belfast, and I won my bout against a much taller D. Allen of Queen's. After the second round, my trainer Michael Long whispered into my ear, 'You have him beaten – keep leading with a straight left arm'. Michael got a great cheer from the crowd when he took out a comb and combed back my fringe from my eyes.

Next day the *Cork Examiner* had a large action shot of Allen and myself. As I am bent down avoiding a punch, it looks like he is killing me!

The *Examiner* had this to say:

> The standard was high, and most impressive were the Cork boxers, who showed the advantage of having a training course under the well-known southern trainer, Mr Michael

Long. There was a good start to the night for the home team when Henry Murdoch gained a well-earned points decision over D. Allen of Queen's University. The Cork boy forced the pace from the start, and he won the first two rounds fairly easily, and then held off a last round challenge by his taller opponent, who though he had a decided reach advantage, could never trouble Murdoch to any great extent.

Under the headline 'UCC Boxers Make History', A P. Mc-Weeney writing in the *Irish Independent* said:

> The showing of the UCC team reflected great credit on their trainer, Mick Long, for they were technically the best team in the championship. The home team captured four titles, the diminutive H. Murdoch and the tall W. Aherne, both using a straight punch in most creditable fashion in taking fly and bantam honours, respectively.

I didn't mind being called a 'Cork boy' by the *Examiner* – even though I was a 'Killaloe boy' – but being called 'diminutive' by the *Independent* was going a bit far. 'Small' yes, but not 'diminutive'!

Declan O'Riordan, who was in my engineering class and very brainy, was a light welterweight, and on the UCC team in the City Hall. Declan had boxing all worked out using engineering principles. He used to do sketches in the Engineering drawing room showing how the human arm moves and the effect of the joints at the wrist, elbow and shoulder. He was up against Ronnie Feely, a brilliant boxer from University College Dublin. They squared up to each other. Declan was shifting his weight from one foot to the other. I could imagine that all those sketches were going through his brain. Ronnie stepped forward, shot out a right hook, and hit Declan just below his left ear. I could see the white in Declan's eyes as he hit the floor. Knock out in the first round is the official result. It doesn't say that there was only one punch thrown. There's engineering principles for you.

·   ·   ·

*The UCC boxing team in 1956. Declan O'Riordan is at left back,
Ted O'Keeffe is centre front, and I am left front*

The members of the UCC boxing team were now heroes. I was catapulted from being a non-entity amongst the 1,300 students to being a leader. I was invited to be President of the swimming club and many of the college societies wanted me to be on their committees. I basked in the glory, while it lasted. It didn't last long. I was now an extrovert.

A month later I had my next and third bout at the finals of the Irish Universities Championships at the Gymnasium Hall in Trinity College Dublin. I was still growing and starting to have difficulty making the flyweight limit. It was the beginning of the end of my short boxing career. I was well beaten by D. Wheeler of Trinity College. The bout was stopped in the second round. I was clearly outclassed.

We were a frugal lot at UCC with very little money. We actually hitched a lift to and from Dublin for our competition at Trinity College.

· · ·

My fourth and last bout was a month later in Perth, Scotland. I was selected to represent the Irish universities in an international against the Scottish universities. It was a daunting occasion. Mine was the first bout. I had been four pounds (1.8 kilogrammes) over the limit at the weigh-in and had to shed those four pounds by skipping for over an hour. But as I looked across the ring at my tall opponent, W. Fox from Glasgow University, my thoughts were that he was like the guy I beat in the City Hall in Cork about five months previously.

Hitching a lift back to Cork on the Naas Road outside Dublin, proudly wearing the UCC scarf

He and I stood to attention as the Irish and British national anthems were played. I was fighting not just for the Irish universities, I was fighting for my country. We won. We beat the Scottish Universities by eight bouts to three. But I lost my bout as did Aherne from Cork and Tulalanba from Trinity.

I was well beaten by a much better opponent. He had my style – a straight left arm. The only trouble for me was that his left arm seemed about twice the length of mine. Every time he thrust it out, he got me straight on the nose. In the middle of the second round, my nose started to bleed profusely. The referee had a close look. At that time it was nearly a requirement that you pleaded with the referee to be allowed continue. It was a badge of honour. The referee must have seen the pleading in my eyes to stop the fight before I was murdered. Thank God he stopped it and I was able to bask in the victory of the Irish team.

I hung up my gloves after that bout. I had had a brilliant boxing career which lasted five months and four bouts. I had won two and lost two. I had made it to the national Irish universities team. I had made great friends such as Joe Hayes (lightweight), Joe Phelan (light middleweight) and Ted O'Keeffe (light heavyweight). I owe a lot to my short boxing career. It brought me out of myself. It increased my confidence. It opened doors for me at the university. There might not have been many at my weight, but I was a 'champion'. And my friends in Killaloe accepted me as a 'champion', even if I was only a 'small' one!

A few years later, in its entry about the Boxing Club the *UCC Student Handbook* (1958–1959), states: 'The outstanding boxers of recent years have been Joe Phelan, Henry Murdoch and Ted O'Keeffe, who attained national and international fame.'

· · ·

In 1959, I was in my fourth and final year in UCC and was honoured to be elected as Chairman of the Engineering Society. The committee comprised of a student representative from each engineering year, both civil and electrical. It was a great committee and very active. We were not aware of it but in our group of engineering students there were two future university presidents in our midst, both then in the second year engineering class – Ger Wrixon and Ed Walsh – who were fellow classmates for years in Christian Brothers' School before going on to UCC. They had both started in the university in 1957 and graduated in 1961, with Ger coming first in that BE Electrical class and Ed coming second. But Ed would be the first to become a university president.

Like some of my classmates, Ed went to the USA and was awarded a doctorate in nuclear and electrical engineering by Iowa State University. He returned to Ireland in 1970 to head up the newly established National Institute of Higher Education (NIHE) in Limerick. Since my time in Crescent College in the 1950s, Limerick had been crying out for a university and Ed Walsh delivered it. In 1989, the NIHE became the University of Limerick, the first university to be established since the creation of the State, and Ed became its founding president.

The publisher's blurb to Ed's memoir *Upstart: Friends, Foes and Founding a University* (Collins Press, 2011) states: 'Along the way, Ed made powerful enemies as he challenged the official cant, traditional academics and clerical humbug.' He has deservedly been recognised with many honours, including being made a Freeman of the City of Limerick. He styles himself as a chartered engineer, a registered silversmith, and an enthusiastic yatchsman (which I believe) and that he plays the violin, piano and clarinet badly (which I do not believe). What is certain is that Limerick and the development of third level education owes an awful lot to him.

Ed Walsh's memoir, 2011

His engineering classmate Ger Wrixon had a slower gestation period to university presidential status, being appointed President of UCC in 1999, a year after Ed Walsh had retired after 28 years at the Limerick campus, and 40 years after he served as the second year engineering class representative on my committee in 1959. Ger returned to UCC in 1974 after a very successful career in the USA where he was awarded a doctorate at the University of California (Berkeley) and worked in Bell Labs, world leading academic and research establishments.

Ger is married to a Quaker, as is my son Breffni, so it is not surpris-

UCC Engineering Society committee members at the Engineers' Ball in February 1959 with lady friends. L-R back: Barry Macken, Gerard Wrixon; front: Des Fitzgerald, and me.

ing that with such a small Quaker community in Ireland the Wrixons attended my son's wedding in Cork in 2003 to Becci Haughton.

Ger had a controversial period as President of UCC, but he was a reforming one. For example, he launched new degrees in architecture, Chinese studies, and sports. He was described by Ed Walsh in 2006 as 'UCC's courageous President'.

> When he was appointed President of UCC in 1999 he lost no time in signalling his determination to bring about change, and awake the sleepy campus. He transformed UCC, attracted talent and, in terms of research funding, made it Ireland's foremost research university.

Even his retirement was controversial. He retired in 2006, only 12 months after getting unprecendented approval to remain in office until 2009, well beyond the normal retirement age of 65.

If I had known in 1959 how important an impact these two junior (to me) engineering students were to have on third level education in Ireland in later life, I might have been more respectful of them then! But, I am now.

. . .

Back in Killaloe in 1959 there was a young boy, a classmate of my brother Laurence in the national school, who was making a name for himself in the world of music – Seamus Connolly. The Connollys who lived on Cross Roads were a very musical family. But Seamus was the star and his musical skills were recognised at an early stage. The *Clare Champion* on 26 September 1959 reported that Seamus, then aged 15, 'added further to his laurels as a traditional violist when he won a cup, 8 medals and 4 certificates at the Birr Fleadh Cheoil'.

Seamus is now recognised as one of the world's most respected master Irish traditional musicians and teachers. He won the Irish National Fiddle Championships an unprecedented ten times. For many years he played with the Kilfenora Ceili Band and travelled with them throughout Ireland and the

Seamus Connolly in 2013 at the National Fellowship
Concert at George Washington University
(photo © Michael G. Stewart, USA)

UK. He emigrated to the USA in 1976 and settled in the Boston area. He holds an endowed Chair at Boston College.

Seamus was the recipient in September 2013 of the National Heritage Fellowship Award in Washington DC. The Fellowship is the highest honour in the USA presented to master folk and traditional artists by the National Endowment of the Arts. Awardees have included Mexican-American accordionists, African-American blues musicians, traditional fiddlers, native American basket weavers, and all types of traditional artists and performers of numerous ethnic backgrounds. Of the 386 recipients of the Fellowship awards since its inception in 1982, only 3 per cent have been Irish-American.

At the Fellowship concert at George Washington University in 2013, Seamus recounted how he had taken up the fiddle in Killaloe:

There was mass emigration around 1950 to 1954. My uncle was a fiddler. They had what was known as an American wake. He was leaving for America. An excuse to have a party in Ireland was a good one. He passed away two years ago. We are getting the fiddle he played. We are putting it into the archives at Boston College. It was the first time I ever saw a fiddle. His fiddle was on the chair. My uncle was saying goodbye to all the neighbours, and I picked up the fiddle. And I pretended to play. And I said to my mother and father that I would like to play the fiddle. So they found one from behind someone's dresser in the kitchen.

He went on to describe how his first job on arriving in America with his family was in a glue factory, but that subsequently he got a 'wonderful job for fourteen and a half years as a legislative aid in the Senate in Massachusetts'. He said that he ended up teaching at Boston College for 22 years. 'America has been good to me,' he said.

In introducing the music he was going to play at the concert, he explained: 'I'd like to play for you a little medley, not melody, beginning with a tune I made up. As we Irish say, we made it up. We do not say compose. We are not like Beethoven or those great composers.'

He concluded, proud of his Killaloe and County Clare roots: 'By the way, Clare is playing in the hurling final tomorrow. Make sure you're watching. Up the Banner!' And Clare won!

· · ·

I bought my 50 cc moped in 1956 with money saved from my six weeks working that summer in Smedley's pea canning factory in Wisbech, Cambridgeshire in the UK. A lot of Irish university students travelled to the UK at that time and manned the canning factories at the peak of the harvesting of the vegetable and fruit crops. Every few weeks I used to travel on that moped the 72 miles (115 kilometres) from Cork to Killaloe. It used to take over three hours as the maximum speed of the moped was only about 22 miles per hour. It was a rough trip because there was no windscreen, so I had to take the full brunt of the rain and wind. And people did not wear helmets at that time.

The moped had a two stroke engine which ran on a mixture of petrol and oil. I noticed that if I didn't use as much oil as was recommended, the moped would go faster. I got it up to 26 miles per hour at one stage. As an engineering student, I should have known that this was a hazardous practice because the oil was providing the necessary lubrication for the engine. But it was great to get the extra speed, even if the result was increased watering of my eyes.

I got another result going through Buttevant, just north of Mallow, on one of my trips home to Killaloe in 1956, when the engine seized and I was thrown over the handle-bars. Luckily I was not hurt, but it was an expensive lesson for me. But I was glad to pick up the repaired moped in Buttevant a few weeks later.

The moped was designed so that you could peddle it if you ran out of fuel, but it was difficult and you could travel only a mile or so. One night just outside Nenagh, well after midnight, I ran out of fuel. It was a good 12 miles (19 kilometres) to Killaloe but I remembered that there was a petrol station about a mile away. So I peddled to it and was exhausted when I got there. Of course it was closed and there were no lights on in the adjoining house, but I had no option but to ring the bell. After a short time, lights came on, and the proprietor appeared in his dressing gown. Initially he appeared to be annoyed to have been woken from his sleep, but when I told him of my plight, I could see a warmth there as if I were his son in trouble. The warmth nearly disappeared when at the petrol pump he asked: 'How much will I give you?' and I responded, 'A half gallon (2.3 litres), that's all it will take, and would you have a drop of oil as well?'

I was so attached to that moped that I brought it with me to England after I graduated. I eventually sold it to a work colleague in 1961 in Lincoln, who wanted the engine for his lawn mower. He told me that it was a perfect replacement.

Thinking of my moped reminds me of Kevin Murphy who was with me in UCC studying engineering, except that he did both degrees then on offer and emerged after five years with two Bachelor of Engineering degrees, civil and electrical. It was to be a good choice as Kevin subsequently worked with Radio Telefís Éireann (RTÉ) seeking out land for their transmitters and subsequently overseeing their construction. Kevin's job took him all over rural Ireland and negotiating in pubs with the owners of those pieces of land on the top of mountains, hitherto of no value and now of some value. He was married to Aileen O'Connor, who previously worked with me in the engineering department in Aer Lingus and subsequently with my wife Davida as an air hostess.

Kevin was a great friend of mine and most helpful to me. He often towed my boat on its trailer because he had a tow hitch on his car. He did not complain when it burned out his clutch retrieving my boat on the slipway in Howth harbour. Kevin died at the young age of 48 in 1985.

My abiding memory of Kevin Murphy is my phone call to him in 1983, two years before he died, when I was appointed by the Minister for Health, Barry Desmond, to be chairman of the National Rehabilitation Board (NRB). I was so proud of myself. It was my first appointment as chairman of a State board. My appointment was also a morale booster as I was still disappointed at not making it as Director General of AnCO – the Industrial Training Authority. My good friend and colleague Malachy Sherlock, who joined AnCO on the same day as I did in 1974, and at the same grade, had been appointed Director General a few months before in October 1982.

I was obviously waxing lyrically about my appointment when Kevin said: 'Henry, never forget that you had no arse in your trousers when you drove through Mallow on your 50 cc moped.' Of course Kevin was right. You should never get above yourself and you should always remember where you came from. Kevin was right about 'no arse' in my trousers when in all those years I had been travelling to and from Killaloe on a machine with a lawn mower engine!

There is no doubt in Ireland that you will never be allowed to get above yourself. There will always be someone to bring you back to ground level. I remember in the 1990s when I was Assistant Director General (Industry) with FÁS, the Training and Employment Authority. It was a senior role which brought me into the public limelight, particularly in introducing the then controversial standards-based craft apprenticehip system. I was attending

In 1977 with Charles Haughey, Minister for Health, at the NRB some years before my appointment as Chairman in 1983 by Garret Fitzgerald's government

a funeral of an old Aer Lingus friend of mine, Captain Joe Barrett. It was over 20 years since I had left Aer Lingus but I knew quite a few Aer Lingus pilots at the funeral. One particular captain came up to me and said, 'Gosh, Henry, it must be a quarter of a century since I last met you. Remember, we met when you were with Boeing in Seattle. What are you doing with yourself these days?'

I responded, 'Oh, I am with FÁS now.'

'Well, that is very interesting,' he said sympathetically, 'and what course are you doing?'

Enough said.

10

MY CORK MOTHER AT UNIVERSITY

*'We will see you at the Pioneer meeting on
Thursday night?' – Canon Bastible speaking to me
across the Quad at UCC (1956)*

During the four years I was at University College Cork, I used to go for lunch every Sunday to my 'Cork mother' Lucy Duggan. She lived in College Road, about a five minute walk from my 'digs' in O'Donovan's Road. She was Professor of Education. She was not married and had no children. If you were an espousing teacher and you needed an 'H.Dip.in Ed' you needed her post-graduate course.

Lucy was a childhood friend of my mother. I believe that the link was developed when my mother was a student in University College Dublin in the early 1920s. Their friendship continued until Lucy's death in the mid-1970s. I knew that when I was being despatched as a 17-year-old down from rural Killaloe to Cork City in 1955, it was in the expectation that my Cork mother would look after me, and she did.

Lucy was a good friend and near neighbour of Patrick ('Pax') Coffey, the Dean of the Faculty of Engineering. Pax lectured on building construction. He was a kind man. He didn't have a stutter but, as he was now in the autumn of his life, he had a hesitation in what he wanted to say. In one lecture, he was saying, 'Here I have a, have a, here I have a, have a ...' and student Johnny Rohan, of subsequent prefabricated houses Rofab fame, interjected, 'You have a fucking brick'. Johnny was right. It was cruel. And worst of all, when Pax Coffey looked up, the only one of us 50 students who looked guilty was Patrick Barron, a mild individual who

My Cork mother,
Professor Lucy Duggan

was shifting in his seat at the time. Life is cruel. But we all loved Pax and enjoyed the enthusiasm he put into his lectures.

In my time at UCC, Lucy never once gave me money – she gave me food. And what food. It was pretty basic by today's standards but it was brilliant. Mostly a beef roast. I would eat enough to keep me going for the week. I got on famously with her. She wanted to know everything about student life. And I talked openly with her about everything. Lucy knew all about my brief boxing career and encouraged me to take an active part in student life. She treated me very much like an only son.

When I graduated in 1959, Lucy was at the graduation ceremony with my parents. It was like having two mothers – my Killaloe birth-mother Greta who had made huge sacrifices to have me there, and my Cork mother who had looked after me during my four year journey. This was the first time Lucy gave me money, £25 (€32), which was a lot of money at the time, being half the university fees for a year.

Graduating BE in 1959, with my
mother and father

And I got a letter from my Dingle grandfather, who wrote:

> Dear Henry, I couldn't tell you how pleased the Murdoch family feels about your success in all your exams. Granda thinks – a little money would be no Load, to help young Henry against the Road. Love from all. Your Granda.

And he enclosed a postal order for £25 as well. I was rich.

• • •

My granddad's letter to me in 1959

I had a great time in UCC. It was a mixture of hard work and hard play, all done on 10 shillings (€ 0.64) a week pocket money. After my first year, my finances were improved with earnings from my summer jobs – Smedleys Canning factory in Wisbech in 1956, Reyrolles who made huge electrical circuit breakers in South Shields in Yorkshire in 1957, Aer Lingus at Dublin Airport in 1958 in the maintenance department, and the Lakeside Hotel in Killaloe in 1959 teaching people to water ski on the River Shannon.

• • •

The Pioneer movement was founded in 1898 by a Jesuit priest, Fr James Cullen, to address the problem of alcohol abuse which was rampant in Irish society at that time. I became a Pioneer when I was a student at the Jesuit-run Crescent College in Limerick. And when I arrived at the door of UCC in 1955 it is not surprising, in this Fr Matthew city, that I became a member of the Pioneer branch in the university and its treasurer.

Fr Theobold Matthew (1790–1861) was the apostle of Temperance. He was known and loved in Cork for his efforts to alleviate distress during the cholera epidemic of 1832 and during the Great Famine from 1845 to 1850. He was also respon-

BE Electrical Class of 1959. Back row: Michael Higgins, Mick Buckley, Tom Gallagher, John O'Neill, Terry Foley. Middle: Kieran Curley, Declan O'Riordan, Jim Barrett, John Thompson, Barry Macken, Kevin Treacy, Kevin O'Brien. Front: Paddy Barron, Tom Skelly, Noel Horgan, Professor Burns, President Atkins, Professor Quinlan, lecturer Christie Synott, and me

sible for the purchase of the botanic gardens in Ballyphehane and the establishment of St Joseph's cemetery on that site. The statue of Fr Matthew, in the centre of Patrick Street, was erected in his memory in October 1864 and is an integral part of the Cork scene. The Catholic church in Killaloe was dedicated to St Flannan in a ceremony in 1837 where the sermon was delivered by Fr Matthew. It is reputed that 20,000 attendees took the pledge at the time. How many kept it is not known!

A Pioneer makes a commitment to abstain from alcohol for life. To the Pioneer, this represents a sacrifice by which great graces are obtained from God for those people suffering from

Logo of the Pioneer Association

the abuse of alcohol. A Pioneer says the following prayer twice every day:

> For Thy greater glory and consolation, O Sacred Heart of Jesus, for Thy sake to give good example, to practise self-denial, to make reparation to Thee for the sins of in-temperance, and for the conversion of excessive drinkers, I will abstain for life from all intoxicating drinks. Amen.

Canon Bastible was the chairman of the Pioneer branch in UCC. He was also Dean of Residence of the Honan Hostel, which was the small student residence within the grounds of the university, and a lecturer on medical ethics, which at the time would have been hugely dominated by the views of the Catholic Church. In effect, he was the religious chaplain to the students.

Following my brief boxing career, I had passed my first year engineering exam in 1956, and had spent six weeks in the summer in Smedley's canning factory in Wisbech, Cambridgeshire. Smedleys was the leading UK brand in canned vegetables in the 1950s. I was now back at UCC starting my second engineering year, when I met Canon Bastible in the Quad (the quadrangle in front of the beautiful college building).

· · ·

Classmate Tom Gallagher at our graduation Golden Jubilee in 2009

Those six weeks in the UK was an eye opener for me. It was my first job. I went across to Wisbech on the *Innisfallen* ferry from Cork to Fishguard with a classmate, Tom Gallagher, who later became an engineering lecturer and professor of engineering in University College Dublin. The *Innisfallen* was affectionately known to Cork people as '*D'Innis*'.

The *Innisfallen* was the third such ship of this name on the Cork to Fishguard route. She was 340 feet overall and 3,705 gross tons, with Denny Brown stabilisers which put her ahead of many ferries at the time. She was built in 1948 and served on the Cork/Fishguard route until 1967. She was then sold and entered service on the Mediterranean for Libra Maritime, until she was scrapped in Brindisi in 1985.

Wisbech was a dull place and so different from Killaloe. In Smedley's factory I worked six days a week and did two eight-hour shifts a day. We all did. Sixteen hours a day and then on to one of 20 beds in a Nizzen Hut, probably salvaged from the last world war, which had ended only eleven years before. But we did not mind. We were seasonal workers and we were making great money – £16 (€17.25) per week). Some nights I was so tired I slept outside the bedclothes with my wellington boots still on.

Michael Smedley with his award winning book What Happened to Smedleys? *in Wisbech in 2013. Michael is the son of the founder of Smedleys in the 1920s*

I had four jobs in the factory in those six weeks. The first was in keeping clear the vast containers which received the peas in their pods from the lorries. I was not impressed to see some of the permanent workers spitting into the containers. I never knowingly ate a Smedley canned vegetable again. My next job was hauling large quantities of peas from one production line, which had broken down, to another line. That was back-breaking work. My next job was the most boring – watching tins of peas on a production line, passing by in front of a mirror, and trying to identify a defective can. In my six hours sleep at night, I would see the cans passing by, one after the other. It was enough to drive you crazy.

But I did not go crazy. I boxed clever. After three weeks working in the factory, I had identified the best job in the whole place. There were 200 beautiful Italian girls working in the factory, all seasonal workers like ourselves from Ireland.

They were all Catholics like us and naturally attracted to us and we to them. Religion is a powerful motivator.

After week three, I went to the managing director. He had an open door policy. In a white lie, I told him that my skills were not being properly utilised, I was a brilliant cook. Not true. My mother had taught me the basics – I could make porridge, fry rashers and sausages, and make scrambled egg. I told him that I should be working in the factory canteen. He agreed to try me out and that is where I spent the next three weeks, on a double shift.

I can tell you that the more beautiful Italian girls got an extra rasher and a wink from me. And Tom Gallagher would point out some girls that he wanted me to favour with an extra lamb chop. I was the most popular Irishman in that factory!

We had one day off every week and that was where the demon drink came in. I broke my Pioneer pledge on Newcastle Brown Ale, but it was all very innocent. We still went to Mass every Sunday. It was nearly like 'you had to'. We were Catholics in a pagan England. It was our stamp of identity. I now know why Irish Catholics living in England wear their Catholicism on their sleeves. And weren't the beautiful Italian girl workers also going to Mass! An opportunity not to be missed.

·   ·   ·

I arrived back in Killaloe with money, something which I had never had before. And here I was back in UCC in the autumn of 1956. Canon Bastible saw me across the Quad. He half shouted, 'Henry, we will see you at the Pioneer meeting on Thursday night?' I couldn't half shout that I had taken to Newcastle Brown Ale, so I went over to him and told him that I had broken my pledge. He was really taken aback. He was a very holy and kind man and I felt in a little way that I had betrayed him.

'Will you come up to see me tonight?' he enquired. 'I would like to talk with you. Would eight o'clock be okay?'

'Fine, Canon. I'll see you then.' I was living in 'digs' (bed and breakfast and evening meal) in Askive Guest House on

O'Donovan's Road at the time. It was less than a five minute walk to the Honan Hostel where Canon Bastible had his flat. I was shown into his sitting room by his housekeeper. There he was, sitting comfortably in front of a blazing fire, having had his dinner.

He welcomed me warmly and asked me how I had come to break my pledge. I recounted how I 'had taken to the drink' (as my father would have said). He thanked me for my contribution to the Pioneer branch in UCC and said that there was nothing wrong with alcohol. He cited the wedding feast of Cana where Jesus had converted the water into wine. It was the abuse of alcohol which was the problem. It was only then that I noticed that he had a large glass of whiskey on a small side table, which he would sip now and again as he was talking to me. He was a kind man but he didn't offer me a drink!

It was over 30 years later in 1986 at a Cork Polio and General Aftercare Association (COPE) function in Cork that I recounted this story to a now elderly Archdeacon Bastible, and now Dean of Cork. He thought it was very funny, but he was concerned that he had been inhospitable in not offering me a whiskey. When I reminded him that I was only an 18-year-old student, he realised that he did not owe me an apology. And he didn't.

In fact, Archdeacon Bastible's presence enabled me to meet the 'real Taoiseach' Jack Lynch (1917–1999) who was at that function. It was the first and last time that I met Jack Lynch, who had been Taoiseach from 1966 to 1973. This was a Cork thing. We might have claimed Killaloe as being the capital of Ireland, but to Cork people, the 'real' capital was Cork and the 'real' Taoiseach was Jack Lynch. He was a lovely man. He talked with me for over 20 minutes, puffing his pipe and sipping his whiskey. It was as if we had been

Jack Lynch – the 'real' Taoiseach – in 1986

Monsignor Bastible when given the Freedom of Cork in 1987.
(photo © Cork Evening Echo)

friends for years and were just catching up on the news. That was his style, and that was why he was the 'real' Taoiseach.

For over a quarter of a century, Dean Bastible guided the development of COPE as its chairman and it was his work with this association and other voluntary bodies in Cork which prompted Cork Corporation to confer the Freedom of the City upon him on 24 January 1987. The following citation accompanied the conferring the Freedom of the City:

> In recognition and appreciation of his long and outstanding services to so many voluntary organisations, particularly those organisations involved in the care of the mentally handicapped, disabled and the poor of the city, and of his magnificent contribution as chairman for 25 years of the Cork Polio & General Aftercare Association and as chairman for 23 years of St. Patrick's Branch Sick Poor Society; and by honouring Dean Bastible to express the gratitude and appreciation of the citizens for the enormous contribution made by all voluntary organisations to the welfare, health, care and housing of the underprivileged, disabled and poor of the community.

Dean Bastible died eight months later on 20 September 1987.

11

CATHOLIC INFLUENCES
ALIVE AND WELL

*'The wrong persons are in the dock. Religion is
above the Courts' – District Justice Gordon Hurley
at Killaloe Courthouse (1958)*

The power and influence of the Catholic Church touched all
aspects of Irish life right up to the 1990s. A good example
was the opposition of the Irish Hierarchy, as they were called,
to the 'Mother and Child' scheme. There was an international
trend after World War II towards the state taking a more active approach in health care. This trend was exemplified by the
birth of the National Health Service (NHS) in the UK. Change
was afoot in Ireland as well.

Dr Noel Browne, who was Minister for Health in 1950, proposed a scheme under which the state would provide mater-
nity care to mothers and healthcare for children up to the age
of sixteen. It was a progressive scheme but not as ambitious as
the NHS.

However the scheme was vehemently opposed by the Catholic Church in Ireland, which regarded it as 'socialised medicine'. The opposition was led by Archbishop John Charles

Dr Noel Browne, former Minister for Health

McQuaid, who feared that it could lead eventually to birth control and abortion. This opposition led in 1951 to the resignation of the Minister, who in his resignation speech stated that the Hierarchy had informed the Government that the scheme 'was opposed to Catholic social teaching'. He said that he, as a Catholic, accepted the ruling of the Catholic Church.

He caused some controversy by giving his correspondence with the bishops to *The Irish Times*, then regarded as a very Protestant newspaper. The Taoiseach, John A. Costello told the Dail:

> I am not in the least bit afraid of *The Irish Times* or any other newspaper. I, as a Catholic, obey my Church authorities and will continue to do so, in spite of *The Irish Times* or anything else.

Another example of the power and influence of the Catholic Church was the ban on Catholics attending Trinity College Dublin, as that university was seen as a danger to a Catholic's faith. A Catholic was required to obtain a formal dispensation before attending at the university. Some did and some didn't. The power of the Church had started to wain but it was still strong in the 1960s.

In 1963, when I attended Trinity College Dublin for the first year of my barrister-at-law course, my mother was quite worried that I had not sought permission. It didn't worry me. Archbishop McQuaid refused for years to appoint a Catholic chaplain to Trinity even though by 1969 it had 1,200 Catholic students. Eventually the ban was lifted in 1970 and a Catholic chaplain (Dean of Residence) was appointed.

. . .

Back in 1956 a local curate in Clonlara, just a few miles from Killaloe, encouraged a group of his Catholic parishioners to beat up two Jehovah's Witnesses who were preaching their religion in the village. The group burned the literature the evangelists were trying to distribute. The curate and ten other people were charged with assaulting the Jehovah's Witnesses. District Justice Gordon Hurley convicted the priest and

Archbishop Charles McQuaid

his ten accomplices, but let them go free without penalty under the Probation of Offenders Act 1907. Extraordinarily, he went on to penalise the two Jehovah's Witnesses, even though they had not been charged with any offence, and were in the court as witnesses for the State. The Justice said that they had sought to destroy the Catholic religion by engaging in blasphemy in the eyes of Catholics. He bound them to the peace on their own sureties of £100 each and two independent sureties of £100 each, or three months in jail.

The prosecuting solicitor, Gerald Goldberg, was enraged with this outturn: 'Your worship's decision is unprecedented and contrary to the law of this country. I say that without fear of contradiction.' He was not the only person to be enraged. Bishop Joseph Rodgers, Catholic Bishop of Killaloe, who was in court that day, had the audacity to write to the Taoiseach, John A.

Gerald Goldberg, solicitor, prosecuting the curate and the parishioners in Clonlara (1956)

Bishop Joseph Rodgers,
Catholic Bishop of Killaloe

Costello, objecting to the conviction of his priest and his parishioners. 'We censure obscene literature, your Attorney General prosecutes one of my priests for doing what I, and all good Catholics here, regard as his bounden duty and right. The matter cannot rest.'

The Taoiseach responded by stating that the authorities had no choice but to allow the machinery of law to take its course, as the action of the priest and his parishioners was *prima facie* contrary to the law. He also stated that if they believed that the Jehovah's Witnesses were guilty of blasphemy, they should have complained to the gardaí. However the Taoiseach added

John A Costello, Taoiseach
(1948–51; 1954–57)

that he appreciated 'the just indignation aroused among the clergy and the people by the activities of the Jehovah's Witnesses'.

This incident was the precursor for a similar incident in Killaloe which took place two years later in 1958. The incident shocked the local population and led nationally to a call for a judicial enquiry. I was 20 years of age at the time. I remember thinking, how was it okay for us to send missionaries to Africa to convert all the black people (and their babies – remember the black baby collection boxes) to Catholicism, and yet it was not okay for other people to try to convert us to their religion. The incident demonstrated how the Catholic Church had influenced all aspects of Irish society at the time.

In the incident, a group of Jehovah's Witnesses were assaulted in Killaloe by a group of 'defenders of the faith' and in the subsequent court case the evangelists were treated as if they were the guilty ones in the dock, just like as happened in Clonlara.

. . .

The incident took place at The Green in Killaloe, which is a large area in front of St Flannan's Catholic Church. At that time and for many decades before, The Green was used for market days and for political rallies. We were glad, living as we were on the Canal Bank, that we did not have to put up with the excrement of the cattle on market days. However, the next day we had to endure the result of the clean-up, when that water-diluted excrement came down Main Street and Bridge Street on its way to the canal and the river.

I remember seeing and hearing Eamon de Valera (1882–1975) on The Green in the general election of 1951, berating Fine Gael and then Taoiseach John A. Costello, and promising that Fianna Fail would not put up the price of a loaf of bread or the pint of stout. De Valera went on to win that election and

Old photo of The Green in Killaloe with
St Flannan's Catholic church behind trees (CCL)

subsequently in 1959 to become President of Ireland and four years later, in 1963, to welcome John F. Kennedy, President of the United States, to Ireland.

Jim Crowe of Main Street, now living in New Zealand, has told me that he also has memories of de Valera speaking on The Green. In fact de Valera was a frequent visitor to their home on Main Street when de Valera was a TD (parliamentary representative) for County Clare. Jim has a vivid memory of meeting de Valera when he was President of Ireland. Jim recalls:

> The last time I saw 'Dev' was a wet Sunday afternoon. I was walking up Main Street when a black Rolls stopped. The driver asked me the quickest way into Limerick. Then a voice speaking Irish came from a man in the the back of the car, who thanked me in Irish and shook my hand. It was only in later years that I realised the significance of what had happened.

Jim reckons that it probably was 'Dev's' last visit to Killaloe.

The black Rolls referred to by Jim was the Presidential car, a Rolls Royce, registration number ZD 5000. It had been purchased specifically for ceremonial occasions but was used by President de Valera for all his travels around Ireland during his presidency from 1959 to 1973. As he became increasingly feeble in old age, he particularly liked the high dimensions of the Rolls, which facilitated his movement in and out of the car. He was permitted by the government to continue to use the car after he retired in 1973, until his death in 1975.

. . .

There had not been any public order problems at The Green during fairs and political rallies over the years. Even the meeting of 1,000 Nationalist Volunteers at The Green in 1914 to commemorate the 900th anniversary of the Battle of Clontarf passed off peacefully, despite the turbulent political times in Ireland at that time, just two years before the Easter Rising in 1916. That is, until the incident in 1958, which culminated in a prosecution in Killaloe courthouse. There were two press reports on the case, the first on 16 September 1958 in *The Irish Times* under a heading 'Religion is above the Courts':

> District Justice Gordon Hurley in Killaloe yesterday applied the Probation Act in a case in which Michael Boland and John (Christy) McKenna, of Ballyloughnane, Killaloe, and Patrick Daly, Killestry, Killaloe, were charged with unlawfully assaulting Robert Glen Lindsay, Samuel Glen Lindsay and Christopher Rowe on June 26th at Killaloe, thereby causing them actual bodily harm. The defendants, who pleaded guilty, were represented by Mr I M Houlihan, solicitor, and Inspector E McDonnell prosecuted

Mr Houlihan said his clients were under great provocation. They were respectable farmers and had been attending a fair in Killaloe when they were confronted by three young men 'vending Christianity'. His clients took offence, as it was the wrong time and place for these men – two of whom, he understood, came from Limerick, and a friend of theirs from England – to go foisting their special brand of Christianity on a people steeped in Christianity.

Furthermore, the position was aggravated by the fact that some time earlier, leaflets had been left in the confessional of the Catholic church in the parish from which his clients came, and the parish priest had protested from the altar, and asked for more vigilance from his parishioners.

Mr Houlihan said that he did not want to associate the complainants with circulating these leaflets for the simple reason that it had not been proved, but it was not the first time that 'pseudo-evangelists' had visited this area.

'The judiciary in England have described those people as a sect of canting humbugs,' went on Mr Houlihan, who added that it was fantastic for these young men from Limerick to come into Clare vending Bible and Christianity on a people who were steeped in it. To say they were preaching Christianity to a people ignorant of it was only adding to the blaze. The

Irish had Christianity since the time of Saint Patrick, and had spread all over the world. Another of his clients, Mr. Boland, he said, was highly commended for coming to the rescue of a member of the Civic Guard when there was trouble before between members of some sect or other and the people.

Inspector E. McDonnell said the men came to Killaloe to hold a religious meeting on the steps of the church. Mr Rowe held the Bible in his hand and this was taken from him by Mr Boland, who gave it a couple of kicks down the street. The guards then had a conversation with the men and they went to their car, but the defendants got around by another street, intercepted them and hit them with their fists and sticks. One of the Lindsays fell from a blow on the forehead and lost two teeth. He was unconscious for about 20 minutes. He was treated by his family doctor and taken to hospital next day. There were no serious injuries, but Lindsay had concussion for some time.

District Justice Hurley said he recalled a similar case in Limerick some time ago. He had gone into the matter very deeply then, and he still held the same views. As he saw it, that case was a precedent for future findings of the court. No costs were allowed. He said:

> Religion is above the courts, the main business of which is to preserve peace. When men come into an Irish village and provoke the people by foisting their views on them, they are abusing whatever rights they have under the Constitution, which guarantees freedom of religious worship. Such action is bound to draw down the rod of the people whose hospitality they have received.

A fortnight later, on 1 October 1958, the *Manchester Guardian* carried a similar report on the case. It is obvious from the Clonlara and Killaloe judgments that the District Justice believed that the wrong persons were in the dock. In the Clonlara case he bound over the victims of the assault to keep the peace rather than the assailant accused. Killaloe was suddenly, nationally and internationally, in the spotlight for all the wrong reasons. There was a call for a judicial enquiry by Dr Owen Sheehy Skeffington in the Senate. And there were public criticisms at the time by notable people such as Mr Justice Black, a retired judge of the Supreme Court, and Dr E Hodges, the protestant Bishop of Limerick.

The Bishop wrote:

> Many members of the community will agree that that street preaching is undesirable. Many will question the adequacy and accuracy of the preaching proposed. These are side issues. The main question is: can the citizen of Ireland depend upon the protection of the law to preserve him from bodily harm if he expresses what are thought to be views unacceptable to the religious loyalties of persons who happen to be present in the public street when the words are used? Apparently not. He can be mobbed and battered with impunity by anyone who is 'provoked' by the words used. Such at least is the ruling of the District Justice involved.

Mr Justice Black said in unequivocal terms:

> The legal way to deal with street preachers – the civilised way – was to tell them to move away. This was what the Guards did. After they had walked away, they were attacked. The district justice applied the Probation of Offenders Act. He let the offenders off without a word of reprimand or without binding them over to the peace, and, for good measure, proceeded to pour the vials of his wrath not upon the miscreants, but upon their battered victims. The critics – and they were many, consisting of both religions – had condemned this, carried away by their indignation with the conduct of the District Justice. They had been so carried away that they had overlooked the most damning feature of the whole scandalous transaction. That was not what the District Justice did, but the last eleven words of his allocution in which he said that this case was to be a precedent for future findings.

There was a call by Tuairim in October 1958 for an inquiry into the circumstances which caused the District Justice to make the remarks he made in the case. Tuairim, meaning 'opinion' in the Irish language, was an intellectual society in the 1950s and 1960s which was to the forefront in challenging orthodoxy and conservatism. One of its distinguished members was Dr Garrett FitzGerald who was later to become Taoiseach.

The Methodist Council issued a statement in October 1958 in which they set out some facts. For example,the preachers were not Jehovah's Witnesses at all; the Bible that was kicked down the street was the Catholic version of the New Testament; when requested by the Gardaí to cease preaching, they did so and went away peacefully; the man who was knocked unconscious had not spoken at all; and the Gardaí tried to offer protection to which the preachers were entitled. The Council added that the preachers did not trespass or offer provocation by standing on the steps of the Catholic church; the steps in question were part of the ground where the fair was in progress, and dealers' stalls and cattle were all around them. 'It is the attempt to silence evangelical preaching by the Killaloe methods that is fantastic,' the statement reads, and concludes with:

> In our view, what was said, and left unsaid by way of rebuke in Killaloe court, reveals a gross ignorance of the spirit of the 1916 Proclamation, where 'freedom' is given a sacred meaning by Pearse, Connolly and others.

The Killaloe case provoked a series of letters to the newspapers. One writer said that the Constitution's guarantee on freedom of religious worship was not worth the paper it was written on, as the District Justice had told the victims, in the clearest possible terms, that they had only got what was coming to them. Eric Benson from Bangor referred to the defendants' solicitor's statement that the preachers were 'foisting their special brand of Christianity on a people steeped in Christianity'. With tongue in cheek, he said that he was relieved that the preachers were not dealing with a people steeped in paganism as the consequences might have been more serious.

A Protestant writer, under the nom-de-plum 'Veritas', said that he was glad to hear that the Constitution now provided him with protection if he wanted to break his Roman Catholic's nose with his Protestant fist 'when he annoys me by foisting his views on me'. John O'Donoghue from Dublin queried whether the actions of the local people in Killaloe indicated that sense of deep security and sureness in their faith which was advanced to excuse their easy provocation. A Northern Ireland writer, 'Fermanagh Catholic', said that District Justice Hurley had given Northern Unionists plenty of material for some time.

A Killaloe resident, D. Woods, however warned of the dangers of 'proselytising societies' who direct their attention on children. He went on to say that the Catholic people of Killaloe, kindly and hospitable though they are, have no welcome for street preachers or tract-distributers, be they followers of John Knox or of the notorious purveyor of 'miracle wheat'. However, Ernest M. Bateman from Dublin asked whether it is to be tolerated that a District Justice should base his decisions on self-formulated and ambiguous generalisations such as 'Religion is above the courts'.

A London resident, J. C. Lawder, drew attention to the fact that in 'pagan' London, open air meetings were held by religious bodies of all sorts, including the very energetic Catholic Evidence Society, without hindrance, with a certain amount of good humoured heckling, but always with silence when the meeting ends in prayer. Liam Flynn from Dublin wrote that it was wrong to challenge the application by the District Justice of the law. He referred to a case nearly 60 years before, where a Protestant lecturer, Mr Wise, put beads around his neck, waved a crucifix and used language likely to insult and annoy the Roman Catholic population of Liverpool. He was bound over to be of good behaviour and failed in his appeal, the judge holding that 'the law does regard the infirmity of human temper to the extent of considering that a breach of the peace, although an illegal act, may be the natural consequence of insulting or abusive language or conduct'.

Brian O'Nolan, who as Myles na Gopaleen, took up the Killaloe case

Even the famous Myles na Gopaleen (1911–1966) was energised by the Killaloe case and write to *The Irish Times* on 29 September 1958 in which he queried why there had not been an instant arrest of the 'ruffians' who snatched the Bible from the preacher's hand and kicked it down the street, and assaulted one of them, knocking him unconscious. Myles na Gopaleen was the *nom de plume* of civil servant Brian O'Nolan for his satirical column 'Cruiskeen Lawn' (meaning 'full small jug') in *The Irish Times*. He was a novelist, a playwright and a satirist. He wrote his novels under the *nom de plume* of Flann O'Brien.

•   •   •

Senator Owen Sheehy Skeffington (known as 'Skeff') moved a motion in the Senate on 10 December 1958:

> That Seanad Éireann requests the Minister for Justice to institute a judicial inquiry into the reported conduct by District Justice Gordon Hurley of the case heard before him on September 15th, 1958, arising out of the assault, on June 26th, 1958, upon three street preachers in Killaloe.

Senator Sheehy Skeffington (1909–1970) came from a socialist-republican background. He championed freedom of thought and encouraged debate on then closed topics. I never met the senator, but I had the pleasure in December 2013 in participating in a Tenancy Tribunal with his granddaughter Patricia Sheehy Skeffington BL, who chaired the Tribunal. Sean O'Faoláin said at Skeff's funeral in 1970:

He was one of the noblest and complete men our country has ever produced, a man undefeated by all the weaklings and cowards who yapped at him while he laughed and fought them, a man who, in a country and time not rich in moral courage, never swerved or changed and who kept his youthful spirit to the very end. Such a man never leaves us.

Cover of book published in 1991 on the life of 'Skeff, written by his wife Andrée

In the Seanad, An Cathaoirleach (the Chairman) ruled that Skeff's motion referred to the function of the Minister for Justice under Section 21 of the Courts of Justice (District Court) Act, 1946, in relation to the setting up of a judicial inquiry. He clarified that the only question before the House was the exercise of that function by the Minister, and the merits or demerits of the conduct of the district justice in question could not be discussed.

It beats me, reviewing these Seanad proceedings 55 years later, how there could be a proper discussion on the setting up of a judicial enquiry without discussing the conduct of the district justice. And of course the senators strayed into this forbidden territory. Senator Skeffington quoted extensively from the reports of the case in *The Irish Times* and the *Manchester Guardian* and the comments of Mr Justice Black and Bishop Hodges.

The Senator also expressed his concern that the report of the case might encourage a repetition of the assaults and he quoted a letter which appeared from one of the people who pleaded guilty to the assault in the Killaloe case, in the *Limerick Weekly Echo* of 25 October, 1958:

> The justice has been very bitterly criticised for applying the Probation Act in our case. It really makes no difference

to us what the judge's decision was. We know our duty and will gladly do it again to-morrow if the necessity arises.

Oscar Traynor, Minister for Justice in 1958

The Killaloe case was raised in the Dail on 29 October 1958 by Deputy Booth and the Fianna Fáil Minister for Justice, Oscar Traynor, replied as follows:

I am aware that various religious denominations have expressed concern lest their rights should be infringed, and I, therefore, wish to say that the freedom of conscience and the free profession and practice of religion which are, subject to public order and morality, guaranteed to every citizen by the Constitution will be safeguarded by every means in the power of the law officers of the State and the Garda Síochána. On the occasion in question, the Garda acted promptly – though they were unable to prevent a surprise attack on the persons who were assaulted and, when the papers were referred to the Attorney General, he at once directed that those concerned should be prosecuted on a charge of assault causing actual bodily harm.

As regards the handling of the case by the district justice and the remarks which he is reported to have made,' said the Minister 'this is a matter on which, I think, it would not be proper for me to comment: to do so would inevitably tend to shake the confidence of the public in the independence of the judiciary.

The Minister indicated that he was opposed to having a judicial enquiry. Only three Senators supported having a vote on the motion and so the matter died.

· · ·

As far as I am aware there were no further incidents of assaults on evangelists and no further controversial comments from District Justice Hurley. It is likely that the President of the District Court would have had a quiet and confidential disciplinary word in the ear of the district justice and that would have been the end of the matter. That is the way things were done in those days and perhaps even today. It might lack transparency, but it is effective.

I met District Justice Hurley in 1959, a year after the Killaloe case, at the Lakeside Hotel in Killaloe. I had a summer job at the hotel, teaching people to water ski. Hurley ordered an after-hours drink at the reception desk from Ms O'Brien, the manageress. She told him that she could not serve him as the bar was closed. 'But you have just served a drink to this young man,' he said, pointing to me. 'Yes I have,' said she 'but he is a resident.' Of course I was a resident, not of the hotel as the district justice was led to believe, but of Killaloe town! Ms O'Brien was a great friend of mine.

In her book *'Tis All Lies, Your Worship* ... (2011), former District Justice Mary Kotsonoris recounts a nice story told to her about District Justice Hurley. Apparently he had a soft spot for an old rascal who frequently appeared before him on public order-type offences and out of generousity and sympathy, Hurley would sometimes surreptitiously pay the fine himself. On one occasion, while deliberating on what fine to impose on the old rascal for a whole series of offences, the defendant intervened helpfully, 'Now don't you be going too hard on yourself, your Worship.'

· · ·

There were a lot of Catholic influences on my mother's side of the family. She had two sisters who were nuns and a brother a priest. Our Auntie Molly (religious name Sister Mary Alice) was with the Irish Sisters of Charity, Auntie Bridie (Sister Albeus) was with the Sisters of Mercy, and Uncle Laurence Lyons was a curate in Cong, County Mayo. When we lived in Killaloe, I was not to know that my Auntie Bridie was going to play a significant part in the direction of my work some 20 years later.

In 1980, I was reasonably familiar with the work of the National Rehabilitation Hospital on Rochestown Avenue in Dun Laoghaire. I was on the board of the National Rehabilitation Board (NRB) which, as a State board, had strong links with this 'voluntary' hospital run by the Sisters of Mercy. While the bodies were separate, Dr Tom Gregg was the Medical Director of both. At the time, the School of Occupational Therapy was the responsibility of the NRB but was situated on the grounds of the hospital. I was chairman of the board of management of the school, so I was a constant visitor to the grounds but not to the hospital itself.

The hospital had an unusual history. In 1935 the Sisters agreed with the Minister for Local Government and Public Health that the hospital would be held by the nuns on a charitable trust for the treatment of persons suffering from tuberculosis. The reason for the agreement was to facilitate (and presumably protect) a grant from the State to extend and improve the hospital. There followed a further agreement in 1949 in which the Catholic Archbishop of Dublin was made a party to the charitable trust and further grants were facilitated.

Then in 1961 an agreement was made with the Minister for Health under which the Archbishop and the Sisters of Mercy would hold the hospital on trust as a rehabilitation centre in association with the National Organisation for Rehabilitation (the forerunner of the NRB) and the treatment of persons suffering from tuberculosis would cease. There was provision for a single Medical Director for both bodies. The Archbishop was the late John Charles McQuaid and the Minister for Health was the late Sean McEntee TD.

In autumn 1980 I had a phone call from Dr Gregg inviting me out to the hospital to have a tour and a bite of lunch. I was happy to accept. I knew that Dr Gregg was the driving force behind the hospital and that he had, in some respects, been inspired by that great medical rehabilitation centre in England, Stoke Mandeville Hospital. The tour went fine. Rehabilitation then was mainly in relation to spinal injuries, amputees, and to a lesser extent acquired brain injury. And there was rehabilitation of children and a school for all ages. Very impressive. We were accompanied on the tour by Sister Josephine Bourke, a stern matron of the 'old school'. You could see the respect in which she was held as we went from ward to ward. The wards were spotless. No hospital acquired infections here. She ruled with an iron hand.

The lunch went fine until she leant forward at the table, looked me straight in the eye and said, 'And Mr Murdoch, what do you know about the Sisters of Mercy?' I thought that it was an extraordinary question to ask a visitor to the hospital who had just done a tour.

What I did not know at the time was that the Sisters of Mercy had de-

Dr Tom Gregg KSG, original medical director of the National Rehabilitation Hospital wearing his Papal Knighthood Medal, presented to him in 1989.

cided to establish a board to run the hospital. Until then the hospital was run by Dr Gregg as the Medical Director and Sr Josephine as Matron. There was terrible industrial relations environment in the hospital at the time. The limb fitters who manufactured the artificial limbs were constantly in disagreement, which on occasions resulted in pickets at the gates of the hospital, preventing supplies, including oxygen, being delivered. The Sisters were at their wits' end.

I did not know that Dr Gregg had recommended me to the Sisters of Mercy as a suitable person to be appointed to the new hospital board, because I was at the time the Director of Personnel in AnCO, the industrial training authority, with its 2,000 unionised staff. He considered that I was an industrial relations expert, just what the new board needed, and that I would sort out the limb fitters. But Sister Josephine was taking no chances. She wanted to meet the person being recommended, firstly to see if he would fit in, and secondly to see if he would bring added value. So I was being interviewed for a position on the board though I didn't know it – consequently, the question about my knowledge of the Sisters of Mercy.

'Well, I know a little about the Sisters of Mercy, but not a lot,' I answered. 'I know that they were founded by Catherine McAuley in Dublin around 1830 to help the sick and the poor. I know that she encountered a lot of resistance but eventually the order was recognised. I think she died about 10 years later. The Sisters of Mercy have made a huge contribution to education and health care in Ireland and around the world.'

I then went on to mention the Mater Hospital in Dublin, St Michaels in Dun Laoghaire, and the school in Baggot Street in Dublin.

'You seem to know a lot about the Mercy Sisters, Mr Murdoch. How is that?'

'Well, my aunt was a Mercy nun, my Auntie Bridie – my mother's sister,' I responded.

'Your aunt was a Mercy nun,' she said almost incredulously. 'And what was her religious name?

'Sr Albeus'.

'Not, Sr Albeus, the music teacher in Baggot Street'?

'Yes, the music teacher Sr Albeus. I attended her funeral in the church in Baggot Street a few years ago and I remember her violin and her music being placed on her coffin.'

There was a pause and then she said: 'You are a nephew of Sr Albeus. Well I never!' I was invited onto the new board and I was delighted to accept.

Dr Gregg told me afterwards that Sr Josephine was gobsmacked. She was convinced that it was divine intervention – I had been sent to help them! He said that it was as if a halo had appeared over my head. I did not like being labelled as an IR expert, because I knew how in this area of management it was easy to be proven wrong in one milisecond.

I learned later that it would take nearly a miracle to sort out the limb fitting problem – divine intervention was needed! But by perseverance on all sides the problem was sorted, and now the prosthetic service is second to none and involves a strategic alliance with a UK prosthetic firm, created and owned by Michael O'Boyle, a former limb fitter from the hospital, following a competitive tender.

The first meeting of the new hospital board took place on 12 December 1980.

The first NRH Board in 1980: (L-R): Back row, Mr Crowley (business-man), Sr Josephine Bourke (matron), myself, Mr Carey (brain surgeon), Miss Moire Corcoran (physiotheraphy manager), Mr Clerkin (chartered engineer), Dr Tom Gregg (medical director). Front row: Mrs O'Connor, Sr Frances de Chantal, Sr Cora Ferriter (superior general of the congregation), Mr Ernest Goulding (chairman), Sr Joseph Sarto, Mr Liam O'Byrne (secretary/manager).

Ernest Goulding was chairman of the board for 16 years He was a fantastic chairman, most industrious, always cour-teous, and passionate about the development of the hospital. He steered the hospital during the economics crisis of the mid-1980s when we had to close the therapeutic swimming pool as we didn't have the funds to heat it. I was his apprentice and he handed over the baton to me in 1996. He remained on the board as an ordi-nary member, and chaired the Ethics Commit-tee, a particular area of interest to him, until he passed away in 2003. Dr Tom Gregg died on 3 December 2013 in his 92nd year. He made a magnificent contribution to the hospital and its

Chairman Ernest Goulding (1980-1996)

patients over many years, firstly as a clinician and secondly as a manager and board member.

The first Annual General Meeting of the hospital board took place on 12 March 1982 with a large number of staff invited, a tradition maintained right up to today, and Sr Cora Ferriter, Superior General of the Sisters of Mercy, thanked the board and the staff.

Over the years there have been many excellent men and women who have served on the NRH Board, including former patients (for example, Arthur O'Daly) who have contributed enormously with their intimate knowledge, from personal experience, of how the hospital operates. One such former patient is Paul McNeive who suffered a horrific car accident in 1983, resulting in both legs being amputated and having severe burns to 76 per cent of his body. But this did not stop him from becoming managing director of Hamilton Osborne King, with its 250 staff, which was sold to Savills in 2006 for €50 million. In his book *Small Steps* (2012), Paul recounts the lessons on positivity, motivation and goalsetting which he learned while in the rehabilitation hospital.

President Mary McAleese greeting Paul McNeive in 2011, with Gay Byrne, Road Safety Authority chairman, and me looking on (Photo courtesy of photographer Bríd Ní Luasaigh)

In his book, Paul says that he does not remember exactly what the President said to him in this iconic photo. I can tell you. I was chairman of the NRH at the time and I was introducing members of the board to the President. I introduced Paul, telling her that he was the first double amputee in the world to gain a helicopter pilot's licence. The President, whose very nature is to be always warm and expressive, remarked, 'Oooooh!'

12

KILLALOE – THE CENTRE OF WATER SKIING IN IRELAND

*'Here comes the quinine kid' (1959) – my father
commenting on my return home from the Lakeside
Hotel at an early hour*

Killaloe was the acknowledged birthplace and centre of water skiing in Ireland in the 1950s and 1960s. The birth was due to the efforts of two formidable characters, Englishman David Nations and Limerick man Hector Newenham. David was from London and had the distinction of being the lone British skier at the first World Championships in 1949. In the next ten years, he went on to win many titles and to set many records. He gradually turned his attention to training, organisation and judging water ski competitions. Hector was the son of Limerick architect Edward Newenham, in 1956 the owner of the historic Lakeside Hotel in Killaloe, who saw the potential for developing water skiing in the stretch of river adjoining the hotel.

So in 1956 Hector invited David Nations, then 34 years of age and already acknowledged as the 'father' of water skiing in Britain, to come over from the UK and to help him promote water skiing at Killaloe in particular, and in Ireland in general.

They both were instrumental in setting up the Irish Water Ski Association (IWSA), as it was then known, in September 1958 and in getting its acceptance into membership of the World Water Ski Union in Geneva.

To get water skiing started in Ireland it was necessary to get a number of competent skiers, drivers and instructors. So David Nations trained many to ski and a small number of drivers and instructors. I was fortunate to be trained by David in 1956 as a skier, driver and instructor. I was to spend the next number of summers in Killaloe teaching beginners to ski. We new inexperienced skiers gave an exhibition of water skiing at the Killaloe Regatta in 1957 and 1958.

An article in *The Irish Times* on 6 October 1958, under the heading 'New water sport at Lough Derg', reported that Brendan O'Regan, Chairman of Bord Fáilte (Irish Tourist Board), had watched a demonstration of water skiing in Killaloe by David Nations and by members of the Killaloe club. David is quoted as saying that some of the Killaloe skiers have the makings of international skiers. He said:

> I have found here an enthusiasm which I have rarely come across before; I think that this lake has endless possibilities for skiing. In fact, I think that, so far, Ireland has failed to exploit her lakes and rivers for this sport. It has become incredibly popular all over Europe in the past 10 years.

He went on to say that ski lessons in Killaloe cost five shillings (€0.32) each while in France such lessons cost more than £3.00 (€3.85).

By 1958 there were already about 70 members of the Killaloe Water Ski Club, skiing every weekend, winter and summer. Most of us wore 'skin-suits', which were specially manufactured rubber suits, which had been developed for use by the French Navy, who were pioneers of underwater swimming and exploration.

Competitive water skiing at that time comprised of three separate events, two of which, 'Slalom' and 'Jumping', are similar to those of the companion sport of snow skiing, except that the power is the tow of a motor boat as opposed to the gravity of the mountain slope. The third event, 'Figure Skiing', bears some comparison to the 'Free Style' event in ice skating.

Both Hector and David recognised that if the sport was to be developed throughout Ireland, there was a need to bring it to the capital Dublin. And so they came up with the idea of a demonstration of water skiing on the River Liffey as part of an international Hotels Catering Exhibition in 1958. With the assistance of Desmond West, a Dublin jeweller, they set up the first exhibition of water skiing to take place on the River Liffey. The programme was impressive. Some of the top skiers in the world would be participating, including 24-year-old Marina Doria from Switzerland who was then the female world champion. There also was Peter Felix the British Champion and Max Salic from Antwerp who was one of the best jumping experts in Europe. And of course there would be David Nations himself, five times a British Champion.

But there were a number of challenges. Firstly, the exhibition was going to be at night in the dark (8.15 pm on 21 October 1958) and would require floodlighting. And secondly, at the insistence of the Irish Tourist Board, there had to be Irish skiers taking part,

Me on a slalom ski off Pier Head, 1958

Catering Exhibition 1958

Water Ski-ing Display

RIVER LIFFEY

TUESDAY 21st OCTOBER, 1958
At 8-15 p.m.

Souvenir
Programme of Events

PRICE - - - - - 6d.

Brochure for first demonstration of water skiing on the River Liffey in 1958

so Killaloe was asked to help. As the brochure for the event states, 'The fourteen skiers from Killaloe are as yet almost beginners – but according to experts, they are progressing at a great rate.'

Desmond West was a flamboyant character, who drove a Rolls Royce, and claimed to be able to drive the twisty 112 miles to Killaloe in 112 minutes. Having experienced his driving myself, I well believed it. Desmond flew over to Paris and collected a whole stock of the Jacques Cousteau invented rubber diving suits for the Killaloe skiers.

Some years later David Nations remembered the exhibition:

> For our take-off point, we stationed ourselves in the Guinness Brewery – that was our first mistake. We'd taught these people to ski and they were to go down, carrying Irish flags, in front of the star performers. There was a remarkable crowd of 50,000 lining the river, even though it was winter.
>
> The parade started, multi-coloured rockets were fired, and off they went. There was about half a mile of darkness and bridges before they came into the limelight, but when the boats appeared, there was not a single Irishman to be seen. They'd had such a wonderful reception at the Guinness Brewery before the start, that they'd fallen off! So we had to turn the boats round and direct the searchlights to find them. A Limerick dentist 'Red' McDonnell, who was wearing a chef's tall white cap and tunic, had sunk while negotiating a difficult turn just above O'Connell Bridge, and he was to sink again before reaching the Metal Bridge.

Then came the jumping. The organisers found it impossible to moor the jump in the middle of the swift-flowing River Liffey, so rather than cancel that most exciting part of the show, the jump was moored against a wall. This made the approach rather terrifying as a sideslip would hurl the jumper straight into that wall. Luckily, there were no accidents.

The report in *The Irish Times* on 22 October 1958, under the heading 'Dublin sees novel sport on Liffey', was equally effusive and strongly supportive of the Killaloe skiers:

Last night Dubliners, young and old, converged on the centre of the city in thousands, by bus, motor car, bicycle and on foot. Their object was a mile-long stretch of the Liffey quays, from O'Connell Bridge to the Four Courts, and soon an estimated crowd of from 10,000 to 15,000 was leaning over the ancient grey walls looking down on the dark waters, crossed at regular intervals by bars of light thrown by specially mounted flood lamps.

The people, as Dublin crowds do, had come in search of entertainment, They were not disappointed. The first water-skiing display ....proved to be exciting, fast, full of thrills – and spills. A Limerick dentist, Mr Redmond J McDonnell, contributed an appropriate touch when he made his run down river wearing a chef's tall white cap and tunic.

'Red,' as he is known throughout the south of Ireland, sank while negotiating a difficult turn just above O'Connell Bridge, and again before he reached the Metal Bridge, but, like a young water ski addict who had also sunk temporarily at the turn, he was rapturously applauded, proving that the crowd was completely with the skiers. Earlier, Mr McDonnell's wife, Mary [Margaret], had made a faultless run down-river, a turn and back up to the start.

During the second part of the programme the crowd saw some of the finest water-skiers in the world, lead by Marina Doria, the 24-year-old Swiss champion. There was also Max Salic, a young Belgian businessman, from Antwerp, one of the current European champions, and one of the fastest jumping experts on the Continent; Peter Felix, the current British champion, and Jack and Jill Morris. As part of one of the best free shows ever staged in Dublin, crowds saw Salic accomplish the rare feat of barefoot skiing at nearly 30 miles and hour.

They saw Marina give a breath-taking demonstration of figure skiing and to prove that expertise does not preclude mishaps, Miss Doria sank twice – on one occasion between O'Connell and the Metal bridges. At the end of the programme the ski-jump was staged. The first to take it was Peter Felix. He jumped faultlessly, but sank on landing. He succeeded on the second attempt. The same fate overtook Salic.

The Killaloe skiers, according to experts, are progressing with amazing rapidity (sic), and Mr Nations, who has helped to found more than a dozen water skiing clubs in England and Scotland, is advising the group preparatory to its entry in European championships. After last night's showing, the group has Dublin strongly behind it.

Everyone agreed that the exhibition was a great success and Irish skiing had been helped a great deal. Less than two months later, in December 1958, the IWSA was admitted to membership of the World Water Ski Union in Geneva, with Desmond West as the President and Hector Newenham as Secretary. *The Irish Times* reported on 12 December 1958 that there were then about 100 persons in Ireland who could ski at that time, and a hard nucleus of 10 who ski all year round and would be skiing in Killaloe on Christmas Day that year. I was privileged to be among that ten. It was not long before there were ski clubs at Balscadden Bay in Howth and in Golden Falls in Wicklow, and eventually around the country.

The following year a further exhibition of water skiing took place on the River Liffey, but this time in the summer and during daylight (12 August 1959). It was held in association with an An Tóstal concert of Irish music and song and the annual Liffey swim. The *Irish Press* next day carried an excellent photograph of a skier emerging from under the arch of a bridge with the caption, 'Water ski experts giving a demonstration on the Liffey last night'. The newspaper noted that Burgh Quay and adjoining streets were jam-packed with an estimated 7,000 people, and that traffic along Burgh Quay was diverted for three hours as the crowds spread along O'Connell Bridge, down Eden Quay and into nearby side streets.

The stage was now set for Ireland to stage its first National Championships which took place at the Lakeside Hotel Killaloe a month later on 19–20 September 1959. The chairman of the IWSA was Oliver Coffey, and Hector Newenham was a member of the committee. The chief judge for the championships was David Nations with his colleague Van der Berg. I drove the boat; I was 21 years of age. There were 27 competitors in the men's competition and 13 for the ladies', from four clubs – Killaloe, Balscadden Bay, Sandycove, and East Coast. Prominent competitors who played a key role in the early stages of the development of the sport included Deirdre Frawley (Killaloe), Fred Waterstone, Desmond West, Noel Treacy (all Killaloe) and David and Roger Johnson (Balscadden but later Golden Falls).

SOUVENIR PROGRAMME

IRISH WATER SKI ASSOCIATION

FIRST

National Championships

Sat. & Sun.
September
19th & 20th
1959

AT
**The Lakeside Hotel,
Killaloe, Co. Clare**

Brochure for the first National Championships in Killaloe in 1959

Driving the boat in a water skiing competition was a very important job. Maintaining a constant speed and course was essential if all competitors were to be treated equally. In the Slalom competition the skier entered the slalom course of six buoys through an entrance gate, went in a zig-zag course around the six buoys and exited through an exit gate. This merited a score of eight if successfully completed. The return

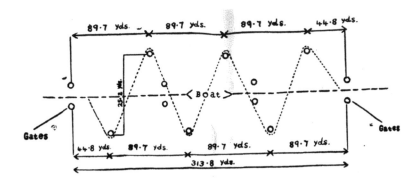

Typical slalom course in 1958

through the course was at a higher speed and this continued until the competitor had a fault, for example, by having a fall after entering the entry gate or a failure to round a buoy. The buoys had to be located with precise accuracy. Irish champion Alan Murray (Sligo) failed to score any points in the national championships held in Killaloe in 1965 when he missed the entry gate, having swung out too far to the side before approaching it.

In the Jump competition a waxed floating timber ramp was used. The boat travelled on a parallel course to the right of the jump and the skier endeavoured to jump the longest distance. Experienced skiers would adopt the technique of 'double cutting' by swinging hard to the right of the boat, and then at the last moment, swinging over and approaching the ramp in a

pendulum-like arc. The skier would ideally hit the ramp at the bottom right and cross the ramp surface diagonally, exiting with a kick or spring at the top left. The skier then had to land and ski onwards for 100 yards (91 metres) to be credited with the jump. The skier would reach a speed in excess of 50 miles per hour when hitting the ramp.

A slight miscalculation could result in the skier running into the side of the jump, which was why a run-off ramp at the side of the jump, called a 'cowcatcher', was recommended. The jump ramp we had in Killaloe in 1959 did not have a cow-catcher. How someone was not killed or seriously injured, I will never know. Also in

The jump ramp at Killaloe in 1959 without side cowcatchers and in 1961 (CCL) with cowcatchers

those days, the way in which we measured the jump distance was very crude and potentially dangerous. We had a floating plank of wood near the likely landing zone, with small vertical poles every foot and larger vertical poles every five feet (1.5 metres). The danger was that someone would land on these distance markers. Fortunately it didn't happen.

The third competition was called 'Figure Skiing', although it was generally known as 'Tricks'. Here the competitor performed a programme of his own composition with the object of achieving the maximum points in the time allotted. There was a defined list of approved tricks, each with a points value based on difficulty. For example, a simple two ski 180 degree turnaround got

The dangerous jump distance markers in 1959

30 points, whereas a single ski 360 degree turn in the air, off the wake, with the tow rope held in a foot-hold, got 300 points. Tricks could not be repeated and a fall terminated the run, but points awarded up to then were credited. This was by far the most difficult competition to judge, because it all happened so fast, and you had to record every trick performed and decide if it had been completed precisely as defined. In later years I devised a shorthand hieroglyphics that looked a bit like ancient Egyptian or Chinese characters, which served me well.

The first National Championships in Killaloe was a great success, and David Nations did a great job as a judge. He was a hard task master who set a high standard but was always fair. David, who was then secretary of the 5,000 strong British Federation, is reported in *The Irish Times* of 21 September 1959 as having praised highly the skill of the Irish skiers, many of whom had only taken up the sport 'within recent months'. Years later he was to recall with a laugh about the inventiveness of the skiers in Killaloe: 'One chap was absolutely convinced

The crowds watching the skiing at Killaloe, 1959

that he should be awarded points for a new trick – juggling three golf balls while skiing.' The first Irish national champions in water skiing in Ireland were David Johnson (Balscadden), narrowly beating his brother and club-mate Roger, and Margaret McDonnell (Killaloe), wife of 'Red' McDonnell, who participated in the Liffey demonstration. Roger Johnson would go on to take the men's overall championship in 1960 and 1961 in Killaloe.

The first championships in 1959 attracted huge crowds who lined both sides of the river and on Killaloe bridge. A brilliant running commentary on the public address system was given by Leslie Thorn, who with his wife Sheila attended most of the early competitions. I remember feeling great pride that our small town with its 900 population, and Ballina with its 140, was again the centre of Ireland, just as it had been in 1002–1014 when Brian Boru ruled Ireland from Kincora. The Championships were rounded off with a dance in the Kincora Hall in Killaloe and a free raffle (using the souvenir programme as the ticket) for a gold wrist watch which was won by Denis Flynn of Criveroe. The Championships were to be the forerunner of many successful ski competitions in Killaloe and elsewhere in Ireland.

For four years, from 1956 to 1959, during the long summer holidays from university, Ann Deakin and I taught people how to ski in Killaloe. It was part of a service provided by the Lakeside Hotel for its guests. Ann was a terrific driver and instructor although she did not ski herself. I remember that my pay from the hotel was free skiing, with Ann doing the driving, and the drinks which were bought for me by satisfied clients. I had at that stage developed a taste for gin and tonic (with

Me coming into the dock at the lakeside 1960. Hector Newenham is driving the speed boat. Cragg Hill is in the background.

quinine) and that tended to become my tip and my tipple. On one occasion I arrived back in our house in Killaloe at an unearthly hour in the morning in a sorry state, to be greeted by my father, 'here comes the quinine kid!'

In August 1959, probably as a forerunner to the first National Water Skiing Championships a month later, a new competition was introduced to Killaloe by Hector Newenham – speedboat racing in ten laps between the Pier Head and the bridge. It was very exciting and drew huge crowds on both sides of the river. There was a neck and neck race between Ann Deakin and Leslie Bradshaw and a brilliant commentary by Leslie Thorn. Noel Treacy from Nenagh lost an engine overboard as its screw bolts came loose due to vibration. In the minor race, with smaller and slower boats, our school friends Michael Crowe and Jim McKeogh came second, and Jim Crowe and my brother Laurence came third. The *Clare Champion* on 5 September 1959 reported that after the races, 'a flawless exhibition of water skiing was given by Messrs Doyle, Johnson and West'.

·   ·   ·

Even though throughout the early 1960s I did win a few trophies in water skiing, I really was not good at it. This photo shows me coming off the ski jump in Killaloe at about 50 miles per hour, but upside down by the time I hit the water – which is not the way to do it. This and other unsuccessful jumps were to result in operations on my right knee in 1963 and 1966. But we were young and had no fear.

Me at the Lakeside Hotel in 1959 – how not to jump!

So like David Nations, I turned my attention to organisation and judging, as did my good friend for many years Cecil Prentice. Cecil was a solicitor, a partner in the prominent Dublin firm of Matheson Ormsby and Prentice (now Matheson). Cecil subsequently became President of the IWSA and I became Technical President, dealing with all the technical issues in relation to competitions.

I was the member of the judging panel in many competitions in Ireland, starting as an assistant judge at the Irish Open Championships held in Killaloe in September 1963. Water skiing had really developed in the four years since 1959. Membership of a club was not that expensive, on average being £5.5s (€6.73) for an individual and £8.8s (€10.77) for a family. At that time, I was earning about £1,100 (€1,410) per annum in Aer Lingus or £21 (€27) per week.

There were 50 entries in the 1963 competition, with competitors from England, Scotland, West Indies, and Ireland (Balscadden, Century, Galway, Glenbrook, Golden Falls, Killaloe, Meteor, and Sligo). Century and Meteor were actually the same club, operating out of Lough Henney in County Down, but more about that later. The senior men's competition attracted some great skiers, including Brian Cullen (Killaloe), who would later buy the Derg Marina in Killaloe, became a pilot and a businessman, chairman of the brilliant Foynes Museum, and whose motto is, 'Growing old is mandatory. Growing up is optional'. There was also Barry Galvin (Glenbrook), who later headed up the Criminal Assets Bureau, John Kelly (Golden Falls) who became a professor and registrar in UCD, and Alan Murray (Sligo) who subsequently represented Ireland at international competitions.

One of the competitors was Aubrey Sheena from the Ruislip in London. Aubrey recounted the story of his flight to Shannon to take part in the competition. In those days of lax airport security, already late, he rushed out to the flight, still wearing his jumping helmet. As he sat in his seat beside a nun – he was Jewish – she placed a hand on his knee and told him not to be afraid, as flying was much safer nowadays!

Also participating in the men's junior competition was a very young skier, Alan Dagg (Glenbrook but later Golden Falls), who would become Ireland's greatest skier ever. Alan and his wife Jennifer emigrated to Perth, Western Australia around 1981 where he has continued to ski and has won state and national competitions in his age group, for over 34s, then over 45s and in 2006 for over 55s. As he approached 60 years of age he decided to give up competitive jumping!

Around that time he told me that when I introduced the grading of skiers

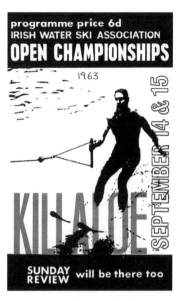

Brochure for Irish Open Championships in Killaloe in 1963

John Kelly at Killaloe in 1962, before he became a university professor

*Alan Dagg lining up a jump
and then executing it*

in the early 1960s, it was a great inspiration for him, as it gave him the determination to get to the next grade, until he finally made it to Grade 1. The system I introduced had a grading scale from Grade 7, which was very basic, to Grade 1, which was at international level. A 'junior' competition was for skiers Grade 4 to 7.

The basic Grade 7 required the skier to swim 50 yards (46 metres); to put on two skis, unassisted in deep water; to swim 5 yards (4.6 metres) wearing skis; to carry out a deep water start; to start unassisted from the dock on two skis; to carry out a series of crossings of each wake; in the centre of the wake, to lift each ski alternatively for three seconds; and to return to the jetty and make a controlled and safe landing. The other grades involved more demanding standards including one-ski routines, ever increasing boat speeds, and minimum jump distances and trick scores. It was the ski equivalent of going from the Junior certificate to a Doctorate level degree.

Notable in the Ladies' competition in 1963 were Deirdre Frawley (Killaloe) and Brenda Anderson (Sligo), who were both brilliant skiers. My sister Hilary Murdoch (Balscadden) also competed. My brothers Laurence and Bill did not take

Ski competition Killaloe 1963 with
St Flannan's Cathedral in the background

up skiing. The 1963 competition, which was sponsored by the newspaper the *Sunday Review*, was a great success, attracting huge crowds and publicity, and was rounded off by a dinner dance at the Lakeside Hotel. The number of spectators was estimated by some newspapers as between 8,000–10,000. There are very few towns that would attract ten times their population to an event.

The Irish Times in its coverage of the event on 16 September 1963, under the heading 'Killaloe was ideal venue', noted 'the combination of excellent organisation, beautiful surroundings and a steady round of excitement'. The reporter went on to state:

> Tony McCleery, a member of Meteor Club Belfast, demonstrated that skis were not really necessary, and proved this by discarding his skis during a fast run and travelling for over a 100 yards using his bare feet as skis. He told me that speed and smooth water were all that were essential for this trick. He takes only 10 ½ size shoes.

The *Limerick Weekly Echo* had this to say:

> There can be no doubt that Killaloe provides a location second to none for this internationally famed sport. Situated in beautiful surroundings with natural grandstands on both banks, it is no wonder that it has won high praise from the visiting skiers.

Cecil Prentice cycling on water in Killaloe in 1963

Raymond Heavey standing on a chair in the early 1960s

The report goes on to acknowledge the initiative of Hector Newenham of the Lakeside Hotel in bringing water skiing to Ireland at Killaloe.

A feature of nearly all championships in those years was the fun skiing demonstrations put on by Cecil Prentice and Raymond Heavey. Cecil became an expert at skiing on a bike. He modified the bike himself and was in great demand at all ski competitions. He attached a ski to the front and back wheels of his bike. It was a wonder to see him emerge from the water as he picked up speed and the skis provided lift. When he was airborne (or should it be waterborne) he would start peddling and it really looked as if he was cycling on water. Unfortunately the bike today is at the bottom of the river Shannon in Killaloe. Cecil loaned the bike to another skier, who unfortunately allowed it to sink, never to retrieved.

Raymond Heavey would demonstrate skiing while sitting or standing on a chair on a round table top. The crowds loved these fun demonstrations and really wondered how they were possible. The demonstrations took a lot of skill, which Cecil and Ray had in abundance.

. . .

I started in the sister sport of snow skiing with Cecil and Ray in 1964. We went to Ehrwald in the Austrian Alps that year and in subsequent years went to other ski resorts, often with other water skiers. We were like one large family and as most of us were not married at the time, we had no other financial commitments. On the few occasions when Cecil did not come with us, Ray and I would pick out the sexiest and boldest post-card, usually with a scantily clad well-endowed female snow skier who would be saying something in German in a bubble above her head. We would send it to Cecil who spoke German, knowing that his prim and proper elderly secretary would be aghast. Cecil often told us that his secretary would come into his office with his post, with a frosty face on her and say: 'Mr Prentice, here is your post. There is another of *those* postcards from those so-called *friends* of yours.'

. . .

Cecil and I had a great time in our involvement in water skiing, trav-elling all over Europe to meetings and competitions. Cecil had a very successful law practice and was well able to afford the expense. And I had a well paid job in Aer Lingus and subsidised air travel.

Alan Dagg and David Johnson jumping together in the 1960s

In 1966 there was a major juris-diction dispute between the Irish Water Ski Association and the Brit-ish Federation. We maintained that the IWSA was a 32 county all-Ire-land body, whereas the British Fed-eration maintained that they had exclusive jurisdiction over the six counties of Northern Ireland. In 1966 the British Fed-eration imposed a ban on their skiers participating in IWSA competitions. They claimed that the IWSA had no right to hold its national championship in Enniskillen the previous July, as Enniskillen, being in the territorial area of Northern Ireland, was under Britain's sole jurisdiction. They further called on the IWSA to compel clubs in Northern Ireland to relinquish their affiliation to the Irish body.

The matter was brought to a head at a meeting of the world body in West Berlin (then a divided city) in 1967, attended by Cecil Prentice and myself. The British Federation had tabled a motion claiming jurisdiction over water skiing in Northern Ireland. We argued against the motion. We claimed that the IWSA had been accepted by the world body as representing a 32-county Ireland. We cited the examples of other sports which were organised on an all-Ireland basis, for example, rugby football and gaelic games (GAA). We were also able to show that we had the support of water ski clubs in Northern Ireland, whose skiers had a greater chance of being selected for a national side in Ireland than in the UK.

Mr Franco Carraro from Italy proposed that the matter be referred to a committee and that the British Federation should lift the ban. This was accepted. Our compromise proposal was subsequently accepted – there should be joint jurisdiction, with clubs in Northern Ireland being eligible to affiliate to either the Irish or the British bodies. This resolved the matter and led to an innovative Irish solution to an Irish problem. For example, in Lough Henney near Belfast, there were two water ski clubs, Century and Meteor. Century was affiliated to the Irish body and its skiers were eligible to ski for Ireland, whereas Meteor was affiliated to the British body and eligible for all the generous UK state grants supporting sports. The two clubs had a common membership and shared the same premises and equipment! An Irish solution to an Irish problem!

.   .   .

Cecil Prentice and I both became officially recognised as national judges, that is, persons who could judge competitions in their own country. But the big prize was to become what was known as *Juge 1 Premiere Classe,* an international Judge of the First Class, recognised by the World Water Ski Union. The jury of judges (there were normally five members) of all international competitions had to be First Class Judges. And David Nations was such a judge. There were only four in the UK and 26 in the whole of Europe, and none in Ireland.

I set out to be qualified as a First Class Judge. The first barrier was to gain experience judging at national level. I eventually achieved that. Then I had to sit a written theoretical test on my knowledge of the rules. I eventually passed that test. But the biggest test of all was the practical. I had to participate as an addition member of the jury in an international competition and score every event, independently of the official jury. My decisions and my scores were then compared with those of the official jury.

Cecil Prentice, Alan Murray, Alan Dagg, me and Denis Long in Trier Germany in 1965, where Cecil and I sat our Judges exams and the two Alans became international champions

This all took place in Trier in Germany in 1965 at the Northern European Championships in which brilliant Irish skiers Alan Dagg (Golden Falls) and Alan Murray (Sligo) participated.

Trier is a lovely city on the banks of the Moselle river with a population of about 100,000. My test was supervised by Ivan Cantacuzene from Switzerland. He was President of the Technical Committee of the World Water Ski Union (WWSU). Ivan, who claimed that he never had a pair of water skis on his feet, was involved in water skiing in an administrative and technical capacity from 1953 until his death in 1987. He was an international First Class Judge for 30 years and was Chief Judge of the 1979 World Championships in Toronto. Ivan was admitted

Alan Murray, Third Overall in Northern European Championships, 1964, in Amsterdam

John Poynton, Raymond Heavey, Doloretta Daly and me, Amsterdam 1964

to the International Hall of Fame of the International Water Ski Federation in 1995 for his long, dedicated and effective service to the sport and in recognition of his calmness in the face of confusion. He was a real gentleman and was very helpful to me, but I never saw him smile. Perhaps it was the Swiss way!

To my surprise, I passed the practical test and in 1965 became the first Irish international Judge of the First Class of the WWSU. I was also appointed as a *Homologateur*, which is the person qualified to certify that the technical facilities comply with the requirements. And Cecil passed his exam as a National judge.

My first international assignment was as a member of the five-man jury at the North European Championships in Amsterdam in 1966. There was a lot of speculation as to who would be going to be on the ski team to Amsterdam to represent Ireland. *The Irish Times* on 19 August 1966 reported that the team would be finalised after the Irish Open championships that September and then stated:

One man who is certain to be in Amsterdam, however, is Henry Murdoch, of Dublin, who has been asked to act on the panel of judges. This is the first time that an Irishman has been asked to judge at an overseas event. Murdoch, a member of Balscadden Ski Club, took an exam at Trier (West Germany) last year and became Ireland's first premier-class judge.

I had a number of other international assignments in 1967, and then in July 1968 I was delighted to be invited to be a member of the judges' panel in David Nation's wa-

U.M.S.N. W.W.S.U.	
Groupe II	est JUGE I (première classe)
	Valable jusqu'au: 31.12.1970
	Le Président du Comité Technique
Photo non obligatoire	est HOMOLOGATEUR
	Valable jusqu'au: 31.12.1970
	Le Président du Comité Technique
	est JUGE II (deuxième classe)
Il est certifié par la présente que	Valable jusqu'au:
Monsieur	Le Président du Comité Technique:
Henry MURDOCH	est JUGE III (national)
	Valable jusqu'au:
Irlande	Le Président de la Fédération ou de la Commission Technique:

World Water Ski Union Judge's Certificate First Class

ter ski club in Ruislip in Middlesex, in which the then current world champion Mike Suyderhoud competed. David was also a member of the jury and the Chief Judge. He was not unfriendly but I got the impression that he didn't altogether welcome this guy from a small Irish town with limited skiing ability. After all, he had been a British and an international champion. All I had achieved was third place in the men's junior Figures competition at Sligo Water Ski Club. I was left to find my own accommodation and transport to the ski location, which was not the norm for the treatment of judges of international events.

Things improved when I was appointed to the same event in 1969 and in 1970, when my accommodation was arranged and I was picked up at Heathrow airport. But 1970 had a number of surprises for me. The first was that I was appointed by the world body to be the Chief Judge of the five-man jury at the Ruislip Northern European Championship. In this capacity, I would assign responsibility for various duties to the other members of the jury, and I would chair our deliberations, and would have a casting vote in the event of a tie. I was a bit apprehensive as this was my first time to act as Chief Judge in an international event, but I had accumulated a lot of experience in that capacity at national level. I was happy that I could handle it.

David Nations (right) with members of the West Indies team (photo courtesy of The Irish Times, 9 August 1963)

When I arrived at the Lido on Reservoir Road in Ruislip I was greeted warmly by David Nations who said to me, reassuringly: 'Henry, don't worry about the competition. You just look after the technical aspects and I'll look after the jury'.

I was flabbergasted. 'David, I don't understand what you are saying. Are you saying that you want me to be a member of the jury and that you will be the Chief Judge,' I enquired politely.

'Exactly, Henry. It is better that way. You have never been the Chief Judge in an international competition and I have been many times.'

He was factually correct but I had been officially appointed by the world body. I searched in my folder for my letter of appointment from Ivan Cantacuzene. Showing it to David, I said firmly but not angrily: 'David, you know as a judge that you must follow the rules. The rules state that the jury and the Chief Judge are appointed by the world body. This letter from Ivan Cantacuzene states that I have been appointed as the Chief Judge of this competition and that you are a member of my team. As Chief Judge, I am assigning you to look after all the technical issues. I am sure we will get on fine.'

I then called a meeting of the jury, the other members of which were from other countries in Europe, and we all got on famously and had a wonderful competition. In a subsequent letter to me, David wrote:

> I am sorry that we raised a bit of dust between us, Henry, but I hope you enjoyed the weekend. It was nice to see you and Cecil, and I look forward to seeing you both at Ruislip again next year.

I suppose in some respects David's reaction was understandable because the apprentice was now supervising his master. David should have been proud of his handiwork, because I would never have been an international judge without the thorough training and example he had given me over the years. David Nations and I never had a problem between us after that.

Five years later, in 1975, David Nations was awarded an OBE for his contribution to water skiing. In 1977, he wrote (with Kevin Desmond) *The Guinness Guide to Water Skiing.* In 1978 he was appointed President of the British Disabled Water Ski Association which he had founded. He died in the mid-1980s. And in 1996 David was admitted posthumously to the International Hall of Fame of the International Water Ski Federation, where he was described as indefatigable, enthusiastic, and totally devoted to the cause of promoting water skiing, and recognised for having been a founder member of the British Water Ski Federation, as well as federations in Ireland, Israel and the Caribbean.

. . .

Water skiing in Killaloe started to go into decline in the early 1970s when Hector Newenham sold the Lakeside Hotel. At that time I used to write an article about water skiing in Ireland in the official monthly magazine of the British Water Ski Federation. In one article about the 1970 Irish Open Championship, I wrote:

Irish Water Skiing Association (IWSA) Crest

> The Irish Open was rated by all as a great social event. The fact that the club at Killaloe is going through a difficult period in its history at this time, militated against a very high technical standard in the competition this year. However, a number of willing hands together made possible a competition,

which at times was in danger of being cancelled or changed to a different venue. The competition that did take place was really enjoyed by competitors and officials alike.

My comments were met with an immediate response from Killaloe. I should explain that the IWSA *modus operandi* was to invite one of its affiliated clubs to run a competition and that club was responsible for ensuring that all the required technical standards were met, on the ground and in the water, for example, correct length of tow ropes and distance between buoys and correct height of jump. At that time the water ski club in Killaloe was part of a larger organisation called the Killaloe Country Club with wider functions, facilities and responsibilities than water skiing.

In his letter to me in January 1971, Captain W. T. Knight, President of the Killaloe Country Club, wrote the following:

> I should like to clarify the situation and to state categorically that the committee of this club decided not to run the event for that year (1970), but that if the Irish Water Ski Association were interested, all facilities and equipment would be at their disposal. The competition was held and every effort was given to the IWSA to make this a successful event, and any standards that were not achieved lies squarely with the IWSA. The Killaloe Country Club has not at any time had a difficult passage and its members at present number over 400. Facilities and assistance have always been available at the Killaloe Country Club, and I should like to state emphatically that there never has been any decline in its attitude to skiing and to those taking part in any of the events held here.

When I investigated the matter, I found that Captain Knight was right about the IWSA being responsible in this case for the technical standards and so I wrote a grovelling apology in the next issue of the magazine:

> The IWSA would like to apologise to the Killaloe Country Club if the impression was given that the Killaloe Club might have been responsible for any poor technical stan-

dards at the Irish Open 1970. The IWSA was fully responsible for the technical arrangements and takes full responsibility for any failure to achieve high technical standards. The Killaloe Club has always been more than generous with the provision of facilities, cooperation and willing assistance.

But Captain Knight was not correct about a decline in interest in skiing at the Killaloe Club. The club's affiliation fee to the IWSA for 1970 was over a year overdue in 1971. The Munster championships, which always took place in Killaloe, had to be diverted in 1970 to Sligo as the Killaloe Club was not in a position to run the competition. The Irish Open in 1971 was offered to Killaloe but again they were not prepared to run it and Golden Falls in Wicklow had to step in at the last minute. Although the Munster championships returned to Killaloe in August 1972, for the first time in three years, and the Irish Open championships were held in Killaloe in 1972 and 1973, no further championships were held there after that date. Around that time the Killaloe County Club was bought by Bill McCormac (Cormac Cruisers) and subsequently bought by water skier Brian Cullen in 1979.

By late 1970s, water skiing, including the jump, had moved from Killaloe to O'Briensbridge. In the meantime clubs like Golden Falls and Meteor/Century in County Down went from strength to strength and are still very active over 30 years later in 2014.

I got married in 1972 and moved to Sligo. Gradually my own interest in water skiing also declined while my attention turned to managing hospitals, changing nappies, paying a mortgage, playing golf, and sailing on Lough Gill and at Rosses Point. I noticed that *The Irish Times*, which had always provided excellent coverage of water skiing in Killaloe, had now turned its attention to the sport of sailing at Killaloe, which was growing in popularity. For example, W. M. Nixon, writing on 2 November 1973 said:

Conditions were pleasant, remarkably so for the end of October with Lough Derg a scene of beauty in Autumn tint. On both days the winds were as steady as could be expected as they blew fairly evenly along the 'fiord' which leads from the lake to Killaloe.

. . .

Cecil Prentice, President of the IWSA, in the 1960s

Back in Dublin and over 30 years later in 2004, I was converting all my old 8 millimetre cine films into electronic format so that they would be saved for posterity. I came across a lot of shots of water skiing, not only in Ireland but also in Amsterdam, Trier and other locations in Europe. There were some terrific shots of Cecil Prentice riding his bike on the water. It was always a stunner with the spectators at water ski competitions. I knew he would be interested in seeing it, so I sent him a DVD. He wrote to me saying that he had to send Nina Ryan, his long term partner, out to buy a DVD player so that he could watch it. I was not to know until after his death some seven months later the sheer pleasure which he got out of the DVD. Nina told me that he would play and replay it on many occasions as it brought back such pleasant memories to him. He was a great guy.

Over the years, Ray Heavey and I talked about having a reunion of all the old water skiers. At each funeral of one of our skiers, we would raise the issue of a reunion again. Eventually in 2005 when three of our skiers died (Brendan O'Connor in January, Lany Bacon in February, and Cecil Prentice in June) we got really serious. We organised a reunion in November 2006 at the Fitzwilliam Lawn Tennis Club in Dublin, which was attended by 28 former skiers and their partners. They came from Cork, Waterford, Wexford and Dublin. We were all delighted that Cecil's partner Nina Ryan attended and Sean Byrne's widow Elaine. And that 87-year-old Eric Timon came all the way from Howth. His boat was called *AMOW* – All My

Own Work! And we remembered our deceased skiers – those mentioned above and Geraldine and Noel Canton, Matt (Toss) Cassidy, Berna Fitzpatrick, Kay Lawless and Irene Wytack.

At the reunion I gave a copy of the DVD to all the attendees and sent a copy to those who were unable to attend. I was able to locate Ireland's greatest water ski champion, Alan Dagg, in Perth in Western Australia and I sent him a copy of the DVD also. The DVD is in effect a visual record of the early days of water skiing in Killaloe and Ireland. Alan was honoured in November 1974 by being included in the Guinness International Sport Roll of Honour for the sport of water skiing.

I also sent the DVD to the President of the now re-named Irish Waterski and Wakeboard Federation (Irish WWF), Des Burke-Kennedy. The IWWF is a non-profit organisation and is the all-Ireland governing body for all forms of waterskiing, wakeboarding, disabled skiing and barefooting. Its members are affiliated clubs. The Federation has 17 affiliated clubs, the four nearest to Killaloe, being Terryglass, Long Island, Limerick and Portumna. (See www.irishwwf.ie.)

Hector Newenham, who brought water skiing to Killaloe and to Ireland, founded the IWSA and was its President, died in Limerick on 28 September 2013. Because of his involvement it is not surprising that the death notice in the newspaper stated, 'formerly of the Lakeside Hotel, Killaloe'. Fifty-four years earlier, on 19 September 1959, the *Clare Champion* said of Hector, 'Killaloe man pioneers water skiing'. The sport of water skiing owes a lot to those pioneers of the sport – Hector Newenham, Cecil Prentice, Fred Waterstone, Desmond West, Joe Acton, Alan Dagg, Alan Murray, the Johnson brothers, John Poynton, Geoff Shanks, and of course David Nations from the UK.

Hector Newenham,
Lakeside Hotel, 1964

13

Leaving Killaloe and Nearly Returning

'You could live in your home town Killaloe'
– Mr Parkes, Chief Engineer, RTÉ, offering me a
job (1962)

Like many people in Killaloe at the time, I headed off to Eng-land in September 1959. I knew I was in a more privileged position than many emigrants, because I had an engineering degree and I was going to a definite job, a two year graduate apprenticeship with a big multinational company – Associated Electrical Industries (AEI) Ltd. I would be getting excellent training and work experience which would, hopefully, enable me to get work back in Ireland. And I would be paid £600 (€770) per annum.

I was seen off at Birdhill railway station by my sorrowful parents. My total assets at the time were the £10 (€12.82), the wristwatch which my parents gave me, and the railway/boat ticket to Rugby in Warwickshire, which the company had sent me. I was to spend the next two years at the company's plants around the UK, in Rugby (large electric generators as used by the ESB), Coventry (aircraft components), Leicester (elec-

Coton House, Rugby, my home in England in 1959 as a graduate engineering apprentice – it was destroyed by fire in 2010

tronic components), Lincoln (selling transistors which were then the innovative part of the transistor radio), and Berkeley Gloucestershire (commissioning a nuclear power station).

I knew that I had an Irish accent, probably a Killaloe/Limerick accent with a tinge of the lilting Cork accent thrown in, but I did not know that I did not pronounce my 'ths'.

In Churchover, near Rugby, all the graduate apprentices stayed in a large rambling eighteenth century Coton House, where the manager (called the warden), a former major in the British army, was in charge. One day I discovered that all my ties had been stolen from my room. So I reported this to the warden. 'A teef has taken my ties,' I told him. He responded incredulously

'A teef has taken your ties? What, may I awsk, is a teef?'

'A robber,' I explained, thinking that he must be an awful eejit.

'Owh, you mean a *thief*,' he said.

I was to learn that pronunciation of the Queen's English was very important amongst the ruling classes in England.

There was a severe outbreak of 'foot-and-mouth disease' in 1960 in the UK during which over 70,000 animals were slaughtered. All Irish citizens were asked not to return to Ire-

My 6' 6" graduate apprentice friend Alex Turner, slightly taller than my 5' 3" in 1961 – in the background is Berkeley Nuclear Power Station

land for that Christmas to prevent the disease spreading to Ireland. I obeyed the request and when one of my pals at AEI, Jim Denningham, learned that I was going to be homeless for that Christmas, he kindly invited me to stay with his family in Dewsbury in Yorkshire. They made me welcome as if I were their own son. He was a Physics graduate of Oxford and had a perfect BBC 1960s accent, perfectly modulated and precise. When we arrived at his home, I was amazed that he spoke in a rich Yorkshire accent with his parents! One accent for work and another for home. I'm afraid I could not subscribe to that, although in Ireland there was a politician who was a European Commissioner and who had an accent which he did not acquire in his native County Tipperary – Richard (Dick) Burke in the 1970s/1980s.

My six month time working on the Berkeley nuclear power station in 1961 was fascinating. I assisted in checking out the electrical circuitry. The power station was built near to the mouth of the river Severn and required a massive tunnel which claimed many lives in its construction, including Irish workers. The station was closed down in 1989 and has been in a state of decommissioning since then. I never thought it would have a shorter life-span than I have had!

There were a number of Irish graduate apprentices with AEI. One was Leo Conway, a UCD graduate engineer, who subsequently worked with me in Aer Lingus, and who went on to have a very successful career in banking and as Director General of the Irish Takeover Panel. I bought my first car in a joint venture with Leo. It was an 8 horsepower 1939 Austin Standard, just a year younger than myself at the time. Old cars were very popular and affordable in post-war Britain – it cost us the princely sum of £13 (€17) each.

I had never driven a car before, but on the good advice of my mother, I had gone up to the Garda station in Killaloe before I left for England, legitimately filled out a form confirming that I knew the Rules of the Road, paid £1 (€1.28) and obtained my driving licence. It was issued in Killaloe and valid throughout the UK. It was a crazy system that you could get a licence to drive without a driving test. As District Justice Gordon Hurley said in Killaloe Court in a traffic accident case on 16 November 1959, ac-

Leo Conway and myself in 1959 with our first car

cording to the *Clare Champion*, 'The real criminal in this case is the system which allows a person to drive a car without first undergoing a test'.

I didn't have a test but I was well trained as Leo Conway taught me how to drive on the M1, the first motorway in the UK. We shared the car on a 'week 'on, week off' basis, when we were in the same location, and when we were in different parts of the UK, the period was three months. It worked out very well. The only problem with the car was the braking system, as 90 per cent of the brake pedal movement was taken up in stretching the brake cable!

There were excellent sporting facilities in Coton House. One thing our English graduate colleagues could not understand was how our hurling skills were so transferrable to cricket, which we played at Coton House. They marvelled at how a person who had never held a cricket bat in his life could just get up there and hit boundaries with aplomb. Of course, the skills were transferrable. I know now that for many years the counties in Ireland which, pre-independence, had a strong cricket tradition, were the ones which subsequently were strong in hurling, for example, Kilkenny.

Two of my UCC engineering class were graduate apprentices with AEI as well – Tom Gallagher, who was a brilliant hurler and went on to become a Professor of Engineering at UCD, and Declan O'Riordan, who did a Masters degree in Cal Tech and subsequently had a very successful career in the US with IBM and Anderson Consulting.

• • •

I came back to Ireland in July 1961. My parents had just left Killaloe for Abbeyfeale, so this became my base for the next six months while I looked for work. I bought a 1950s Morris Minor Convertible, a lovely car but most unreliable.

A Morris Minor Convertible car similar to mine in 1961

I had interviews for an engineering position with Aer Lingus, with the Department of Posts and Telegraphs, with the ESB, and with RTÉ, but no offers. At one stage I would have taken work of any type. I applied for the job of supervisor in a factory in Dublin making ladies bras and knickers. The managing director brought me on a tour of the factory with its predominantly young female workforce. I can still hear the whistles of the girls. I thought I had the job, but a few days later got a letter saying that they would like to have offered me the job, but that I was overqualified, and would likely leave them in a short time. So no job offer.

My job interview with RTÉ in November 1961 was bizarre in one respect. RTÉ, as the national public service broadcaster, was entering an exciting time in its development. It had started radio broadcasting in January 1926 and was now planning a television service to commence on 31 December 1961. They needed a number of engineers but it was not clear where they would be stationed. The chairman of the interview panel was Mr Parkes, RTÉ's chief engi-

RTÉ logo in 2014

neer, who was English. I thought the interview went very well. We talked about my time in Killaloe, in Cork at university, and my recent graduate apprenticeship in England. Then there was a bizarre episode. In all my previous interviews, I had never been asked a question to test my technical knowledge. It was presumed that if you had been conferred with a degree in a technical subject, particularly an honours degree, you had the technical skill.

'Mr Murdoch, do you know the formula for the area of a circle?' asked Mr Parkes.

Though surprised at the question, I responded, 'Of course, 'pi r squared.'

'Right,' said he, 'and how would you prove this?'

'By calculus,' I responded knowledgeably.

With that he put a sheet of paper and a pencil across the desk in front of me and said, 'OK, prove it'.

I was really taken aback. I didn't know what to do. I was not sure that I could complete the task there and then. I still don't know what thought processes were responsible for my response: 'Mr Parkes, it is six years ago since I got honours in honours mathematics in the Leaving Certificate. If you had asked me then to prove the area of a circle by calculus, I could have done it without batting an eyelid. In the last six years, I have studied engineering at university and completed a post-graduate apprenticeship. In that time, I have learned that what is important is not necessarily knowing how to do something, as knowing where to source the required information, understand it and apply it, by doing it.'

He seemed to have been genuinely taken aback by this response. 'So you are not going to do it now?' he asked.

I responded emphatically: 'That is correct. If at any time in my job I needed to prove that the area of a circle is 'pi r squared' I know exactly where to get the information, to understand it, and to apply it.'

With that he terminated the interview and I left thinking that I had blown all prospects of getting the job. But at least it was better than being put through the embarrassment of endeavouring to prove something on paper in front of a three-person interview panel and failing.

Aer Lingus logo in 2014

The Aer Lingus interview in August 1961 was more traditional. I thought my strong points were the fact that I had worked with Aer Lingus in the summer of 1958, my interest in aircraft as demonstrated by building model airplanes as a teenager in Killaloe and being a founder member of the Kincora Model Airplane Club, and my post-graduate apprenticeship with AEI, particularly my time in Coventry in designing aircraft components. I was delighted in December 1961 to be offered an appointment by Aer Lingus as Electrical Systems Development Engineer at Dublin Airport, with a start date of 8 January 1962. I accepted it immediately. The money was good – £900 (€1,154) per annum. Later that month I received an offer of an engineering post with the ESB and with the Department of Post and Telegraphs which I turned down.

Shortly after I joined Aer Lingus, and to my amazement, I was offered an engineering post with RTÉ. So my bizarre episode at interview may not have done me any harm after all. However, the RTÉ offer was not specific about location and as I was now committed to Aer Lingus, having just completed a three month training course on the Boeing 707 jet aircraft, I turned the offer down.

The next thing that happened was even more bizarre. A short time after I had turned down the RTÉ offer, I got a letter from Mr Parkes asking me to telephone him, which I did.

He said that they were impressed with my answer to the 'area of the circle' question. All other candidates had attempted to prove on paper 'pi r squared' and had failed. I had neatly side-stepped the question. He asked me to reconsider my rejection of their offer.

He also said that they had now finalised the location of the engineering posts and RTÉ could confirm that my job would be based in Killaloe in County Clare. I would be responsible for all the transmitters in the area, which would include the mountain tops of Tountinna, Woodcock Hill and Maghera. He told me that I would have one technician on my staff and I would have a jeep assigned to me for accessing the transmitters, and it would be available to me for personal use.

It was a very attractive offer. He kept emphasising what a terrific job it was, a good salary, permanent and pensionable, living in my home town, with all the things I was interested in, for example, fishing and water skiing. While my parents were now in Abbeyfeale, my father would be retiring in less than six years and would likely settle in Killaloe, having already lived there for 12 years (1949 to 1961). It was a difficult call. If the RTÉ offer had come in before I had accepted Aer Lingus, I probably would have accepted it and might have spent my whole career in Killaloe. But it was not to be. I was committed to Aer Lingus, so I turned down the RTÉ offer.

With Aer Lingus hostess Mary Frayne at the roll-out of the first Jumbo jet in Seattle USA (Boeing 747) in 1968

I was to spend ten years in Aer Lingus in a variety of posts, initially in the engineering area, then at the Boeing Airplane Company in Seattle, and finally as Aircraft Leasing Manager.

. . .

My Aer Lingus identity card in the 1970s signed by then general manager Michael Dargan

I was passing through Kennedy Airport in New York on my way home after a business meeting in the United States in July 1972, when I met Tony Ryan. This was my last trip as an Aer Lingus employee as I had resigned from the airline to take up an entirely new career in the health services. It was going to be a far cry from my work in the previous 10 years in the airline business, firstly as an aircraft development engineer, later as a general aeronautical engineer, and more recently as the manager of the aircraft leasing business of the airline.

I had spent the previous three years, other than a nine-month absence to do an MBA degree, travelling the world, endeavouring to lease the spare capacity of the airline. I had been involved in successfully completing aircraft leases to Air Algerie, Nigeria Airways, Flying Tiger Airlines in the USA, and Trans Mediterranean Airways in the Lebanon. And I was responsible for managing the previously negotiated lease of two Boeing 747s (Jumbo) to Trans Caribbean Airways.

I was now getting married and wanted a different life. I was going to be in charge of all the general hospitals, the psychiatric hospitals, and the nursing homes in Counties Donegal, Sligo, and Leitrim in the newly established North Western Health Board. This meant leaving Dublin and living in Sligo, which was better than living out of a suitcase, travelling the world.

I knew Tony Ryan, but not well. He was 36-years-old and the Station Manager at Kennedy Airport. I was two years younger and the Aircraft Leasing Manager at headquarters in Dublin. I met him frequently in my travels, and we regularly had, as was described at the time, a 'two stroke' conversation. A not unfriendly 'hello' and 'how are you'. And that was it.

It was different this time. After our initial 'two stroke' exchange, Tony said that he would like to have a chat with me, and would I like to join him in the VIP lounge for a drink. In my 10 years in Aer Lingus, I had never been in that lounge.

As I enjoyed my complimentary gin and tonic, Tony told me that he had been offered my job as Aircraft Leasing Manager back in Dublin, and he wondered if he should take it. I initially thought that his potential career change was less disruptive than mine.

Tony Ryan – Ireland's Aviator

He was staying in the same industry and was going to manage a smaller number of employees. I was changing industry and going from managing two persons to managing 1,600 staff. So his change was no big deal. But Tony had told me at this stage that it would involve moving his family, his wife and children who were then well settled in New York, back to Ireland – a big disruption.

'Tony, if I were you, I would take the job. But only for three years, as I have done. You will live out of a suitcase, because you have to be ready to follow up every lead. You will have no social life. You will get a great buzz out of clinching a deal. But when you get fed up of international airports and international hotels, as I have, it will be time to quit.'

Well, Tony took the job, moved his family back to Ireland in 1972, and made a success of the job which I could never have done. His first success and the pre-curser to the founding of the aircraft leasing firm Guinness Peat Aviation (GPA) was the lease of a Boeing 747 (Jumbo Jet) to Air Siam in 1973. I had sourced Air Siam a year earlier in 1971. It was an independent airline in Thailand owned by the royal family and run by Prince Varananda. They had no money but they had valuable routes to the west coast of the USA. I was told by the Boeing company that they might be interested in a lease.

So I headed off to Bangkok in 1971 with Don Gleeson from the Aer Lingus maintenance department. Don was the brother of Neil Gleeson, my boss, assistant general manager commercial. Don liked his drink on flights and insisted on sitting at an aisle seat, to facilitate the supply. I was happy to sit at a window seat and sleep. We eventually made it to Bangkok and had a series of excellent meetings with the Prince and his advisors. We were wined and dined in the best of restaurants, usually perched high in the sky with magnificent views of the city.

After three days of negotiations, we agreed the terms of a lease for a Boeing 747 and signed a Letter of Intent. Up to then I had converted most Letters of Intent into a formal lease. Although I was over the moon on the progress Don and I had made on this occasion, I was not as confident in converting this one, because Air Siam did not have any money.

'Air Siam wants to lease an airplane from us and defer the lease payments until they have the funds?' queried Michael Dargan, general manager of Aer Lingus.

'Yes,' I replied, 'but the routes they have are potentially very profitable and they will be able to pay us in time.' But I was not able to convince him. The risk was too great. So regretfully I had to inform Prince Varananda.

Two years later, Tony Ryan was in my job in Dublin and he read the Air Siam file. He went out to meet Prince Varananda

The Aer Lingus Boeing 747 on lease to Air Siam

and satisfied himself, just as I did, that there was great potential in the Air Siam routes and that a lease was worth the risk. Tony was able to convince David Kennedy, then deputy general manager, that the risk was worth taking. However, as a precaution, David insisted that Tony should live in Bangkok for the duration of the lease and in effect live with the airplane.

This he did and the lease was a huge success. And it created in Aer Lingus's and Tony Ryan's minds the concept of linking a financial institution with aircraft leasing, which lead to the creation by them in 1975 of GPA. It was to become the largest aircraft leasing firm in the world and had revenues of $4 billion. However, the flotation of the company on the stock market in 1992 was a disaster following a dip in confidence in the sector because of the 1991 Gulf War. GPA was restructured and taken over by outside investors in 2000. But Tony had made his money out of the business by that time.

Tony Ryan founded Ryanair in 1985 with his sons Cathal and Declan, and Liam Lonergan of Club Travel. Ryanair was to grow from a single 15-seater airplane on the Waterford to Gatwick London route, to being Europe's biggest low-cost airline in 2013, operating 1,611 routes, with over 1,500 daily departures, out of 57 bases and 180 airports in 29 countries, carrying over 81 million passengers per annum in 303 airplanes, with a revenue

Ryanair logo

stream of €4,884 million and profit after tax of €569 million. Some achievement!

Tony Ryan's links with Killaloe were limited to his ownership of Matt the Threshers pub and restaurant in Birdhill in 1982, and his positioning of a Shorts Sandringham flying boat in Ryanair livery on the Shannon at the Lakeside Hotel in Killaloe in 1989.

• • •

In 1994, I was to have contact with Tony Ryan again. I had been appointed Chairman of the European Commission on Vocational Rehabilitation. The Commission was established by Rehabilitation International, an international organisation concerned with persons with disabilities. I needed sponsorship funds to run the office of Chairman. I approached a number of organisations, mainly banks, with success.

The Lyons Demesne, set on 600 acres in County Kildare, bought by Tony Ryan for £3.5 million in 1996, which he lovingly restored and transformed in a €80 million project, for which he was awarded the Europa Nostra in 2001. The house was built in 1785 by wool merchant Nicholas Lawless.

At this stage Ryanair was doing nicely, having previously nearly gone under. Perhaps Ryanair would provide some sponsorship funds? So I wrote to Tony Ryan at Ryanair, in his capacity as a non-executive director, and reminded him of the good advice I had given him 22 years before! Apart from an acknowledgement of the value of that advice, the next paragraph in his letter of reply was blunt and to the point. Ryanair, as a low cost airline, did not sponsor anything, no matter how meritorious. The next paragraph went on to say that he personally admired the work of Rehabilitation International and the work programme of my Commission and that he was enclosing his personal cheque in support of that work. Hardly the ruthless, hard-nosed businessman which was sometimes his reputation.

Tony Ryan died in October 2007 at the age of 71 after a long illness. His family fortune was estimated at €1.2 billion. He had a profound and positive impact on aviation business worldwide. Not bad for a guy who started life in 1936 as the son of a train driver in Thurles, County Tipperary, and who joined Aer Lingus as a dispatch clerk.

Eleven weeks later Tony's eldest son Cathal, who was a pilot and captain, and only 48 years of age, died from cancer. He had a daughter Claudia, with Michelle Rocca, a former Miss Ireland, but they had a very public and acrimonious split in the early 1990s. On Cathal's death, Michelle issued a statement in which she said that they had had a very good relationship over the past number of years and that Cathal had been a wonderful father to Claudia. I had an unintentional link with the former Miss Ireland. I owned a lovely 1988 Mercedes 280 SEL car right up to 2003 which had been previously owned by Michelle Rocca. I used to point out to people the nail polish stain above the passenger door. Ireland is a small country.

. . .

In 2002, The Liffey Press published *Pioneers in Flight: Aer Lingus and the Story of Aviation in Ireland*' by Niall G. Weldon. Niall was General Manager – Corporate Affairs with Aer Lingus until his retirement in 1988. He had this to say about Tony Ryan (page 228):

Niall Weldon's book on Aer Lingus (2002).

Tony Ryan started off as a traffic clerk in Aer Lingus and after getting to know the business of servicing passengers at ground level, he quickly moved up the ranks to become Manager (Aircraft Leasing). Interestingly, this was a position which he virtually created for himself, by dint of the fund of knowledge he accumulated on the world's airlines' fleet movements and aircraft availability. He brought a new dimension to Aer Lingus's on-going search for profitable opportunities to optimise fleet usage on a year-round basis.

I think that Tony himself would agree that profitable aircraft leasing had been well established in Aer Lingus before he took up the position in 1972, and he would acknowledge the groundwork and contacts made by the previous holders of the post from 1964 to 1972 – Con Calahene, Dermot McKeever and myself.

Siobhán Creaton in her book *Ryanair: How a Small Irish Airline Conquered Europe* continued the myth that Tony Ryan somehow originated aircraft leasing in Aer Lingus. In relation to Air Siam she states: 'In his travels, Ryan stumbled upon Thailand's Air Siam, which was just about to start up and was looking for aircraft.' Though of course he didn't stumble upon Air Siam. I had opened the door and he had gone through it and created a successful lease. And he had convinced the powers-that-be in Aer Lingus to take the risk, and more power to him, because I was unable to convince them.

Siobhán Creaton's book on Ryanair

Richard Aldous in his superb book *Tony Ryan: Ireland's Aviator* (2013) is more accurate in that he acknowledges that before Tony Ryan came back to Dublin in 1972, 'Aer Lingus by 1972 had developed a certain amount of in-house expertise on the legal financial and operating complexities of leasing out aircraft.' We certainly had. In fact, Aer Lingus was then acknowledged in the airline industry as 'world experts' in aircraft leasing.

But Aldous is inaccurate in giving the impression that Tony Ryan came back to Aer Lingus head office in 1972 from his job as station manager at JFK airport, cap-in-hand, 'unsure what awaited him at the Aer Lingus headquarters'. The facts are that he had been offered and accepted my job as Aircraft Leasing Manager before he left New York. Tony would not have been stupid enough to uproot his family once again, after all the previous moves to Shannon, London, Cork and Chicago,

Richard Aldous's book on Tony Ryan

without a definite job offer. While Tony Ryan may have had his faults, one of them was not stupidity!

Tony Ryan was a visionary who deserves the title 'Ireland's Aviator'

· · ·

Don Gleeson, who was with me in Bangkok in that initial contact with Air Siam, died suddenly five months later in April 1972. He was in his late forties. He was a larger than life character and a great contrast to his brother Neil, who was my boss, and a chartered accountant. Don was an aircraft mechanic, who had worked with the RAF and saw action in North Africa. He was gregarious, full of fun, adventurous, and a bit of a rogue. I really liked him. He was a great travelling companion and full of stories. My abiding memory of Don is waking up on that long flight to Bangkok in 1971 for breakfast, to be handed a Jameson whiskey by Don, who assured me it would improve the breakfast. I cried at his funeral.

14

AFTER KILLALOE

'We never really left Killaloe. We are still there and
Bill's ashes are scattered on Lough Derg.'

When my parents moved to Abbeyfeale in 1961, that could have been our last contact with Killaloe as we kids had flown the nest. My sister Hilary had qualified in England as a nurse and midwife, and was now an air hostess with Aer Lingus and living in Dublin. My brother Bill was on the high seas as a radio officer in the merchant navy. My brother Laurence was in University College Cork studying medicine. And I was finishing my two year graduate apprenticeship in the UK, having qualified as an engineer from University College Cork.

But the impact Killaloe had on us all in those formative years as children, teenagers, and young adults had a huge magnetic effect. Throughout the 1960s, Hilary and I were back in Killaloe nearly every weekend, as we were both involved with water skiing in the capital of water skiing in Ireland, Killaloe. And when Bill got his feet on dry land again, he was a constant visitor to Killaloe, particularly during the 'mayfly' period, when the trout fishing would be at its best. And my brother Laurence was back in Killaloe to a lesser extent.

Dad retired in 1967 after 46 years' service in the Provincial Bank of Ireland (AIB) and my parents moved to Dalkey, County Dublin. They would have returned to Killaloe, but at this stage we were all in Dublin. They had a long and happy retirement. They took up bridge again and were founding members of a bridge club in Dun Laoghaire, where members still play for the Murdoch Cup. They had a beautiful garden which they enjoyed caring for.

Our parents in retirement in Dalkey, County Dublin, 1972

Our mother died in 1984 at age 82, seventeen years after their move to Dalkey, and while I was attending a conference in Portugal. She suffered a massive heart attack and died in the ambulance on the way to Vincent's Hospital. She had been a very heavy smoker all her life and the only person I knew who smoked right through a cold.

And at their 50th wedding anniversary celebration at Bill's house in 1983

In her later years she had beautiful white hair, which had a tint of brown in the front, due to the rising cigarette smoke. Her last words just show how addictive smoking is, because when she momentarily regained consciousness in the ambulance, and had been told by my father that she had had a 'turn' and was on the way to hospital, she asked, 'Did you bring my cigarettes and lighter?' And when he told her he had she was relieved. She died minutes later.

Our mother was a remarkable woman. She showed great courage and tenacity in taking on the Provincial bank and the Catholic Church. All the location changes in the family home must have been very hard on her, moving from Killarney, to Cavan, to Carrick-on-Shannon, to Kilkee, to Killaloe, to Cork, and to Abbeyfeale. She worked very hard to protect and provide for her family. She was an entrepreneur, with her commercial strawberry production, and her laying hen cages, mushroom plots and vegetables. And she ensured that we all got the opportunity of a third level education.

My sister Hilary (left) with colleague air hostesses admiring a new Aer Lingus Boeing 707 in the early 1960s

When my sister Hilary became an air hostess in Aer Lingus and I was an engineer with the airline, my mother was so proud. As far as she was concerned, Hilary kept all the passengers happy by serving them the best of food and drink, and as a nurse could look after them if they became ill. And I kept the passengers safe by ensuring that the aircraft were all airworthy. You would swear that we were running the airline between us.

At that time the parents of Aer Lingus staff were entitled to concessionary fares, usually a 90 per cent reduction on the full fare. It was called 'staff travel' but the only difficulty was that you were on 'standby' and only got on a flight if there were vacant seats. You also had to wait until all normal passengers had checked in. It was a pain-in-the-butt for the Aer Lingus check-in staff because these standby passengers would be constantly coming up to the check-in desk enquiring about how many seats were still vacant.

When our parents retired to Dalkey in 1967, they started to use the 'staff travel' extensively and travelled all over Europe in the following years. I will always remember my mother recounting her experience in checking in at the Aer Lingus desk at Barcelona airport. She handed in her ticket to the obviously jaded check-in girl, who, seeing the ticket, said despairingly, 'Oh, you are staff'.

To which my mother proudly proclaimed in a huffy manner: 'I am not staff. I am the mother of staff!' This was as if to claim a higher status, having brought two Aer Lingus staff members into the world, who would not be there except for her.

Our parents on holidays in Sitges, Spain, in 1971 on their Aer Lingus 'staff travel'

My dad lived on for the next 11 years after my mother died. He lived on his own in Dalkey, which was about a half mile (0.8 kilometres) from our house in Glenageary, so I got to see him a lot. And when I was abroad, I rang him every night at 10.00 pm, irrespective of where I was in the world. In my generation, fellows were close to their mothers and not to their fathers. I had the privilege of getting close to my father during those 11 years. He would not come and live with any of us, his children (although we all offered), as he did not want to be a burden on us. And he would not go into a nursing home. When he was about 85 years of age, he got pneumonia and was brought to St Vincent's Hospital. I was abroad at the time and was told by one of the family that he was dying and that I had better get home quickly. which I did.

When I got to see him, he was lying in bed, hooked up to a whole series of tubes and monitors, and when he saw me he was delighted, and he said with a twinkle in his eye: 'Henry, do you know what I had this morning? I had a bath with two pretty nurses!' I should explain that, at that time, not being able to lift himself out of a bath at his home and not having a shower, my father for many years would wash himself with a face towel, standing vertically in the bath tub. So a real bath was a luxury and, with two pretty nurses, a bonus! I was happy to ring the family that evening and tell them that with that twinkle in his eye, there was no way he was dying.

Around this time, my father's local doctor in Dalkey had died. This was his fourth doctor since he had come to Dalkey in 1967. They had all died before him. So I suggested to him that he should use my doctor, a relatively young man in his forties. He was happy to get a younger man, as he was concerned that all the people advising him on how to stay alive were themselves dying!

One evening, when my dad was 90 years of age, he had a terrible cough. 'Has Dr Maughan been up to see you?' I asked.

'Yes, he has, and he wants me to go to Vincent's, but I'm not going,' he said.

'And why not?' I asked.

'Well, I asked Dr Maughan,' he said, 'if they would be giving me tests which were not available when he qualified from medical school and when he responded that they would, of course, I told him that he would just have to treat me, as if he had just qualified.' Dr Maughan told me subsequently that this posed a huge challenge for him as the only equipment he had was his stethoscope, thermometer and blood pressure gauge. But he did a great job as my dad lived healthily for another two years.

About six months before my father died in 1995 in his 92nd year, he asked me to get him into a nursing home near me and to sell the house. It was as if he knew the end was near and he wanted to put his affairs in order. The nursing home, 'Altador' on the Upper Glenageary Road, about 300 metres from our house, was a brilliant and caring nursing home. My father liked a drink – a beer and a chaser of whiskey. Before he went into the nursing home we would go out for a drink once a week, usually to Finnegan's in Dalkey (the watering hole of the late Maeve Binchy and where Michelle O'Bama had her lunch in 2013). His big disappointment was that, increasingly, alcohol did not agree with him and he missed the outings.

When I sold his house and Mark McParland, his solicitor, delivered the cheque to him at the nursing home, he asked me to see him so that he could tell me where to deposit the proceeds. He was so delighted with the cheque and that his affairs were now in order that he took out a bottle of brandy from under the bed and we drank it between us. At the time he really enjoyed it, but next day he was 'dying' and I wasn't feeling too good myself!

The nursing home was excellent, but my father was not happy there. He really missed the independence he had in his own home and the food that he cooked himself. He passed away in his sleep during the early hours of 21 October 1995. I had been up with him the night before and had arranged to bring him shopping next morning. He was in great form and his brain was a sharp as ever, interrogating me on what interest his money on deposit was getting.

I delivered the eulogy at the funeral in Dalkey. As I was speaking for us all, I had to remind myself to use the expression 'our dad' and not 'our father' as that sounded too much like the prayer. I was quite emotional and nearly broke down a few times. A work colleague of mine said to me afterwards, 'you really loved your father, you must have been very close'. We were.

·　·　·

In 1966 my sister Hilary married Brendan O'Connor whom she met through water skiing. Brendan was studying for the Bar in 1962 when I first met him and he was responsible for me becoming a barrister. Before they were married, Brendan and I shared a wooden hut, on the cliff edge off Balscadden Road in Howth, County Dublin, while Hilary shared the adjoining cottage, 'Strand Villa', with two other air hostesses. Our wooden hut, with the grandiose name of 'The Chalet', cost us £50 (€64) per annum which we shared between us!

Brendan was a great character. One day in 1963, I took up one of his books on criminal law and was soon engrossed in reading about murder, incest, infanticide and treason. I found it all very interesting. 'Why don't you study for the Bar,' Bren-

'The Chalet', Balscadden Road, Howth

*In 1966 with Brendan (left)
when I was called to the Bar*

dan said encouragingly. 'You can do it part-time and I'm sure Aer Lingus will give you time off.' Which they did. Brendan told me subsequently that I was responsible for him passing his law exams, because I was just a year behind him and he couldn't let me catch up with him. So that drove him to study when he didn't feel like it.

When Brendan qualified and was called to the Bar, he got a job as a lawyer in the Land Registry where he stayed until he retired. Hilary and Brendan had five children: Ciaran, Diarmuid, Orla, Rory and Fergal. Brendan died on 15 January 2005. He was always very helpful to me throughout my career. I was privileged to carry his coffin with his sons.

· · ·

My brother Bill fulfilled his teenage ambition to be a radio officer and to sail the High Seas. Once he had got that out of his system he returned to Ireland at the age of 25 in 1961. He applied for and got an 'adult matriculation' (based on his work and life experience, which made him eligible for entry to university), applied to University College Dublin to do a B.Comm (our mother's degree) and was accepted, bought a Vespa scooter and whisked around town, and wore a Hitler style moustache.

At university he took a great interest in student affairs and was a student colleague of Gerard (Gerry) Collins TD, later to be Minister for Justice and who performed the official launch of the first edition of my law book *A Dictionary of Irish Law* in 1988.

At university, Bill was decidedly 'left wing', but over the years moved gradually to the right, so that by the time he retired he was decidedly 'right wing'. After graduating with a B.Comm degree in 1964, he started as an investment analyst in a stockbrokers in London, returning to Ireland to take up a job as a financial journalist with *The Irish Times* in 1968. He was later to become the business editor with the paper.

Bill married Bernadette Patchell in 1969 and they did not have any children.

Bill could analyse the financial details of a company's annual report better than any journalist I have

Bill, centre bottom row, with some of his Crescent College Leaving Cert classmates 1954

My brother Bill's graduation with a B.Comm in 1964

ever met. At the start of his career with *The Irish Times* it would take him three or four hours to do the analysis and then to prepare the 1,000 word article for the next day's paper. In later years, he would do the same in 20 minutes. When he retired in 2001, *The Irish Times* asked him to write a monthly column.

Bernadette and Bill in 1979

He would labour over each article, trying to choose a subject which was topical and yet not something the present journalists were already writing about.

On occasion, I would get a phone call from Bill: 'Henry, I was thinking of writing an article on health insurance and community rating and using the opening sentence like this .... what do you think?' On the first occasion, I remember responding, 'Bill, in all the 30 years you were with *The Irish Times*, you never asked for my opinion on any article you were writing, so why now?' To which he said 'Well, you see, I have the time now!'

Bill loved his fishing in Killaloe, particularly the mayfly. He loved good food and good wine. He was a great cook himself and was meticulous about the way food was presented. He died after a long illness on Wednesday 16 April 2008, aged 72 years. My wife, Davida, and I were in London for my 70th birthday, to escape any 'surprise' birthday party when we got the news. We rushed back for the funeral.

It was great to see so many of Bill's journalist and business colleagues at his funeral in Kilquade, County Wicklow, and so many of my friends. Fr Liam Belton described Bill as a 'very hospitable, generous and kind man' with many interests beyond the world of financial journalism. Music was provided by soloist Colette Grant, Bernadette's sister, accompanied by her husband Michael on the organ. *The Irish Times* reported the funeral under the heading: 'Former *Irish Times* journalist lived full life.'

Bill was very well known throughout Ireland. I had a huge number of phone calls and Mass cards, all recounting how they had regularly read Bill's writings in *The Irish Times* and that they would now miss them. Jim Crowe from Main Street in

Former 'Irish Times' journalist lived full life, mourners told

FORMER *Irish Times* business editor Bill Murdoch was a man who "pushed a lot into his life", Fr Liam Belton told mourners at his funeral on Saturday.

Addressing the congregation at the funeral Mass in St Patrick's parish church, Kilquade, Co Wicklow, Fr Belton described Mr Murdoch as a "very hospitable, generous and kind man" with many interests beyond the world of financial journalism in which he worked for more than 30 years.

brothers Laurence and Henry and his sister Hilary.

Music at the ceremony was provided by soloist Colette Grant, Mrs Murdoch's sister, accompanied by her husband Michael on organ.

Among the mourners were many former colleagues from *The Irish Times* and other media, including *Irish Times* managing editors Eoin McVey and Joe Breen, business editor John McManus, former property editor Jack Fagan, former news editor

Bill Murdoch: "a very hospitable, generous and kind man"

McDowell, economics lecturer at University College Dublin.

Mr Murdoch, who had been ill for a short time, died on

Irish Times coverage of Bill's funeral.

Killaloe, now living in New Zealand, told me about the day in 1959 when he and Bill caught so many fish, below the Killaloe bridge in a hole near where the canal ends, that they had to stop from tiredness. The *Nenagh Guardian* of 19 September 1959 carried the story:

> PERCH GALORE: Bill Murdoch and James Crowe, Killaloe, had a record catch Thursday landing 110 perch and 6 pike, when fishing on the Shannon below Killaloe. Several of the perch weighed 4 to 5 lbs each. Many locals, who were relaxing on the Killaloe bridge, had their Friday (fast day) menu problem solved, through the generosity of those young anglers.

I even had a letter from Tony Scallan in London, a Crescent College Limerick classmate of Bill's, in which he said:

> Bill and I were good pals in the Crescent and I particularly remember how our science teacher Fr Hurley mentioned William Murdoch, the 19th century inventor, to the great glee of the class. Later on I visited Bill on board ship in Limerick Docks. A few years elapsed, and one day while he worked in London he approached me on a station platform. He subsequently visited Eileen and myself, before he returned to the Irish Times in 1968. Our next meeting was Adare for the reunion.

The reunion Tony referred to was the 50th year reunion of Bill's 1954 Leaving Certificate class of Crescent College which was held in 2004 in the opulent Adare Manor Hotel, near Limerick. There was a large turnout for the event, which included spouses and a few interlopers from other years, for example, my 1955 Leaving Certificate classmates Tony Darcy and Jim Bradshaw. The reunion commenced with Mass at 6.00 pm celebrated by one of the classmates, Fr Brian O'Leary who became a Jesuit, and was followed by a sumptuous dinner with the best of wines. My 50th year class reunion in 2005 was a more modest affair, with no spouses – a game of golf at Ballyneety Golf Club near Limerick, followed by a club dinner and house wine!

· · ·

The Irish Times published an Obituary on 26 April 2008 which read as follows:

> Bill Murdoch, who died aged 72 on April 16th, was one of the best regarded financial journalists of his generation. He came into financial journalism when it was still in its infancy and, as business editor of *The Irish Times*, he established a reputation for thoroughness and accuracy which raised standards in his own pages and in those of rival publications.
>
> Bill Murdoch was born in Cavan town on March 1st, 1936, the second child of Archie and Gretta Murdoch. His father was an employee of the Provincial bank of Ireland (later to become part of AIB) and the family subsequently moved to Kilkee, Killaloe and Carrick-on-Shannon as his father climbed the promotional ladder to manager. Bill's principal schooling was with the Jesuits in Crescent College, Limerick. He had three siblings, Hilary, Henry and Laurence.
>
> Having an absorbing interest in travel, spurred on perhaps by weekly trips to the cinema in Killaloe, Murdoch decided to complete a radio officer course in Cork after which he

worked for British merchant navy vessels and travelled throughout the world.

At age 25, he returned to Ireland and, with money saved, he put himself through the B.Comm in UCD, qualifying in 1964. He then moved to London where he worked as an investment analyst for a stockbroking firm.

After four years in London he decided to return to Dublin, and secured a position as a financial reporter with *The Irish Times*. The business editor at the time, Valentine Lamb, was only the third to hold the post (in succession to Nicolas Leonard and Hugh O'Neill) and financial reporting still had to gain acceptance, not from the readers of the newspaper but from the financial and business community, who regarded it with suspicion bordering on hostility.

Murdoch left the newspaper for a brief period. He went into investment and then in 1975 became the founding editor of *Irish Business*, which was established by Kevin Kelly. He returned to the newspaper and in 1978 was appointed business editor in succession to the late Richard Keatinge. As business editor, he was precise, demanding in a good-natured way, and very competitive. He had good contacts in the business community which appreciated that while he may write stories that they wished he did not write, he would be fair and accurate at all times. He was particularly good at financial analysis and regularly expressed views at odds with those of the company in question, but which turned out to be correct.

He was always impeccably dressed, a person who liked good food and wines but wisely decided not to make friendships with those that he would be writing about. One exception was the late Noel Griffin of Waterford Glass.

Very much an outdoors man, Murdoch was a keen fisherman and an accomplished shot. He was particularly fond of cooking and gardening and, in retirement, discovered the wonders of digital photography which, being adept at computer technology, did not faze him in the least.

He married Bernadette Patchell in November 1969 in the University Church on Dublin's Stephen's Green, where his parents had married 36 years previously. He took ill last year and spent a considerable time in hospital while tests were carried out. Eventually, he was diagnosed with the rare disease vasculitis. Last Christmas, as his extended family gathered for his and Bernadette's traditional dinner, he expressed confidence that it had been caught in time, but his relative health proved to be just a remission. He is survived by Bernadette.

It was an excellent Obituary, detailed and balanced, mostly factually correct, and a fitting tribute to a great financial journalist. Bill's love of Killaloe was demonstrated by his decision that his body should be cremated and his ashes scattered on Lough Derg. So now, every time I am on Lough Derg, I think of Bill and how for many years of our childhood in Killaloe, he was the 'fountain of knowledge', having his hand on the pulse of everything.

. . .

My brother Laurence, the youngest in the family, married Claire Kirwan in 1972. They are experts in the card game bridge, following in our parents' passion. Laurence and Claire became the All Ireland National Husband and Wife Bridge Champions in 1975. Following his medical studies, Laurence worked in pharmaceuticals, retired early and became a computer expert. I can attest to that, as a few years ago my desktop computer crashed with irreplaceable wedding video footage on the damaged hard disk. Despite paying €150 to supposed experts, whose final diagnosis was that nothing was

Claire, Laurence and family in 1982

retrievable, Laurence got all the data back for me. Don't ask me how he did it, but he did.

Claire retired in 2009 as assistant Director of Nursing at St John of God Hospital, Dublin. They have four children – Keith, Gregary, and Olga who all have university degrees in computer science, and Nichola in financial services. And there are now two grandchildren, Jack and Oisin.

Most of the people I have met in Killaloe, while researching this book, remember Laurence as the 'great swimmer', which he was. But he was also a great fisherman.

·   ·   ·

That leaves me. If you have read the previous chapters, you probably have a good idea of what happened to me after leaving Killaloe in 1959. I have been fortunate to have had a very interesting and varied career, and a long and happy marriage. I canned peas in the UK and sold transistors. I was part of a team which commissioned a nuclear power station. I worked as a chartered engineer and as a barrister. I maintained airplanes and leased them around the world. I managed hospitals, general and psychiatric, as an executive and as chairman of the board, I established the AnCO training centres (later FÁS and now SOLAS) around the country and was the executive primarily responsible for the introduction of the standards-based apprenticeship system.

In July 1972, I got married to Davida Franklin. We had a quiet wedding. Davida and I went on to have three children, Maeve and twin boys Breffni and Joe. In Chapter 2, I describe how infant Joe did not survive and now has a 'seat' in Trinity College.

Maeve went on to obtain a degree in languages and business and worked in Frankfurt in the office of the President of the European Central Bank. She married Ahmed Al-Dam in 1998 and they now live in Hamburg in Germany where Ahmed is a maxillo-facial surgeon in the Hamburg University Hospital. He was born in Saudi Arabia but educated from his late teens in

Our children Breffni (3) and Maeve (5) in snowy winter 1978

Germany. His father is from Palestine and his mother is from Egypt. The wedding, which took place in Frankfurt, was a fantastic affair and very different from an Irish wedding. Maeve has become a Muslim and they have four children – Amira, Nabil, Malik and Tamara.

Breffni obtained a degree in Computer Science and works as a software engineer. He married Rebecca (Becci) Haughton in Cork in 2003. The Haughtons were a well-known Quaker family in Cork with a builders' providers business, run by Becci's grandfather Alan Haughton, who played tennis for Ireland in the Davis Cup team in 1932. Breffni and Becci's wedding was in the Quaker meeting house in Cork and again brilliant and very different from an Irish Catholic wedding. They now have three children – Daisy, Luke and Bonnie.

So Davida and I now have seven grandchildren, four Muslims and three Quakers, As far as we are concerned, we have no problem with this, as long as they are healthy and happy, and being brought up with a proper set of moral values, and they are. On top of that, they are all very different children and great fun.

I have been fortunate to have lived at a time of great entrepreneurship and in different cultures. I worked in different countries – mainly the UK, USA and Ireland. I worked in the public and the private sectors. I was an employee, self-employed and an employer. I was made redundant twice and was unemployed at one stage for over six months. I worked with and for politicians, local and national, including ministers and taoisigh. I met in an official capacity all Presidents of Ireland, except Douglas Hyde.

In semi-retirement since 1999, I have had the opportunity of being a founding director of Skillnets, an enterprise-led training promotion organisation, a non-executive director of a mortgage bank First Active plc, as well as a similar position in London with City & Guilds. That active retirement included participating on Mental Health Tribunals (reviewing the involuntary admission of patients in psychiatric hospitals), on Tenancy Tribunals (adjudicating on disputes between landlords and tenants), and long may it continue. At 76 years of age, I have no intention of stopping working.

But it has not been all work. Along the way I have enjoyed myself enormously, playing tennis and golf, water and snow skiing, sailing and boating. And I wrote a few books – the most successful of which is *Murdoch's Dictionary of Irish Law* which in November 2013 was 25 years old and at over 1,400 pages and over 1 million words, in its fifth edition, with a sixth edition on its way, updated by solicitor Dr Brian Hunt.

．　．　．

When 2013 dawned, I did not know what a momentous year it was going to be in my life. In March that year, I was fit as a fiddle. I had been playing a lot of tennis and golf and had enjoyed 75 years of great health. My father had lived to 92. I was invincible. I would live to 120. Here I was in Obergurgl Austria with my 80-year-old skiing friend Raymond Heavey, skiing at 10,000 feet and at minus 17 degrees Celsius. I had a cold and was having trouble with my right knee, which I had injured while water ski jumping in Killaloe in 1963 and 1966, but which, after two operations in the 1960s, had stood up well to a lot of punishment in the following 50 years. Ray achieved his goal of skiing at 80 and being 'free' on the gondola lift system.

Back in Dublin on 12 March 2013, I was experiencing a loss of hearing in my left ear and still had the cold. I went to my local GP who sent me for an xray to St Michael's hospital in Dun Laoghaire. On 14 March he diagnosed pneumonia and the onset of Bell's Palsy, which was beginning to distort my face. On 19 March I was delirious, slipping in and out of unconsciousness and brought by ambulance to the emergency department of the Blackrock Clinic, with great assistance to my wife Davida from old friends Kieran and Olive Dooley. In five minutes the clinicians in the Clinic had diagnosed that in addition to the pneumonia and Bell's Palsy, I had the killer meningitis.

In the four weeks I was to spend in that hospital, the clinicians and nurses did a great job in curing the pneumonia and the meningitis. The Bell's Palsy would not kill me, so that was rightly disregarded. I have no memory of anything from five days before going to hospital and for about three days afterwards. In those early days, I had a terrible fever, a racing heartbeat and a terrible pain in my head. The clinicians could not figure out how a 'ski fit' person could have been engulfed by three different illnesses all together. I had every test, xray and scan under the sun, including a cerebral scan over in Beaumont Hospital. I had two lumber punctures, a bone marrow procedure and a number of blood transfusions. I was hooked up to all types of monitors and was being fed antibiotics straight into a main artery. My daughter-in-law Becci (Breffni's wife) came up from Cork and was a great help to Davida during all that traumatic time.

The most frightening time was at the start, when I was obviously seriously infectious, and everyone coming into my room in the hospital was robed accordingly and with a face mask. And then there was the time when the main Consultant, Dr John Fennell, pointing to his watch, asked me 'Henry, do you know what this is?'

'Of course I know what it is,' I responded, 'it is a ... a ... a ....' I knew it was a watch but I just could not articulate the word. He then held up a pen, and asked me to name it. Again, I responded, 'It is a .... a ...' I could not articulate the word, even though I knew it was a pen. Having spent most of my life reducing complex things down to their simpler parts, the thought that I might have to spend the rest of my life not being able to communicate the simplest of messages nearly overwhelmed me.

But I gradually improved, day after day. The pneumonia and the meningitis were bad enough, but being hit with the Bell's Palsy as well, I thought, was a bit cruel. It paralysed the left hand side of my face and prevented me from chewing. So I lived on liquids, particularly yogurts, during my four weeks in hospital. It also affected my speech – words beginning with 'b' and 'p' being particularly difficult. And as my left eye was no longer blinking, it had to be regularly moisturised during the day, and taped closed at night. I was a mess.

When I left the Blackrock Clinic on 16 April 2013, I was in a quite weakened state. I had lost 18 pounds (8.2 kilogrammes) and was back to my 1956 university flyweight boxing weight but could not walk 50 metres. My balance was badly affected. In my 33 years on the board of the National Rehabilitation Hospital (NRH) and 17 years as chairman, I never thought I would be seeking their help. I didn't go to them – they came to me – Derek Greene, the CEO, Eilish Macklin, the Director of Nursing, and Dr Mark Delargy, Consultant in Rehabilitation Medicine.

I stepped down temporarily as chairman of the Board. My old friend Kieran Fleck SC took over as Deputy Chairman, and I became an out-patient in my own hospital. It was to give me a unique insight into the marvellous work done in the hospital. In the next three months I underwent an intensive physical fitness regime under chartered physiotherapists Maeve Turner (general physio, pilates and the paralysis in my face), and Lorenza Cafolla (sports physio). They certainly put me through my paces. I used to joke with them that the extra kilo they put on the weights, or the extra friction on the bike, was their way of getting back at management!

I got to meet other out-patients and was able to admire the progress that they made. The one abiding feature that impacted on me was the 'positiveness' of the whole approach. Every 'tiny' bit of progress was acknowledged by the rehabilitation staff and that engendered great hope of further progress.

When I came home from the Blackrock Clinic in April 2013, I was in defiant mood. I was physically drained but I felt mentally strong. I was delighted to be still alive and wanted to do something to demonstrate my confidence in the future. Why not buy a new car? I had not bought a new car in the previous

40 years – I had always bought a good quality second-hand car about three years old, usually a Mercedes, and kept it for a long time. My 13-year-old Merc was on its last legs, but why buy a car when I could not drive it ? I rationalised that if I had a new expensive car out the front door, which I could not drive because of my disabled condition, that would be a huge motivator for me to get better quickly. And that is what I did. Less than two weeks after I was discharged from hospital, I was the proud owner of a new 131D registration Skoda Superb, parked outside our front door, which I could not drive but it was waiting for me.

My recovery owes many authors, including my 1972 MBA classmate Chris Park, and his wife Ella, who post-discharge, brought me on many occasions back to the Blackrock Clinic; my 1955 UCC Engineering classmate Sean O'Connell and his wife Elaine, who came up from Cork on two occasions to lend me support, as did Raymond and Helen Heavey and Michael and Pat Burke; my golfing friends who encouraged me to come back to the golfing scene despite my disfigurement, including Niall Quinn, Brendan Murphy, Owen Fox, Douglas Clarke, Michael Wright and Michael Kennedy; my many friends who sent 'get well' cards, including one signed by all my tennis pals from the Tuesday evening 'organised play' in Fitzwilliam Lawn Tennis Club. There was one very amusing card from my tennis pal Mona McGarry. It showed a man in bed with his golf clubs near the wall, being examined by his doctor, and his wife is talking on the phone, saying, 'He's been much better since the doctor told him that he was just under par'.

I made great progress in the three months that I was an outpatient of the NRH. We spent a month in Killaloe from mid-July to mid-August 2013, and I messed about on my boat *Curlew*, a 23-foot Trusty 23, which is built like a lifeboat. Even though it was one of the best summers on record, I could not do much boating as my left eye was wide open from the Bell's Palsy and I had to protect it from the wind. When we came back to Dublin, I played my first game of golf since my illness, with Michael Burke and Edmund O'Sullivan on 14 August 2013. They were full of sympathy for me on the first tee with my black patch over my eye. The sympathy quickly disappeared when I scored 19 points in nine holes and won the money.

In late August 2013, my face was still very distorted from the Bell's Palsy. The left-hand side was still paralysed. While I could move my left upper eye lid, I could not move the lower lid and could not close my left eye. And my mouth was distorted, with the left side lower than the right side. I had got my strength back but I looked a right mess when I shaved every morning and saw my reflection in the mirror. I thought of the *Hunchback of Notre Dame*. It was all disheartening.

My Bell's Palsy face in August 2013, five months after onset of the paralysis. The tape on my left cheek was to lessen the distortion!

On Friday, 23 August 2013, I was down in Killaloe researching this book and strolled into Killaloe that afternoon. I stopped at the Marian Shrine as I always do, but this time instead of the little prayer to my parents, I said, partly jocosely and partly seriously:

> Mary, you would not be up there if my father had not contributed ten shillings back in 1954, which he couldn't afford, and if my great friend Jim Ryan had not donated the sand and the gravel. So what about doing something about my face?

The next Tuesday I had a review meeting with physiotherapist Maeve Turner at the NRH and she told me there was a definite change taking place; she could see movement in my lower eye lid and my mouth and lips were straightening out. The following week I had a prearranged EMG (electro myro graph) test carried out in the Blackrock Clinic by Dr Connolly which confirmed that signals were getting through from my brain to the left side of my face. And two weeks later on 17

September 2013, in a dramatic change, I was able to close my left eye and my face had straightened out, and I had my first game of tennis in seven months at Fitzwilliam LTC.

A miracle or an intervention by Our Lady? Maybe, maybe not. A dramatic change in

My Bell's Palsy face in late September 2013, six months after onset. The muscles in the forehead above my left eye are still paralysed

my condition after I talked to her? Definitely yes. Was that change going to happen anyway, with all the physiotherapy intervention I had received and the continuing self-administered one-hour-a-day electric stimulation which my facial muscles were receiving? Probably. Well, whatever the truth, I am prepared to give the benefit of the doubt to Our Lady and give her credit for speeding up my recovery. And so I thanked her on my next visit to Killaloe and continue to do so.

•   •   •

I returned to duty as chairman of the National Rehabilitation Hospital in November 2013, managed two board meetings, and on 31 December 2013, after 33 years on the board and 17 years as chairman, I retired as chairman. I felt it was the time to pass on the baton, just as the former chairman Ernest Goulding had passed it on to me back in 1996. And I was so pleased that Kieran Fleck SC, who had acted as chairman during my absence, was prepared to take over from me and that the Sisters of Mercy and the board agreed to his appointment. I should point out that the board members and the chairman are not paid and serve in a totally voluntary capacity, as do many other persons managing charities in Ireland which, in many cases for historical reasons, are doing the State's work.

The board presented me on my retirement from the hospital with what has become an iconic photo which is being used by the hospital in its fight to eradicate hospital acquired infections, such as MRSA. The photo was taken during a visit to the hospital in June 2012 by the Tánaiste Eamon Gilmore and James Reilly, Minister for Health, to announce formal government approval of the first phase of a replacement medical rehabilitation hospital on the current site.

We were about to make a visit to the wards before the formal speeches and as we had recently, in our fight against MRSA, introduced a strict 'bare below the elbow' policy in all clinical areas, we were told to take off our jackets, roll up our sleeves and remove any watches or rings, before we entered the wards. The action was caught on camera in a superb action shot by photographer Bríd Ní Luasaigh. It wasn't rehearsed or anticipated. You might well ask, why are we all laughing so much. Hygiene and hospital acquired infections are no laughing matter. Well, I do remember saying to the politicians at the time,

Iconic photo of the implementation of the NRH 'bare below the elbow' policy by the Minister for Health, James Reilly, Tánaiste Eamon Gilmore, and me in 2012 (Photo courtesy of photographer Bríd Ní Luasaigh)

in a slip of the tongue, that this was the hospital's 'bare below the waist' policy! That might have triggered the laugh – or it might have been the ribald comment I heard at the time from an onlooker, who said that this was the coalition government parties about to 'square up to each other' – but then why was I also getting involved?

I was not surprised that the photograph got a lot of publicity in the press, particularly the medical press. The *Medical Independent* in its issue of 14 June 2012, under the heading 'Nothing up their sleeves', reported that we were on hand to announce a significant capital development on the campus of the NRH, a new 120-bed facility with integrated therapy services, a partnership between the HSE and the NRH Foundation. The article went on to say:

> As the Ministers rolled up their sleeves, for a moment it seemed as if they were about to abandon their busy schedules to start work on the development themselves. In fact they were simply adhering to the hospital's 'bare below the elbow' policy.'

The 'Think Hand Hygiene' campaign of the NRH

The *Medical Independent* ran a caption competition, inviting readers to send in their appropriate (or inappropriate) captions for the photo. Mary Rogan submitted the winning entry, playing on the cockney dropping of the 'h': 'We're 'armless but beware the fella with the beard!'

And while I was absent from the hospital during most of 2013, Rosemarie Nolan and her communications team at the hospital came up with the idea of using the iconic photo as part of the ongoing drive in the hospital to improve hand hygiene. She approached the Tánaiste and the Minister and they agreed to the photo being used for this purpose, as I did as well. I was not surprised, because the Minister for Health told me during that 2012 visit, that in all the visits he had made to hospitals over the years he had never been asked to 'bare below the elbow'. The poster is now located at the entrance to every clinical area in the hospital. Full marks to the NRH.

I am indebted to the staff of the Blackrock Clinic for curing my pneumonia and meningitis. And I am particularly indebted to the NRH for getting me back to full fitness again. That is why all my author's royalties of this, and the sister book *My Killaloe*, go to the NRH Foundation for the benefit of the patients of the hospital.

Appendix

Population of Killaloe and Ballina (1926 to 2011)

Census Year	Killaloe	Ballina	K+B Sub-total	26 Counties	K+B/ Ireland 1926 as 100
1926	904	180	1,084	2,971,992	100
1936	890	176	1,066	2,968,420	98
1946	890	136	1,026	2,955,107	95
1951	901	134	1,035	2,960,593	95
1956	888	260	1,148	2,898,264	109
1961	835	273	1,108	2,818,341	108
1966	816	319	1,135	2,884,002	108
1971	871	336	1,207	2,978,248	111
1976	*cancelled due to economic circumstances*				
1979	975	424	1,399	3,368,217	114
1981	1,022	451	1,473	3,443,405	117

Census Year	Killaloe	Ballina	K+B Sub-total	26 Counties	K+B/ Ireland 1926 as 100
1986	1,033	507	1,540	3,540,643	119
1991	956	477	1,433	3,525,719	111
1996	972	598	1,570	3,626,087	119
2001	*cancelled due to foot and mouth disease*				
2002	1,174	1,185	2,359	3,917,203	165
2006	1,035	1,861	2,896	4,239,848	187
2011	1,292	2,442	3,734	4,588,252	223
Year 2011 Population as % of Year 1926					
	143%	1357%	344%	154%	

Note: The population of Ireland (26 Counties) increased by 54% between 1926 and 2011. During that time the population of Killaloe increased by 43%, marginally less than the growth of the national population, while the combined population of Killaloe/Ballina more than tripled, due to the phenomenal growth in the population of Ballina.

Source: Central Statistics Office, Ireland 2013

Bibliography

Aldous, Richard, Tony Ryan: Ireland's Aviator (2013), Gill & Macmillan

Bassett, William, *The Bassett Directory for County Clare* (1875-76), further details in 1880-81

Bradley, John, *Killaloe Archaelogical Survey 1988*, (1988), Office of Public Works

Bulfin, William, *Rambles in Eirinn* (1920, seventh impression), M H Gill & Son Ltd

Clare County Council, *East Clare Local Area Plan 2011–2017*

Coleman, Marie, *The Irish Sweep* (2009)

Creaton, Siobhan, *Ryanair: How a Small Irish Airline Conquered Europe* (2005), Aurum

Cronin, Mike, *Does Time Fly? Aer Lingus – Its History* (2011) Collins Press

Crosson, Sean and Rod Stoneman, *The Quiet Man ... and Beyond* (2009), The Liffey Press

Duffy, Sean, *Brian Boru and the Battle* of Clontarf (2013)

Edmonds, Phil, *Reconnecting with the Soul of Ireland* (2009) philwhistle@gmail.com

Finn, Tomas, *Tuairim, Intellectual Debate and Policy Formulation in Ireland, 1954–1975* (2012) Manchester University Press

Forbes, John, *Memorandums made in Ireland in the Autumn of 1852* (1853)

Geraghty, Rebecca and Patrick Grey, *The reception of William Bulfin's Rambles in Eirinn: 1901-1904* (2009), Society for Irish Latin American Studies

Grey, RC, Pamphlet condemning the killing of four IRA Volunteers in Killaloe (1920)

Kearney, Katie et al., *Killaloe local history, 1739-1997* (1998), Clare Local Studies Project

Kierse, Sean, *Historic Killaloe: A Guide to its Antiquities* (1983), Boru Books

Kierse, Sean, *The Famine Years in the Parish of Killaloe 1845–1851* (1984), Boru Books

Kierse, Sean, *Education in the Parish of Killaloe* (1987), Boru Books

Kierse, Sean, *History of Smith O'Brien GAA Club, 1886–1987* (1991), Boru Books

Kierse, Sean, *Portraits of Killaloe* (1995), Boru Books

Kierse, Sean, *Priests and Religious of Killaloe Parish* (2000), Boru Books

Kierse, Sean, *The Killaloe Anthology* (2001) ,Boru Books

Kierse, Sean, *Land and People of Killaloe Parish* (2008), Boru Books

Kotsonouris, Mary, *'Tis All Lies, Your Worship: Tales from the District Court* (2011), The Liffey Press

Laheen, Kevin A., *The Jesuits in Killaloe 1850–1880* (1998), O'Brien

Lewis, Samuel, *A Topographical Dictionary of Ireland* (1837)

MacCarty, Carthach, *Archedeacon Tom Duggan: In Peace and in War* (1994), Blackwater Press

McHale, Des, *The Complete Guide to The Quiet Man* (2000), Appletree

McHale, Des, *Picture The Quiet Man* (2004), Appletree

McHale, Des, *A Quiet Man Miscellany* (2009), Cork University Press

McHale, Des, *Ripples in the Quiet Man* (2013), ebook, Amazon

McNeive, Paul, *Small Steps* (2011) Ballpoint Press

Ni Mhaonaigh, Maire, *Brain Boru: Ireland's Greatest King?* (2008), Tempus

O'Connell, Pat, *The Fishmonger* (2013) The Liffey Press

Owen, Edwin, *St Flannan's Cathedral Killaloe: A Short History* (1992), Ballinakella Press

Rothery, Sean, *The Shops of Ireland* (1978)

Tipperary County Council, North Tipperary County Development Plan 2010–2016

Walsh, Ed, *Upstart: Friends, Foes and Founding a University* (2011), Collins Press

Weldon, Niall, *Pioneers in Flight: Aer Lingus and the Story of Aviation in Ireland* (2002), The Liffey Press

Went, Arthur, Irish Fisheries Investigations – Series A (Fresh Water) 1968 Stationery Office

Westropp, Thomas J., *Killaloe – Its ancient Palaces and Cathedral* (1893), Royal Society of Antiquaries

INDEX